JOCKOMO

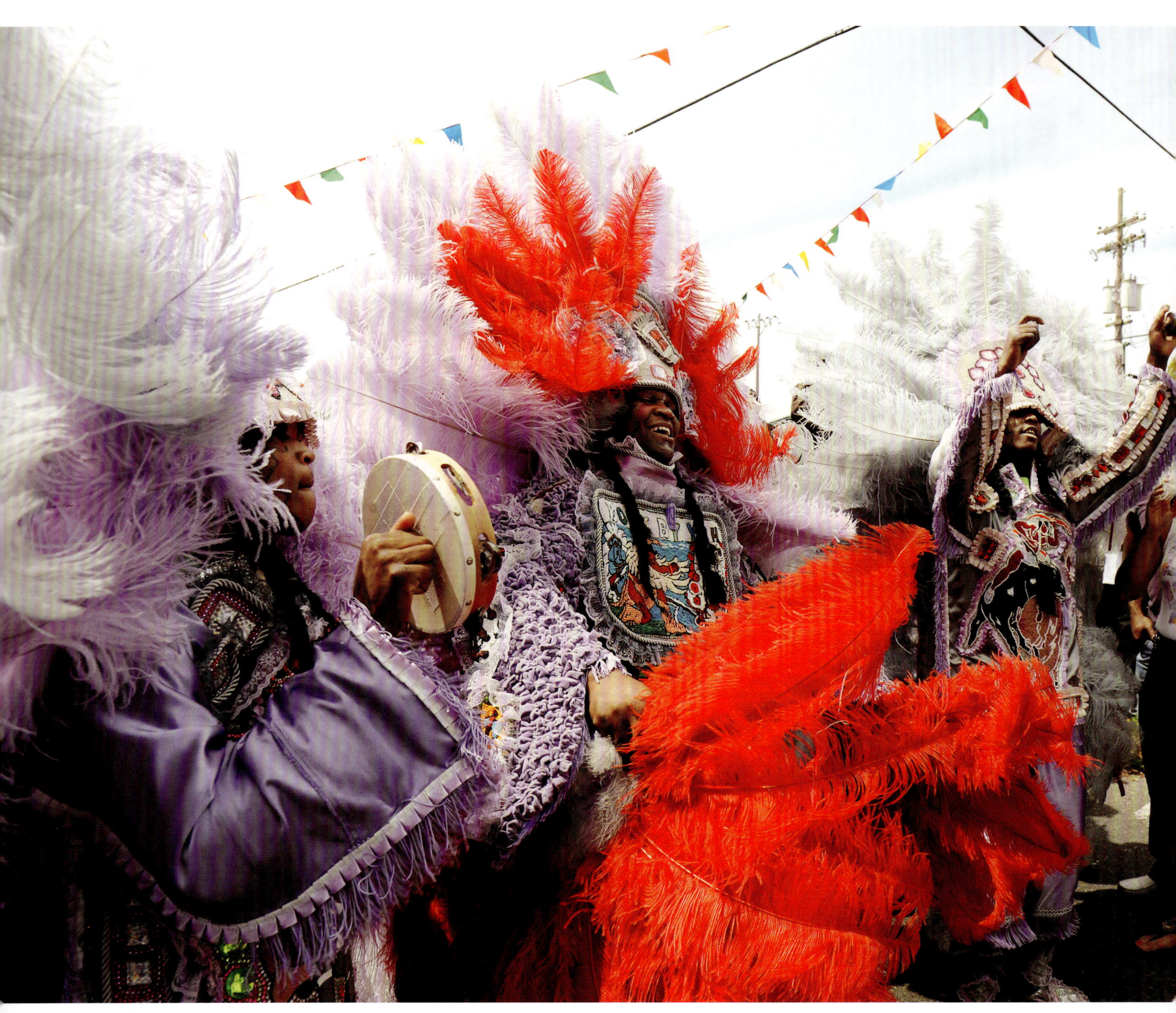

JOCKOMO

The Native Roots of Mardi Gras Indians

Shane Lief and John McCusker

University Press of Mississippi ◆ *Jackson*

The University Press of Mississippi is the scholarly publishing agency of the Mississippi Institutions of Higher Learning: Alcorn State University, Delta State University, Jackson State University, Mississippi State University, Mississippi University for Women, Mississippi Valley State University, University of Mississippi, and University of Southern Mississippi.

www.upress.state.ms.us

The University Press of Mississippi is a member of the Association of University Presses.

Text set in Warnock Pro and Hadriano Light

Material from Chapter 2: Balbancha was originally published in *The Jazz Archivist*, Vol. 28, 2015.

Printed in China

First printing 2019

∞

Library of Congress Cataloging-in-Publication Data

Names: Lief, Shane, 1971– author. | McCusker, John (John P.), 1963– author.
Title: Jockomo : the native roots of Mardi Gras Indians / Shane Lief and John McCusker.
Description: Jackson : University Press of Mississippi, [2019] | "Material from Chapter 2: Balbancha was originally published in The Jazz Archivist, Vol. 28, 2015." | Includes bibliographical references and index. |
Identifiers: LCCN 2019008121 (print) | LCCN 2019020347 (ebook) | ISBN 9781496825919 (epub single) | ISBN 9781496825902 (epub institutional) | ISBN 9781496825926 (pdf single) | ISBN 9781496825933 (pdf institutional) | ISBN 9781496825896 (cloth : alk. paper)
Subjects: LCSH: Mardi Gras Indians—History. | African Americans—Louisiana—New Orleans—History.
Classification: LCC F380.N4 (ebook) | LCC F380.N4 L54 2019 (print) | DDC 976.3/35—dc23
LC record available at https://lccn.loc.gov/2019008121

British Library Cataloging-in-Publication Data available

CONTENTS

ACKNOWLEDGMENTS

Thank you to the following people, who have offered intellectual companionship and loving feedback during the creation of this book:

First and foremost, Sarah Shelton, whose support has been manifold and well beyond words; Dona Lief, for unstinting enthusiasm in rallying the troops for public lectures; Tom Lief, with his inspiring commitment to Native cultural practices; Will Buckingham, sharing keen insights and courageously facing the maw of the academic meat grinder; John Joyce, always there with a sense of wonder; Russell Desmond, generous with his erudition; Cooper Wiley, for many enriching conversations; Jeffery Darensbourg, for sharing his experiences and leading the way to a deeper view; Lynn Abbott, Bruce Boyd Raeburn, Alaina W. Hebert, all three playing a key role in bringing our research to light; and also to so many others who have helped in various ways, including Pete Gregory, Daniel Usner, Kathleen DuVal, John Barbry, Donna Pierite, John Mayeux, James Andrew Whitaker, Kathryn Hobgood Ray, Nick Spitzer, Dan Sharp, Kyle DeCoste, Olanike Ola Orie, Judith Maxwell, Nathalie Dajko, Greg Waselkov, Greg Lambousy, Robert Sullivan, Luther Gray, Tosin Gbogi, Joshua Rogers, John DePriest, Evan Parker, and Jack Stewart, as well as other family members and friends.

For research assistance and support: Elizabeth McCusker, Ellen McCusker, Scott Aiges, Eliot Kamenitz, Kathy Anderson, Doug Parker, Lolis Eric Elie, Norman Dixon Sr., Alfred “Bucket” Carter, Belva Misshore

Pichon, Joyce Montana, Katy Reckdahl, Natalie Pompilio, Chris Gray, Ashlye Keaton, Laura Paul, David Sager, Sherri Miller, and Joseph Makkos.

Mardi Gras Indians, both living and dead, who generously gave of their time, including Big Chiefs Robert "Robbe" Lee, Allison "Tootie" Montana, Victor Harris, Tyrone Casby, Clarence Delcour, Alphonse "Dowee" Robair, Estabon "Peppy" Eugene, Juan Pardo, Wallace Pardo, Walter Cook, Howard Miller, Al Womble, Kevin Goodman, Alfred Doucette, Cyril "Iron Horse" Green; and Queens, Flag Boys, Spy Boys, Wild Men, Drummers, and Needles, including Mercedes "Merk" Goodman, Dow Edwards, David Dejan, Ivory Holmes, Irving Scott, Issac Kinchen, Greggory Hawk, Thomas "Bo" Dean, Greg Perkins, Michael Green, Derrick Hullen, Thomas Watson, Darrell Lee Preston, Jay Williams, Jack Robinson, Irving "Honey" Bannister, Raymond Perique, Cherise Harrison-Nelson, and Ronald Lewis.

Finally, we offer thanks to all the people whose lives we wish to celebrate, recognizing our debt to those who came before us and who helped shape the world we inhabit.

Of course, any errors or lacunae in this book are our own responsibility. Nonetheless, we hope these will provide openings for future conversations.

PREFACE

We are all too aware of the contours of American history, which includes a long and bizarre record of attempts to capture a "vanishing race" of indigenous people or somehow encapsulate the spirit of a people or even the essence of America—however that may be imagined. There are notable examples of painters, photographers, and writers who have tried to do so. Although we also offer a collection of words and images, we do not claim that our book can fully represent any group of people or cultural tradition, and our work does not provide a conclusive statement about human nature. Instead, as a manifold of other people's experiences as well as our own, recorded in various ways, this book gives a range of views about the past and present, and especially how language and music make the past alive in the present. Most of all, this book grows out of our love for our hometown of New Orleans. As the city marks three hundred years of existence, it is intrinsically worthwhile to ask questions about the meaning of this special place that has influenced so many lives. We find that the Mardi Gras Indian cultural system in New Orleans is a particularly compelling point of departure for asking such questions.

One of the peculiar aspects of New Orleans historiography is the relative absence of Native Americans from the story of the city. In the spirit of offering some balance in perspective, our story includes numerous encounters between indigenous people and others who came to this land later, as well as their descendants. Given the gaps in knowledge, many of which come from systematic erasures of people and public memory, we are confronted with the limits of language in discussing these many different cultural groups. Language usually fails to encapsulate the complexities of people, not only in terms of the intricate webs of family ties, but also in how people relate to others outside their kinship groups, and how everyone deals with others they might perceive as "outsiders." The terms used in this story are themselves descendants of complex legacies of usage, and flow back and forth between "Indian," "Native American," "indigenous group," and other expressions. Please note that, while "White Man's Indian" is an unequivocal reference to the way that Europeans and their descendants in North America have perceived Native Americans, the term "Indian" is also sometimes used in this sense. The particular history of that term alone is worth several volumes and is best discussed at another time and place. In the meantime, though, we believe it is good to continue exploring questions about the ambiguity of the word "Indian," how this relates to New Orleans specifically, and what the more general implications are for all people and places.

Even though a range of terms are used for the group of artists, performers, and community leaders who are the focus of this book, including "black Indians" and "Indians," since we are often discussing outside perceptions in addition to the people themselves, we also use the term "Mardi Gras Indians." This helps to ground the reference in an artistic and ceremonial context.

When it comes to discussing language itself, we have chosen a less technical route. Although we analyze words and phrases and discuss their usage, in several places, in lieu of a technical term or a "scientific" transcription, we went with a more common formulation. Once again, we reserve a more nuanced linguistic discussion for another time and place. Suffice it to say that words are mutable, slippery entities, and as we see with the quotes from manuscripts and newspaper accounts, spelling can be a creative art.

Back to the peculiar aspects of historiography: the odd myopia attending most discussions of the past becomes more explicable when we consider how political ideology and the practice of history are tightly bound together. Economic disparities and social hierarchies—often collapsed into the terms "class" and "race"—introduce selective distortions, not only in any given individual's experience of events, but also in recollection and the storytelling that happens afterward. A little more than a century ago, this complexity tended to be buried beneath the notion of objectivity in history, the hubristic belief that we can reconstruct the past by arranging empirical facts in a crystalline lattice of exactitude. Over the past few decades, it seems the pendulum has swung away from the obsession with objectivity to complete subjectivity. This has entailed the abandonment of the ideal of impartial judgment, and in its place, a passionate embrace of idiosyncratic views. Instead of a window into the past, we can't help but see through a prism, brilliant and colorful, fragmented by the fractals of individual perspectives, yet relentlessly dictated by one's membership to a social group, whether assigned by others or self-imposed. At best, this is tantamount to methodological alienation, and at worst, an infinite regress of re-othering.

If there is one idea that can be said to guide our historical essay—with the momentary risk of seeming abstraction—it is a humanism that recognizes difference but refutes mutual exclusivity. In this vision, human beings are never merely a means to an end, which in historical terms would mean reducing individuals to symbols or representations. Instead, we recognize the human condition as mutual rediscovery. Alive within a greater world that must always remain partly unknown, people are nonetheless able to experience and imagine a more encompassing significance together, so the strange can become familiar. In the realm of artistic creation, which can be synonymous with spiritual ceremony, the world takes on a protean quality. To paraphrase Schopenhauer, the cosmos is a vast dream of one being, yet also dreamt by all of the dreamt beings.

This story does not seek to explain all the meanings that are possible in connection with Mardi Gras Indian cultural practices. However, we offer several threads—historical accounts, phrases, images, and family lines—which might help people understand and appreciate a little more the complex cosmos of interactions that have taken place near the mouth of the Mississippi River, yielding a unique spectrum of voices in New Orleans.

JOCKOMO

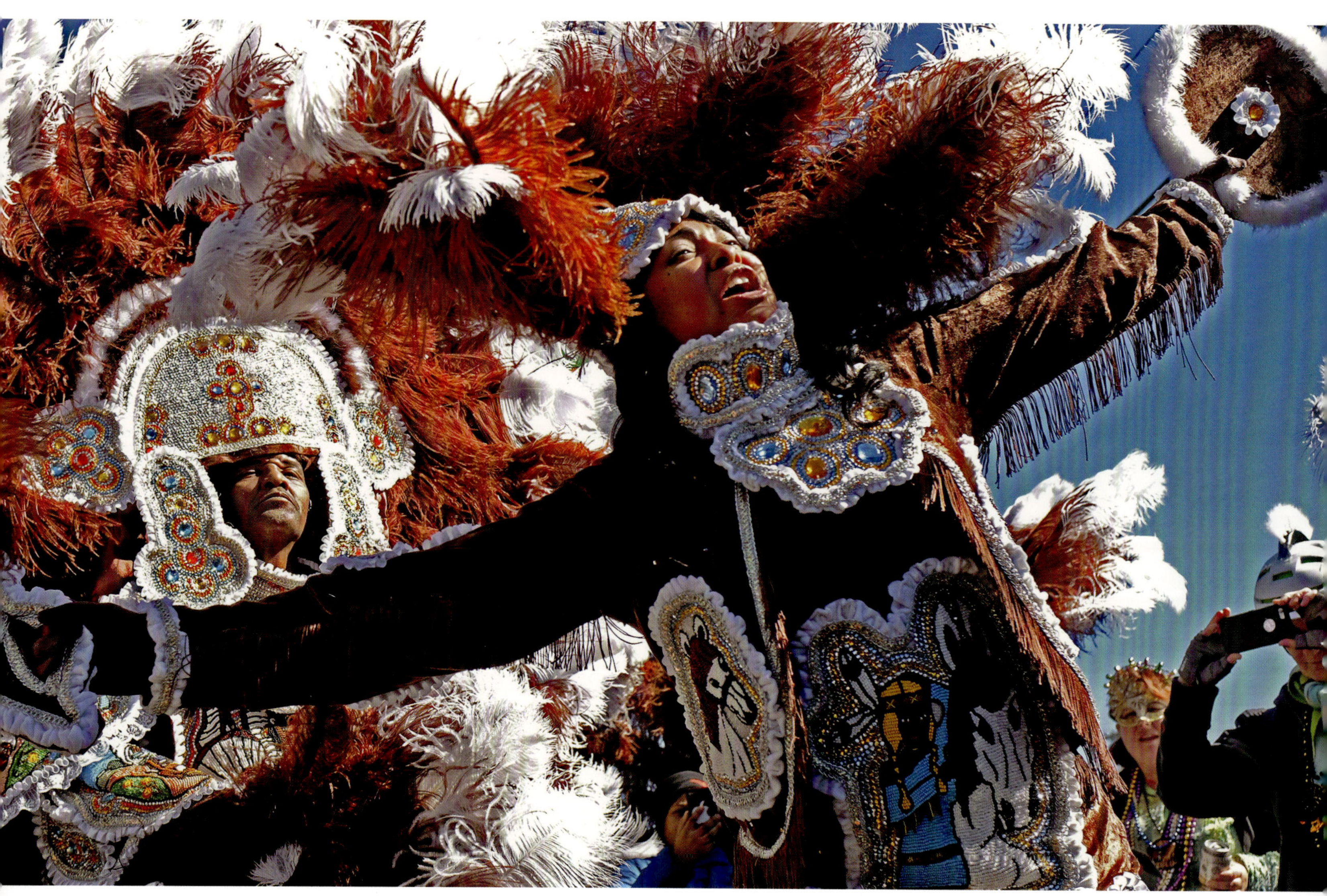

Big Chief Al Womble, *left*, and Queen Angelique Briscoe and the Cheyenne tribe sing "Indian Red" on Dryades Street on Mardi Gras 2016. Photo by John McCusker/ New Orleans Advocate.

CHAPTER ONE

Indian Red

First, in the distance, you hear the beat of approaching drums. Then come the layers of call-and-response singing accompanied by the jangling of tambourines. An Indian flashes by, feathers rippling, the top of his headdress, or crown, projecting plumes that hover seven feet in the air. Soon you're caught up and carried by a sudden flow of people, in the thick of it, moving with the crowd, lost in the spirit of the moment. Your sense of time is changing in this electric event, your eyes dazzled by color as Indians go past in this public gathering of people singing and dancing in the street together. It is a joyous assault on the senses. While every public ceremony in New Orleans tends to have a unique texture, the most strikingly different—the one that involves the deepest sense of connection between the ancient past and the living present—is the experience of the Mardi Gras Indians.

The term "Mardi Gras Indians" applies to groups of contemporary African Americans in New Orleans who make elaborate costumes annually for Carnival, or Mardi Gras Day (Fat Tuesday), when they take to the streets and search out other Indian tribes or "gangs" in similar attire. Among other things, the point of the search is to compete aesthetically with other Indians to see who is "the prettiest." But this is no mere costume contest. Instead, for the participants, it is just one of a complex web of activities including sewing, dancing, drumming, engaging in public processions and private rituals—as well as special structural elements such as phrases, songs, a distinct social hierarchy and spirituality—all of which is more

Jay Williams, Spy Boy with the Buffalo Hunters, races down Third Street in search of other Indians on Mardi Gras 2013. Photo by John McCusker/New Orleans Advocate.

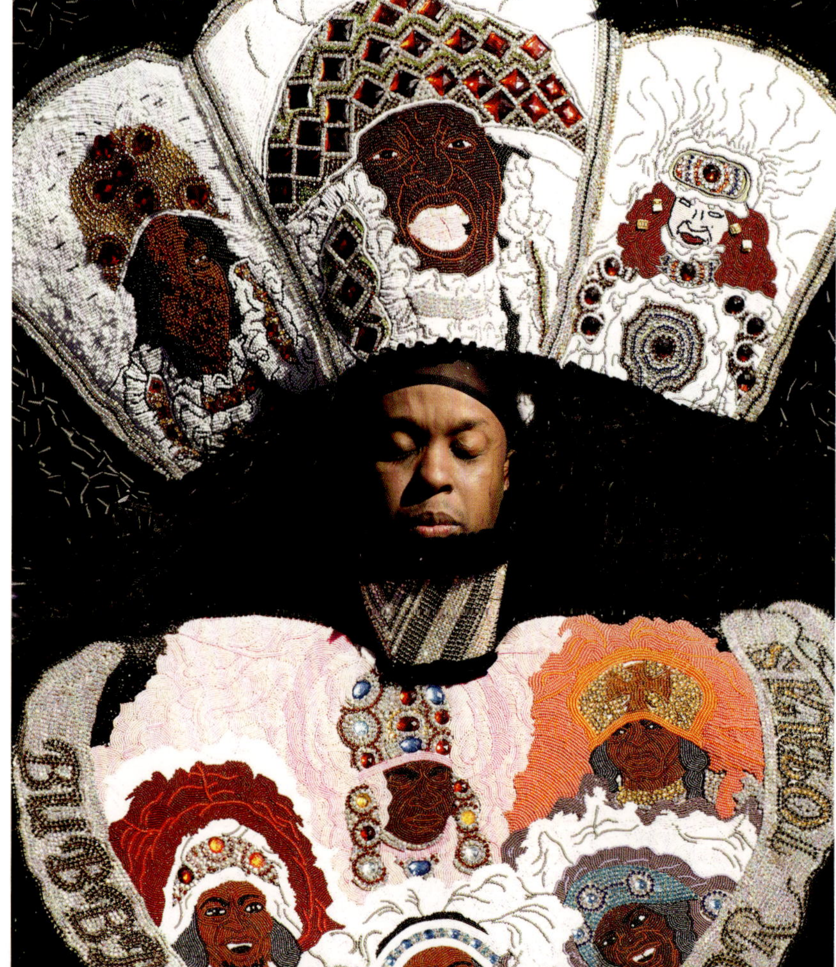

Big Chief Bo Dollis Jr. closes his eyes for a moment before crying out "Madi cu defio," the opening line of "Indian Red," the prayer song that the Indians sing before taking to the streets in search of other Indians, in 2016. Dollis leads the Wild Magnolias as his father did for decades. Photo by John McCusker/New Orleans Advocate.

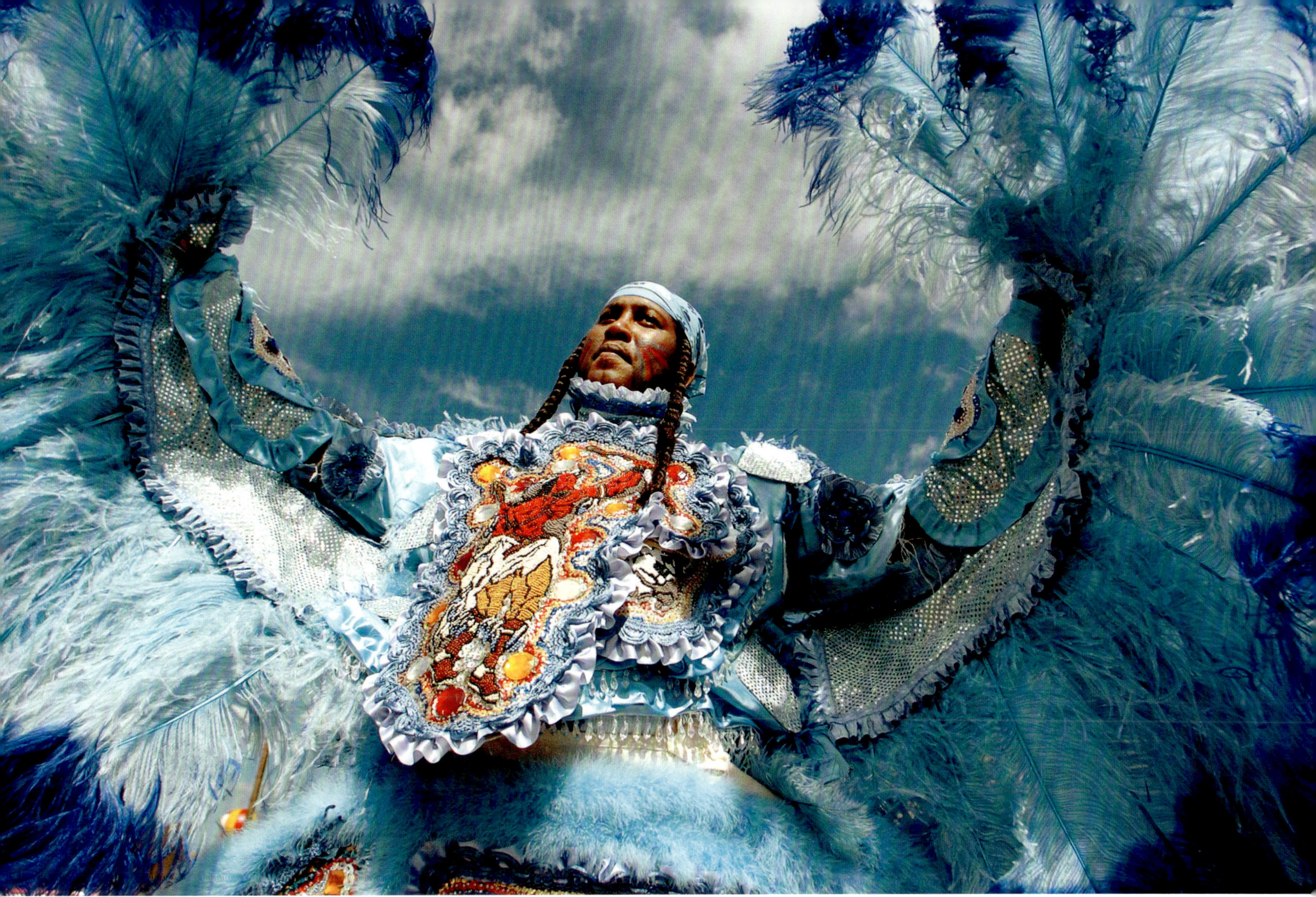

accurately described as a cultural system. Being an Indian means gathering all these strands of tradition and responding creatively in a complex, interwoven combination of inherited and improvised actions. It requires committing oneself to a collective identity with its own priorities, beliefs, and dynamic social order. Despite the public displays for which they are best known, Mardi Gras Indians form a community that is exclusive and even secretive.

Like the braided streams that flow to form the Mississippi River, where different groups of people have gathered to dance and sing for centuries,

Gang Flag Thomas Watson spreads his wings as he and the rest of the Golden Blades take to the streets on Mardi Gras 2006, the first carnival after Hurricane Katrina. The Golden Blades had numerous members displaced by Katrina. Some sewed in evacuation cities like Atlanta, Memphis, Dallas, and Houston and showed up Mardi Gras morning to reclaim their place. Photo by John McCusker/The Times-Picayune.

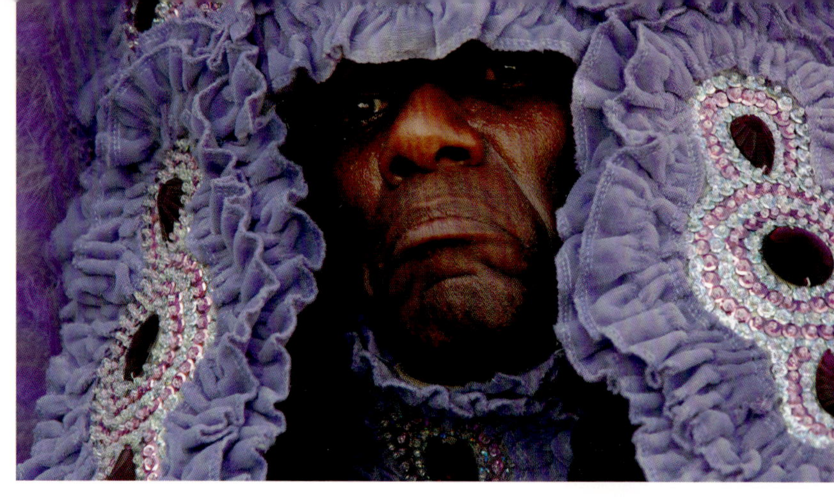

Second Chief Irving Scott, of the Golden Comanche, brings his game face to Dryades Street on Mardi Gras 2006. Photo by John McCusker.

Tribes face off on Super Sunday, uptown, 1997. Photo by John McCusker.

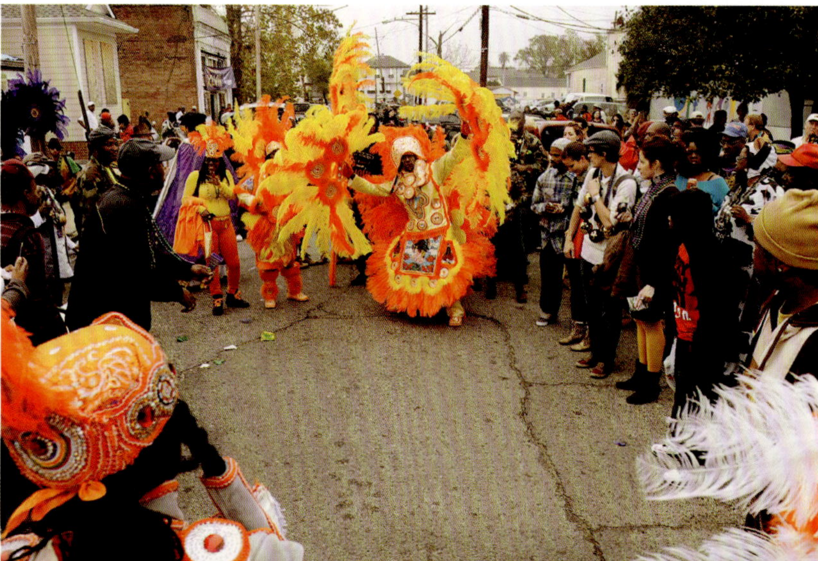

Big Chief Irving Scott of the Buffalo Hunters opens up the crowd on Dryades Street as his group travels through uptown in 2013. Photo by John McCusker.

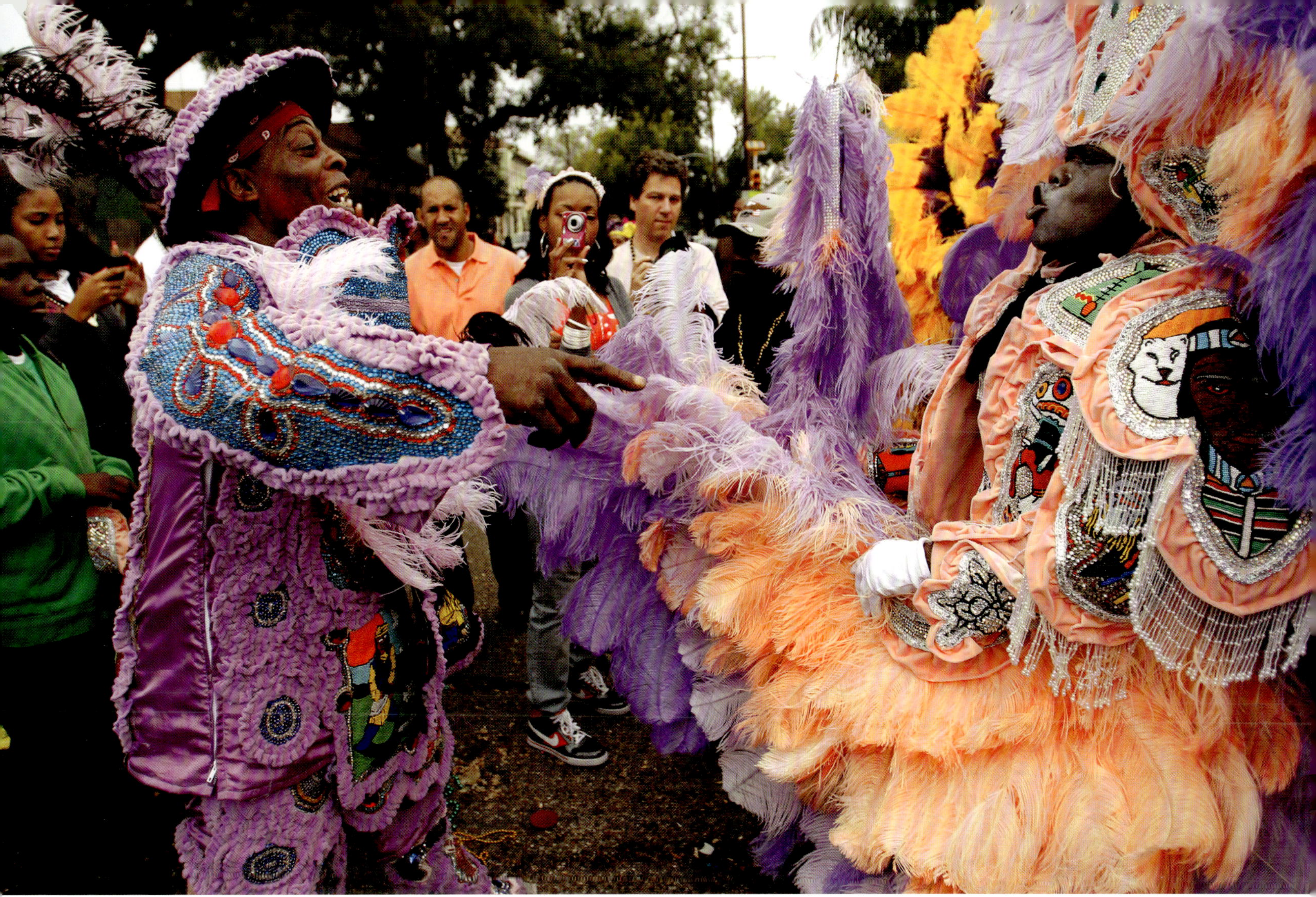

Walter Sandifer, *right*, First Spy Boy of the Creole Wild West, turns away Timothy Washington as he makes his way down Jackson Avenue on Mardi Gras 2011. Photo by John McCusker/ The Times-Picayune.

this culture arose from a series of blended traditions. Three hundred years ago, people from three major parts of the Earth—Africa, Europe, and North America—all found themselves in the place that has become New Orleans. This story is about recovering and remembering those who have come before us, taking up the various threads of memory and experience of different individuals and cultural groups, so we can have a greater understanding and appreciation for the people who have had a hand in creating the intricate costumes, the complex ceremonies, and the music that flows in the public spaces of the city on Mardi Gras.

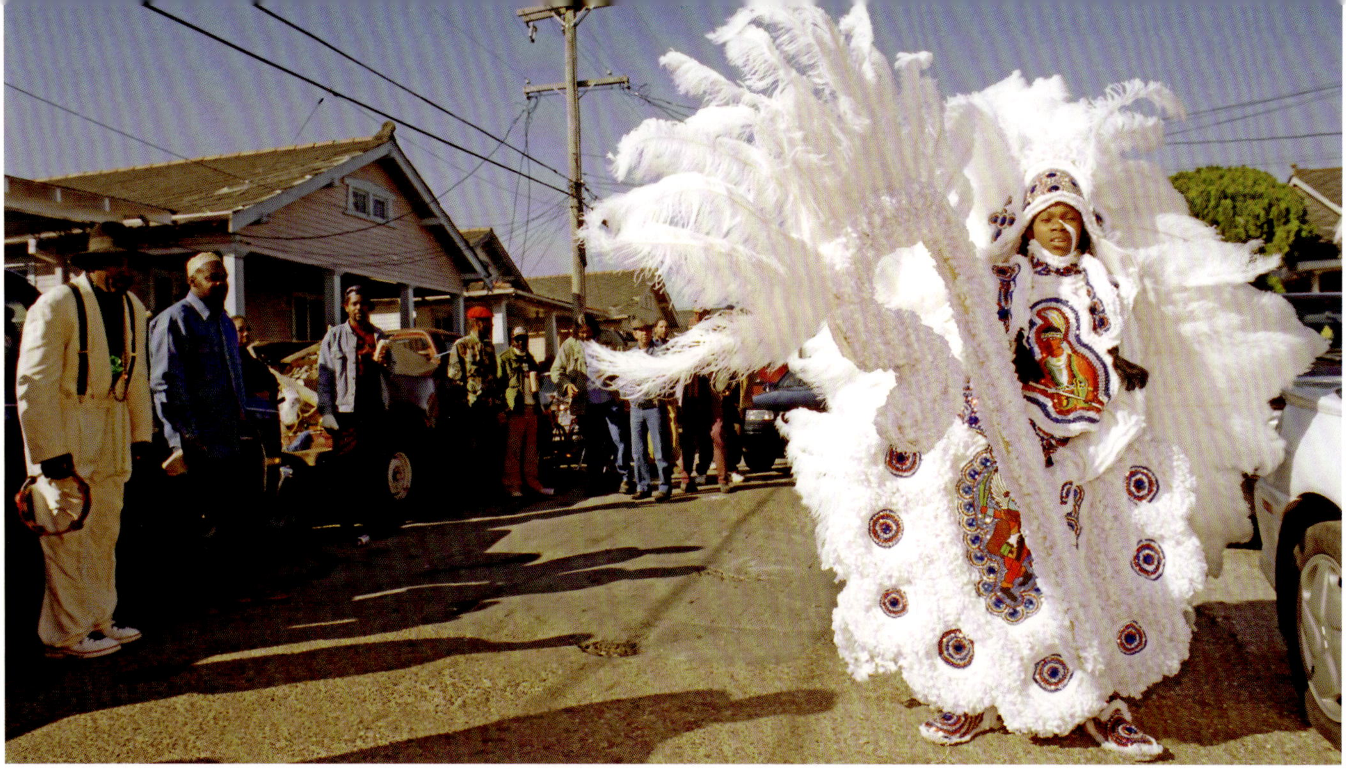

Ryan Goodman of the Flaming Arrows takes to the streets in the Eighth Ward, 1997. Photo by John McCusker/The Times-Picayune.

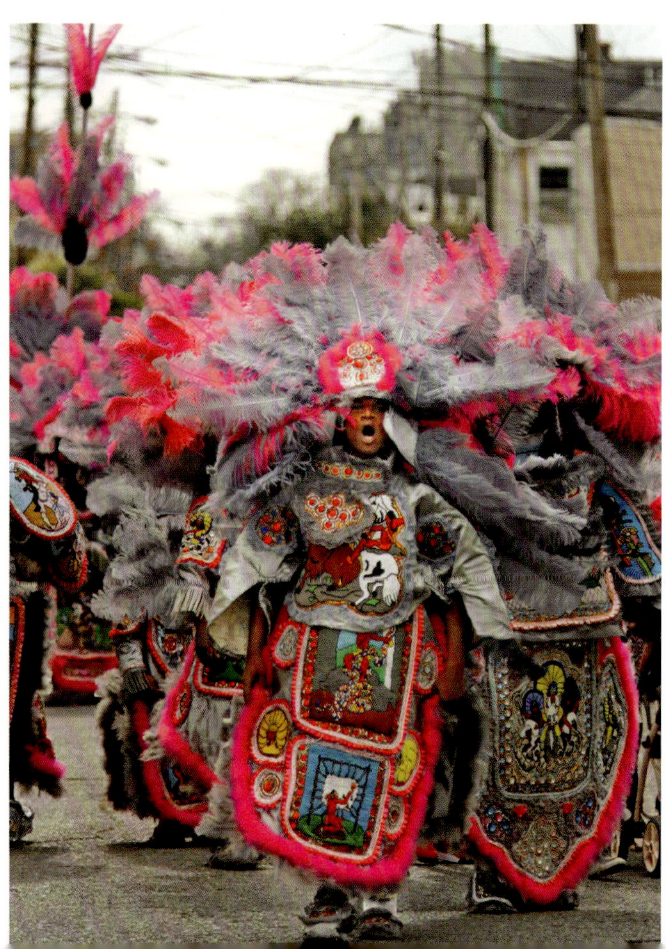

The Cheyenne occupy Second Street with a dozen Indians in matching feathers in 2011. Photo by John McCusker.

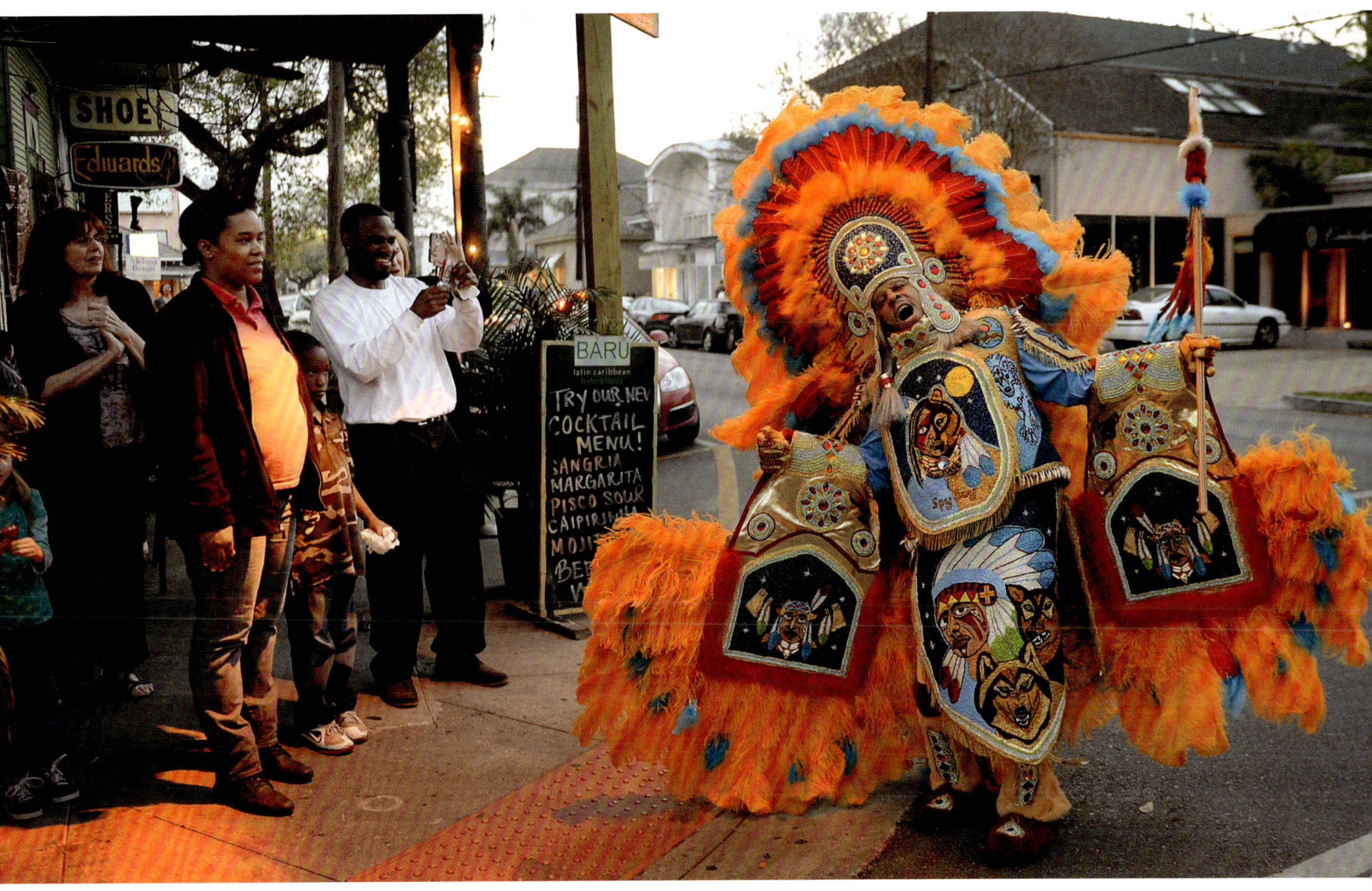

Spy Boy Dow Edwards of the Mohawk Hunters emerges onto Amelia Street near Magazine on St. Joseph's Night in 2013. Photo by John McCusker.

The Indian tradition is sometimes described as New Orleans culture at its most African, and this is a theme that has attracted much attention.[1] Of course, it deserves further exploration. However, another path of inquiry, substantially less traveled in popular and academic literature, involves exploring how much of Mardi Gras Indian cultural tradition, on the one hand, reflects Native American legacies, and on the other, how much of it represents the projection of the "American Indian" icon. From what inspirational wells did the earliest Mardi Gras Indians draw for their music, language, dancing, sewing, and other practices?

But first, a snapshot of the Indians today.

Michael Green emerges onto Jackson Avenue and declares to the assembled crowd, "I'm a Flag Boy, Creole Wild West!" He is wearing a bright magenta suit of ostrich plumes and a single chest patch depicting an Indian man holding his bride. He carries a Mirabeau-lined cutout of a rifle that served as his flag staff that reads "Flag Boy, CWW." His moccasins are each topped with the face of an Indian. A big man over six feet tall, his imposing presence is made more striking by the immense Indian suit as he moves through the carnival throng.

Inside, Big Chief Howard Miller is preparing to sojourn the streets that the Creole Wild West have followed for over a century. It is a process of spiritual immersion. "The transformation is coming long before that morning. It starts from sewing. Once you put it [the suit] on and the spirits should be coming into you. Guys who truly sew with their heart and soul and the right intentions I guarantee you they will tell you. Such a feeling coming over you as you pull it on. Now you're who you're supposed to be. It's the spirit. How powerful is my spirit? Is it strong enough to lift these people and now can lift my tribe? And now we can go," Miller said.[2]

That same morning a few blocks away, the Cheyenne take to the streets of Central City with a dozen Indians in matching gray, pink, and burgundy feathers led by Big Chief Al Womble. As each tribe emerges, they gather to sing their prayer song, "Indian Red." The song begins with three strikes on the tambourine followed by the lone voice of the Big Chief crying out: "Madi cu defio." The tribe responds, "En dans dey, end dans day." They repeat this call and response and then sing in unison:

We are the Indians, Indians, Indians of the nation
The wild, wild creation
We won't bow down (We won't bow down)
Down on the ground (On that dirty ground)
Oh how I love to hear him call my Indian Red[3]

The song is a declaration of existence, belonging, importance, and pride. In a few short lines of verse, black New Orleanians disappear behind a veil of what historian Angela Pulley Hudson calls "Indianness."[4] "You go into another place. It becomes emotionally overwhelming. Let the spirit go, and go where it pleases. Your warrior nature is awake. You're in an alternate state," said Big Chief Juan Pardo of the Golden Comanche.[5] Beyond the suits they wear, the essential piece of being an Indian is projecting identity to other Indians. Who is the most Indian? Gazing upon the faces of the tribe, their immersion into their spiritual Indian identities is clearly evident as they sing together Mardi Gras morning. After "Indian Red," another song from the Indian canon will be pulled out, like "Iko Iko," "Sew, Sew, Sew," "Shoo-Fly," or "Let's Go Get 'Em."

As the Indian tribes begin their journeys across the city on Mardi Gras, traveling from uptown to downtown, or downtown to Algiers, they typically frequent gathering places in the old neighborhoods that have been used for generations. Shakespeare Park (now A. L. Davis Park), Second and Dryades streets, and under the Interstate 10 at Orleans Avenue downtown in the Treme neighborhood have endured as battlefields between those seeking to be the prettiest.

While on the path, the Spy Boys search out other Indians, serving as the eyes and ears of the Big Chief. Typically, a Spy Boy's Indian suit is lightweight, with little in the way of a crown in comparison to the elaborate, often expansive ones worn by a Chief. This allows him to run ahead of the others and then report back. If the Spy Boy spots the approach of another tribe, he will signal the Flag Boy, who will alert the Chief and wait for directions. As the name implies, Flag Boys carry pennants attached to long staffs that are sometimes cut into the shapes of rifles or tomahawks. Their suits may be bulkier than that of a spy, but they too require the ability to move quickly. If, at the direction of the respective Big Chiefs, the tribes choose to meet, the parties will converge. The Wild Man then steps in to clear an opening in the crowd of spectators so that the battle may be joined. Wild Man costumes can vary widely, but they typically incorporate animal horns or antlers, hides, Spanish moss, and perhaps a

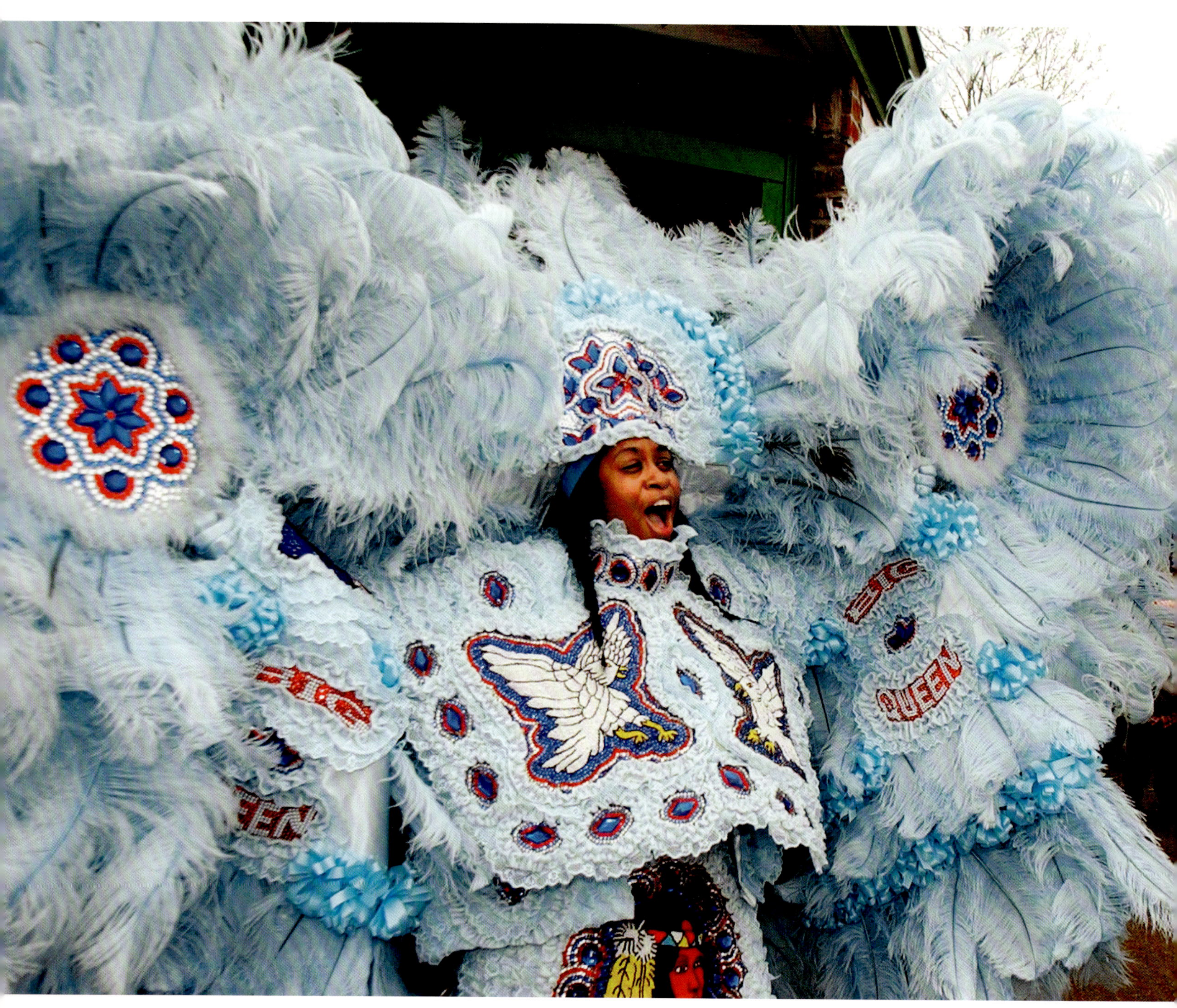
BIG
QUEEN

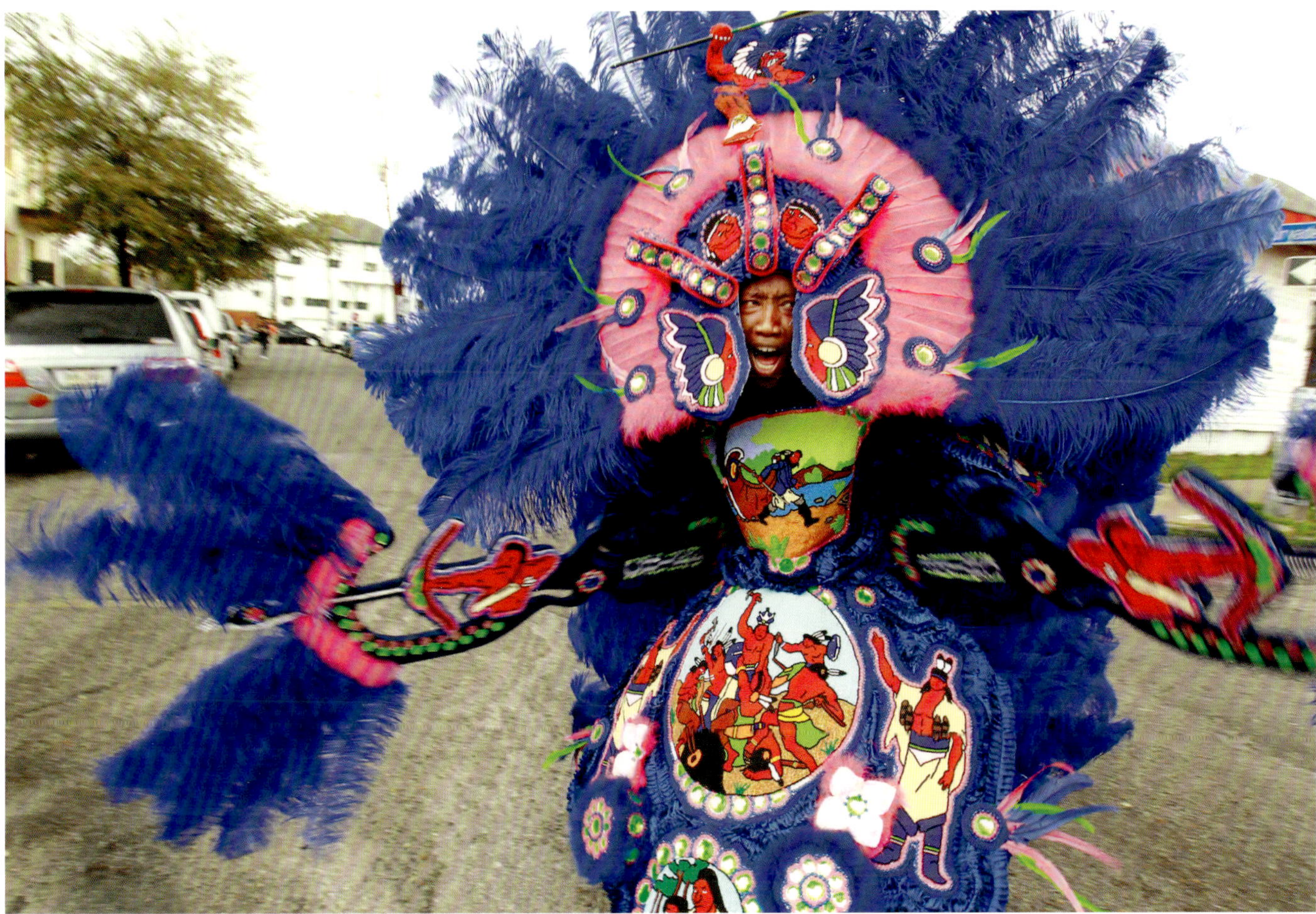

Juan Pardo of the Golden Comanche lets out a whoop on Dryades Street as he travels with his gang, or tribe, to Second Street on Mardi Gras 2012. Photo by John McCusker/The Times-Picayune.

(Left page) Patricia Johnson, Big Queen of the Wild Magnolias, emerges onto Dryades and Second streets, Mardi Gras afternoon 2004. Photo by John McCusker.

decorative tomahawk or staff. Once the crowd is pushed back, the stage for the face-off is set and the Indians prepare their minds for battle.

"I'm sizing up what tribe it is. What's the reputation of the guy in front of me? What is he known for? I read his actions. Who's level headed? Who's into libations? I look at what he has on. I'm 5'5". I'm a realist. I'm never gonna wear a 7-foot suit. My edge can't be beads or size. There's no winning that. At that point you have to know how to play to him. Your focus is him. I go in winning, that's my thought process," said Pardo.[6]

When tribes meet, the hierarchical structure again plays out—Spy Boys vs. Spy Boys, Flag Boys vs. Flag Boys, and so forth—climaxing with

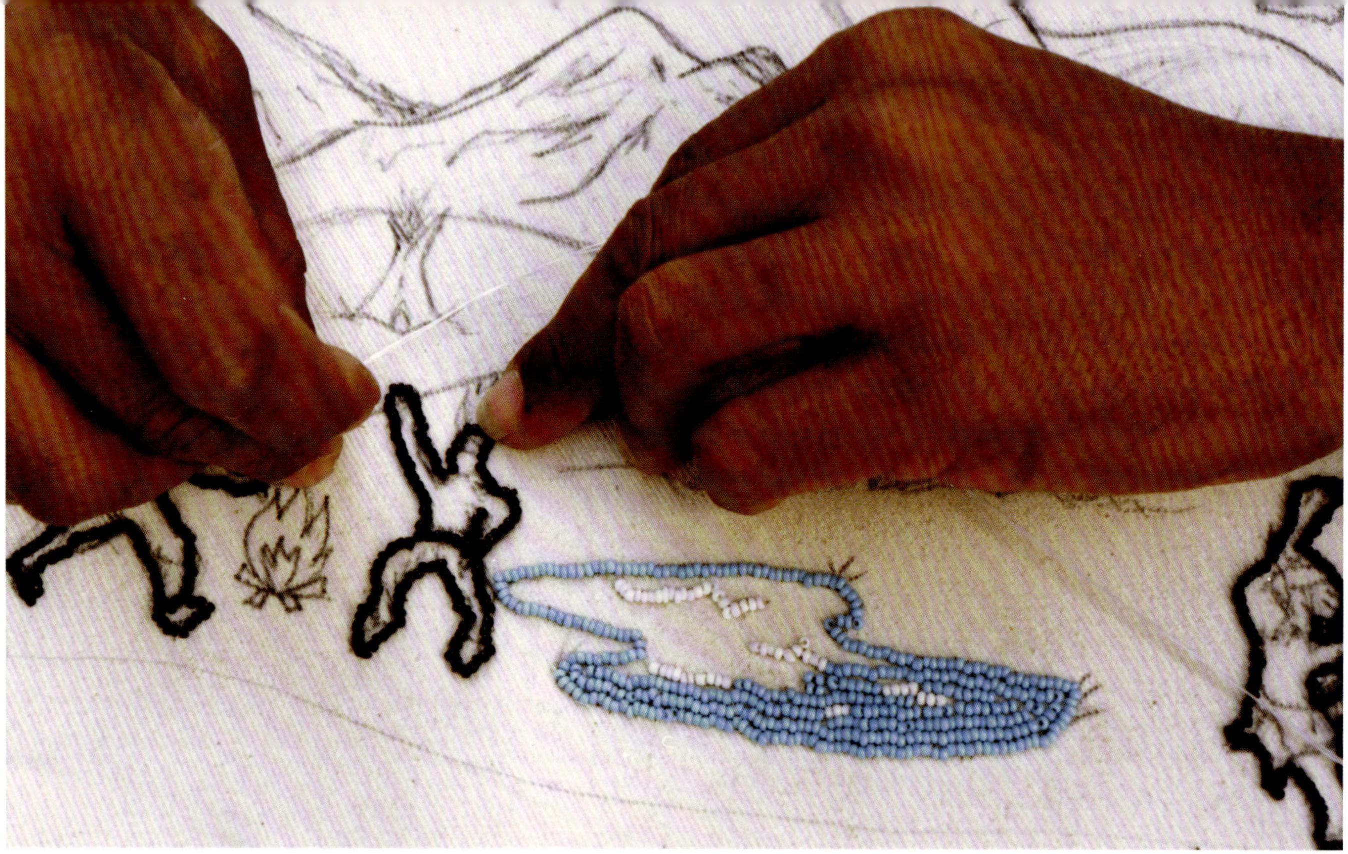

Alfred Doucette of the Flaming Arrows sewing an Indian suit in 1996. Photo by John McCusker.

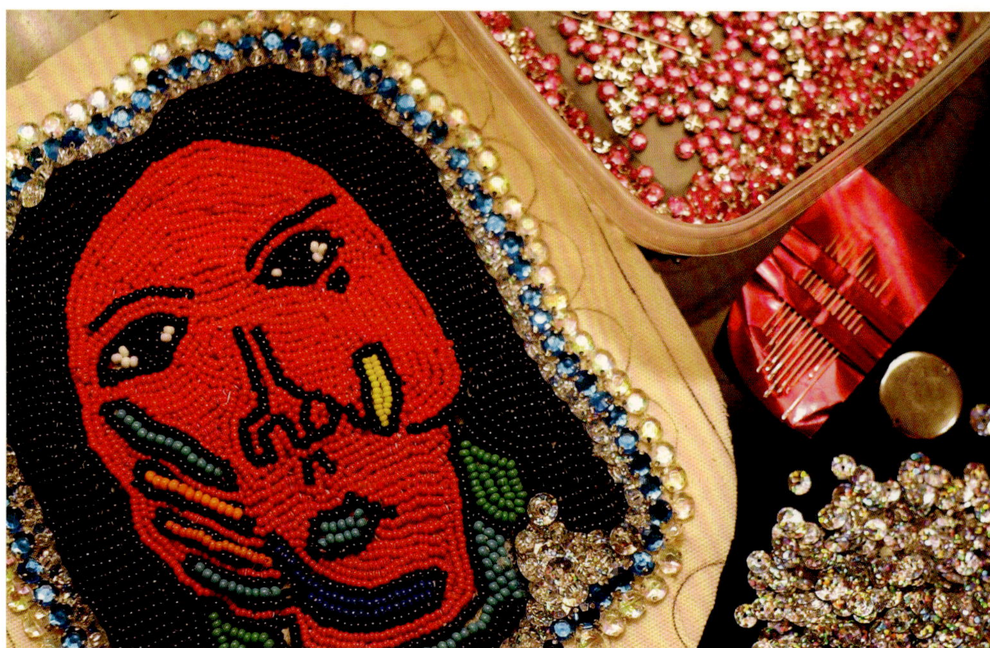

Flaming Arrows Big Chief Kevin Goodman's sewing table in 2004. Photo by John McCusker.

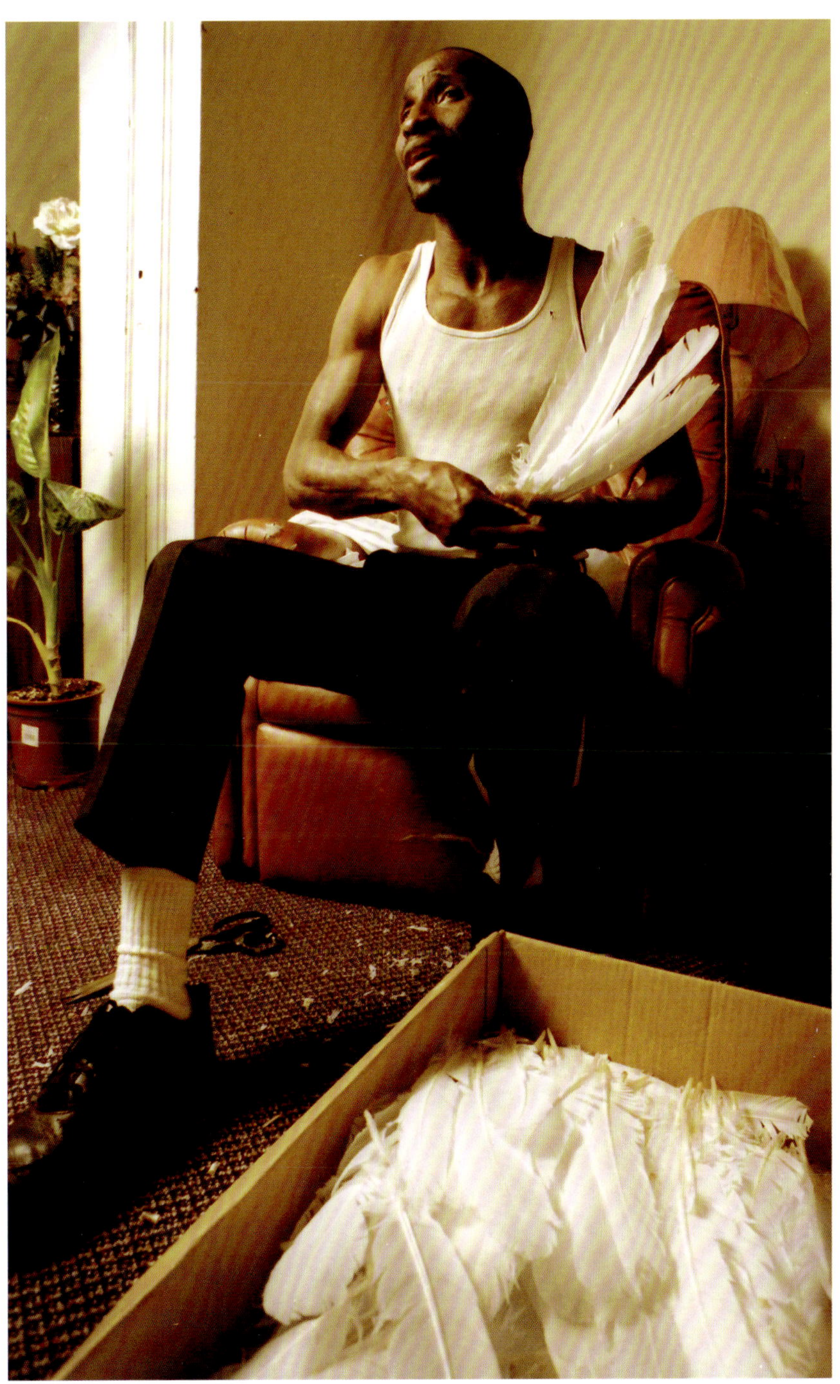

Estabon Eugene, known as Big Chief Peppy of the Golden Arrows, in 1996 breaking feathers. Photo by John McCusker.

the meeting of the Big Chiefs. As the drums pound in the background, the competitors face each other at a distance of about ten to fifteen feet. The ritual combat begins with time-honored etiquette, as each announces his rank, Spy Boy or Flag, etc., and his tribe with shouted boasts and cries of Indianness in a powerful, wailing voice: "I'm a pretty Spy Boy, Flaming Arrows. I walk through fiyo on a burning biyo, Spy Boy got boom, boom in the mornin'!" His opponent responds with his own introduction, boasts, and blood-curdling cries. With that, the battle is joined. They throw hand signals, shout, whoop, wail, and strive to show who is the most Indian. They dance at each other and back again, swerving from left to right, feathers slicing through the space, in an aggressive display of pride in one's self and tribe. It often concludes with an embrace between the competitors signifying respect at combat's end. The battles continue until the members of both tribes have faced down their opposite number. This ritual warfare is repeated throughout the day for hours as tribe meets tribe across the city.

Eventually, after every battle has been fought, the weary Indians retreat to a bar or gathering place. Another Mardi Gras has passed but there will be little rest for the weary; another set of challenges lay ahead.

That's because the sight of an Indian on the streets on Mardi Gras morning is the result of countless hours of often solitary sewing, a process that begins months earlier with a commitment to the Big Chief that one will sew a suit that year. It is a massive undertaking of creative personal sacrifice where costs can reach well into the thousands. Each Indian suit is made of numerous parts, including the crown, the apron, bib and sleeves, and sometimes wings. Each is adorned with various combinations of tiny, colored, hand-sewn bead patches, sequins, and Mirabeau. All this is topped off with feathers or ostrich plumes. Shipped in boxes, the feathers need to be sorted to left or right leaning and must have imperfections bent out. The Indians call this "breaking." This entire process is repeated each year.

Sometimes starting with inspirations sketched out on a pad, patch designs are outlined on canvas, leather, or even cardboard, and needles and thread are pushed through, securing a colored bead in place. This process is repeated thousands of times in the creation of just one patch. A typical suit will often feature half a dozen patches. Some subscribe to the "downtown style," sewing nonrepresentational, sometimes three-dimensional designs, while the "uptown style" typically features scenes and vignettes of heroic Indians triumphing against their enemies or dying heroically in defeat. Many combine the two. The patches, when completed, are cut out and sewn into place on the suit. On a crown, a patch is usually placed on front across the forehead with feathers projecting rainbow-like around the face. A giant patch or a series of patches will be sewn into the apron and bib sections.

For much of the twentieth century, Indian suits were simple affairs. The earliest known picture of an Indian tribe was made in 1903 for the *Times-Democrat* newspaper. Some men wear shorts while others have knee pants with colored knee-high socks. Some are draped in a tunic and skirt made from a single fabric pattern. Others wear buckskin or body suits topped with decorations. The crowns, or head pieces, range from simple feather headbands to turbans sporting a few feathers or plumes. One wears an Iroquois-style crown that could have come off the Indian image that graced the US currency at that time. Another Mardi Gras Indian wears a giant headpiece that features no feathers and has no obvious Indian imagery behind its styling. Some men wear braids, others flowing straight hair. One of the figures could be mistaken for an African in his style and attire. The costuming variety displayed within just one turn-of-the-century Indian group shows that inspiration for suits has always drawn on diverse images of Indianness.

In his memoirs, Jelly Roll Morton did not describe elaborate Indian suits, saying only that "[t]hese people, they had the idea that they wanted to act exactly like the old Indians did in years gone by. And they wanted to live true to traditions of their style."[7] A 1940s-era picture of Indians shows men wearing silk shirts with vests featuring sewn patches, fringed buckskin trousers, and ribbons hanging down on both sides of each headdress of turkey feathers. Big Chief "Robbe" Robert Lee recalled a time when he might snatch a loose button or bauble while visiting a girl's house. "I'd just snatch it," he said.[8] It was a simpler time.

This approach began to change in the sixties and came into full effect in the seventies. Sewing became more complex, accessories like extension pieces got grander, and "the suit" became a defining feature of Indianness. This was a natural development of shutting down violence that once existed among tribes. Decades ago, being the baddest Indian was the goal. Nowadays, the emphasis is on being the "prettiest." Miller of the Creole Wild West notes, "The seventies is when suits started to become more elaborate. About the mid-seventies or so. When people got away from mainstream Indian suits. Before then I made a suit in 1969. I'm only 13 years old. Maybe it wasn't . . . but it was a Mardi Gras Indian's suit. I was able to say I was a Mardi Gras Indian. Today that's not gonna happen."[9]

Indeed, the late Big Chief Tootie Montana is often credited with elevating suit making to a new artistic level, incorporating three-dimensional designs topped with exquisite beadwork. In recent decades, Spirit of the Fi-Yi-Yi Big Chief Victor Harris has further pushed the boundaries of Indian suit making, incorporating designs that pay homage to African and African Diaspora decorative aesthetics. His beadwork includes conch shells, dried grass strands and, unlike most other Mardi Gras Indian tribes, beaded masks that are evocative of Bahamian Junkanoo dancers.

"I was always a person of humanity. I'm not talking about white, black, orange. I saw awful things as a child and was even treated bad as a kid. I never understood that. When I got a little older I wondered why are we being deprived? So, it made me start tracking my history. So I had to go back to where they took the people from, the origin. So that's how I went back, and I went into that culture, went back to Africa. To slaves. They went there and they brought slaves here. But then I thought about it. We had this culture before we was taken. So, it's not just an Indian thing that people are looking at. We had [Africa] in our DNA. We were descended from Africa," Harris said.[10]

Harris also speaks of his sewing hand being guided by a spirit of fire, a notion echoed by Big Chief Juan Pardo of the Golden Comanche. "When I come up with an idea, I draw and I sketch. I may start working on a suit I don't finish. Spiritually that may not be the suit I'm gonna wear. The spirit may guide me to something different. I have remnants of suits from where

Robert "Big Chief Robbe" Lee, called the chief of chiefs. Photo by John McCusker.

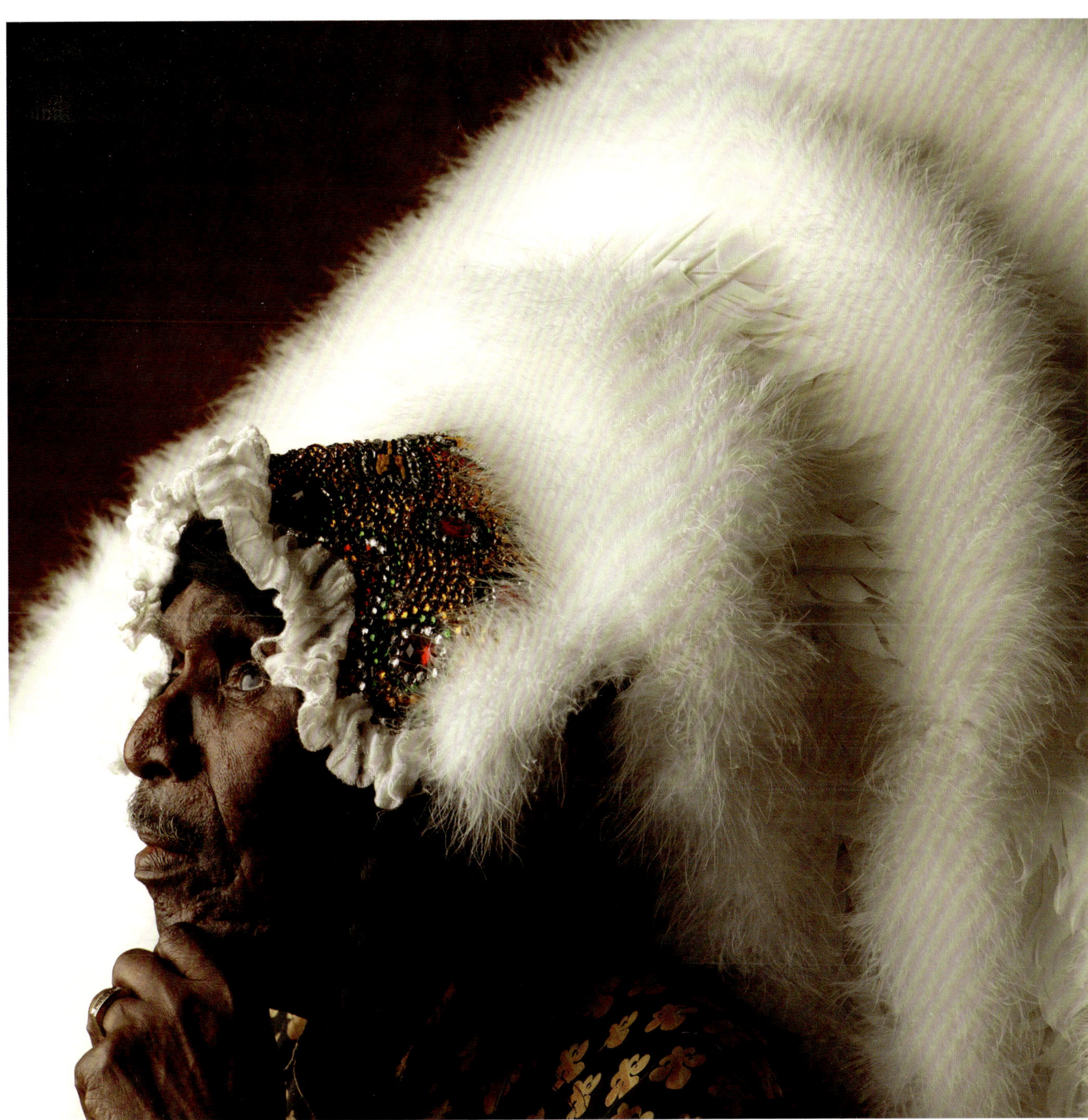

Mardi Gras Indians Irving Bannister and Robert Mayo sew the Indian suits they will wear with the Creole Wild West Indian gang in 2003. Bannister was the Tribe Flag in the group, Mayo the Flag Boy. Photo by John McCusker.

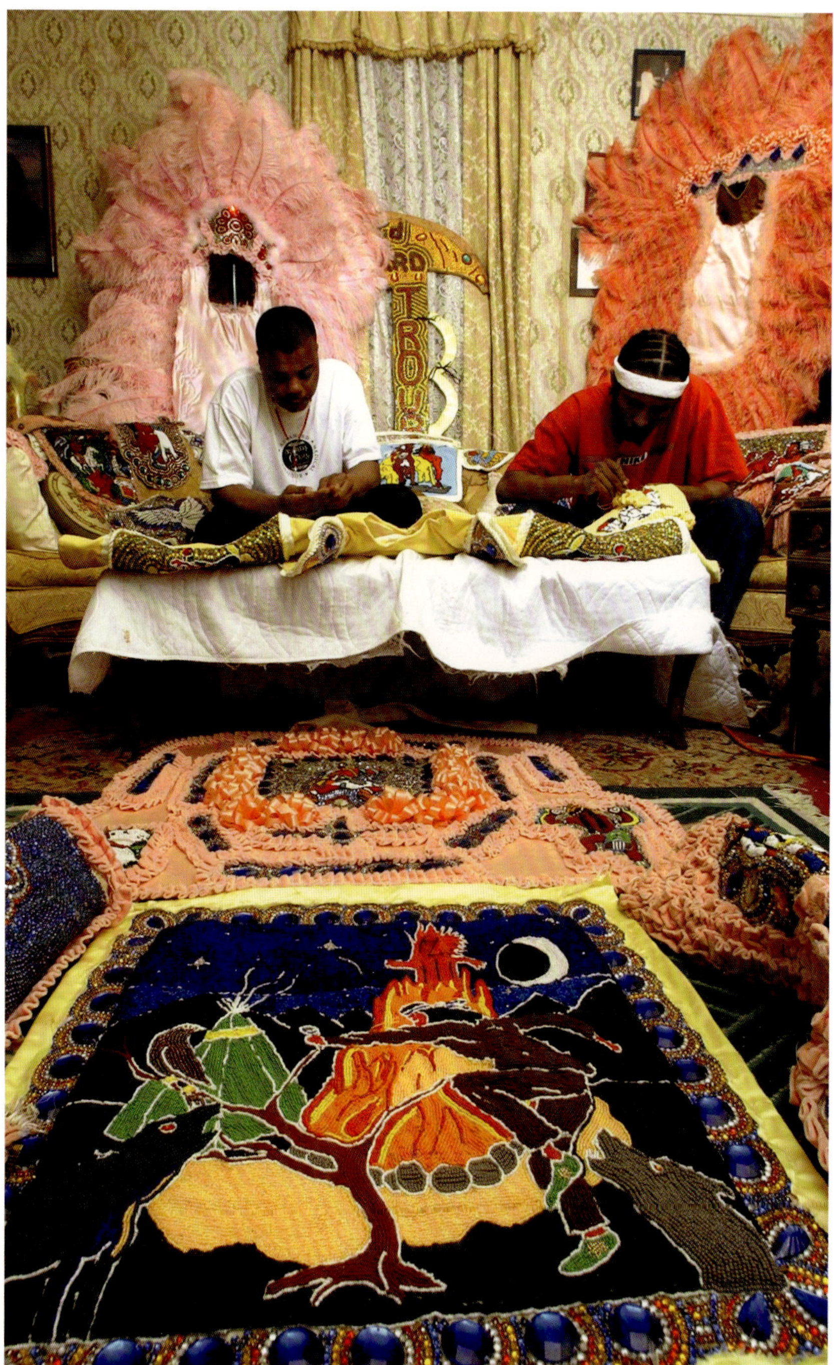

(Right page) Cyril Green, known in the Mardi Gras Indian community as "Big Chief Iron Horse," was laid to rest Tuesday, April 2, 2013, after a service at Our Lady Star of the Sea Church on St. Roch Avenue. Green was handicapped but came out as an Indian in his wheelchair. Indians from around the city gathered to escort his casket as it was brought out of the church. Photo by John McCusker/New Orleans Advocate.

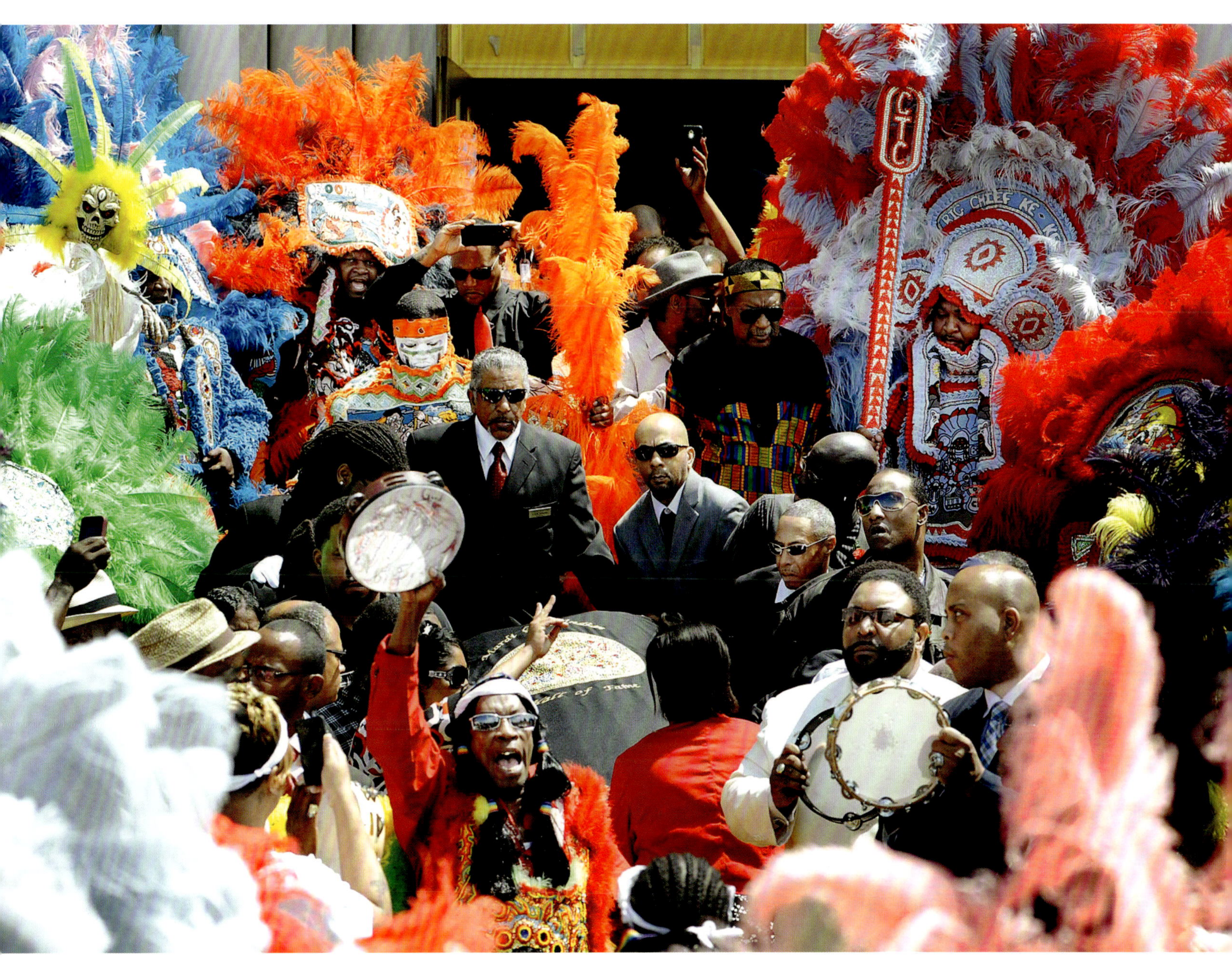
CTC

I've started a suit that wasn't right for that year. Listen to your inner voice and that spirit guides your hand."[11]

Big Chief Howard Miller of the Creole Wild West too speaks of the role of the spirit, not only in guiding his sewing hand, but as his base inspiration to being an Indian. "The designs we come up with and the creations, it's a spiritual thing for uplifting the people. When Indians are around, people are joyful and happy," Miller said.[12]

INDIAN PRACTICE

"The suit is not the whole thing. [The Golden Comanche] mask beyond the suit. For me the suit is not more important than the Indian. Never will I require a guy to mask at this suit level of greatness more than I want him to mask in his greatness as an Indian," said Pardo.[13] By Indian greatness, Pardo means an Indian who will do what the Big Chief asks. Indians have to be straight on language, throwing signals, and being able to dance and sing the Indian song canon.

Sunday evening Mardi Gras Indian "practices," which often occur in neighborhood bars, are the place where these Indian skills are honed. Some of the practices feature African and Western style drums while others are driven by tambourines, clapping, and the clacking of keys against beer bottles. After a song begins, twenty minutes may go by before it is finished. The first song is always the same: "Indian Red."

The drums or tambourines stake out a rhythm against which the Chief will improvise verse against the tribe's persistent response line. Lead singers will trade off but the song continues.

As the dance commences, members of the tribe, sometimes wearing Indian braids, journey out onto the crowded barroom floor and open a space. If Indians from another tribe are spotted, competing Flag Boys, Spy Boys, Wild Men, and others line up and wait their moment to meet their adversaries on the dance floor. The dancing is competitive and aggressive, and the participants face each other directly throughout. The dance and music are punctuated by defiant whoops and cries from the

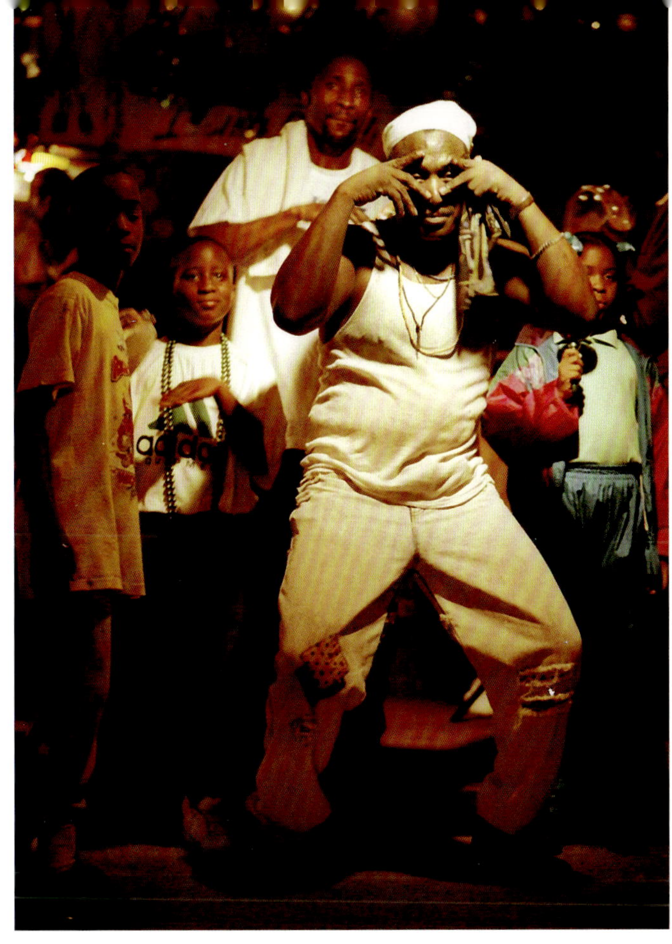

Indian practice at Kemp's Lounge with Ivory Holmes of the Golden Arrows, 1996. Photo by John McCusker.

Indian practice, Kemp's Lounge, 1996. Photo by John McCusker.

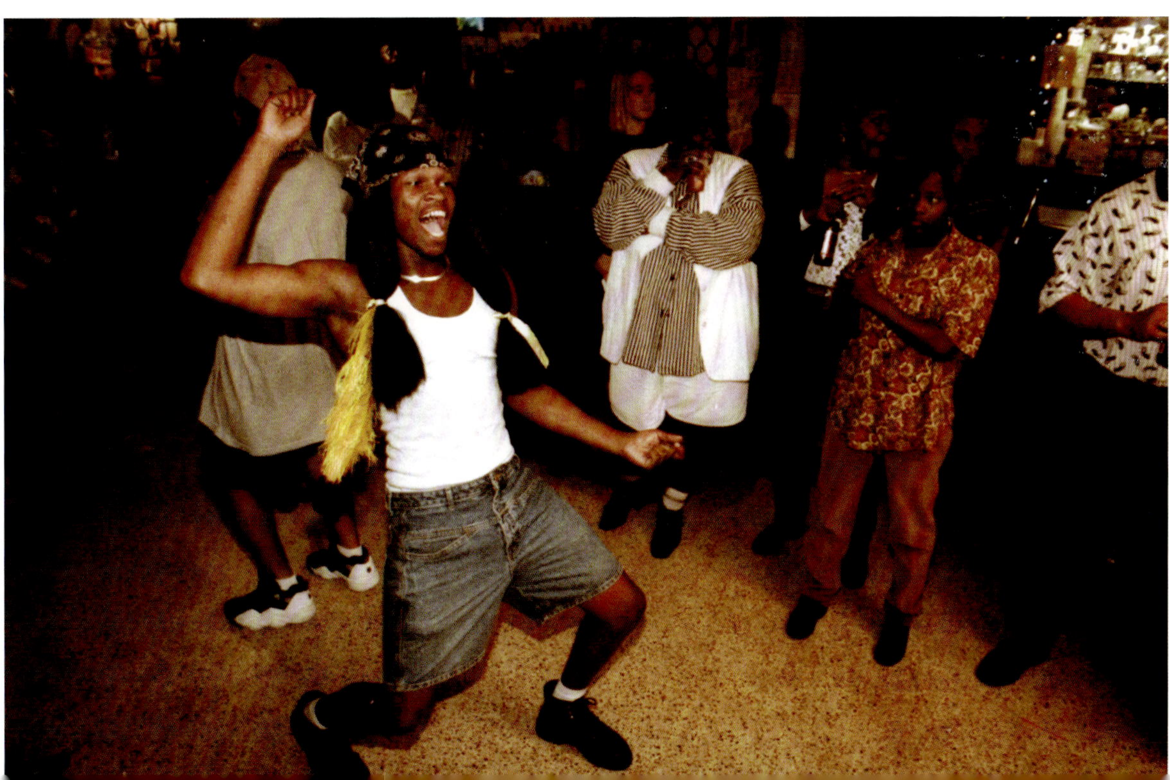

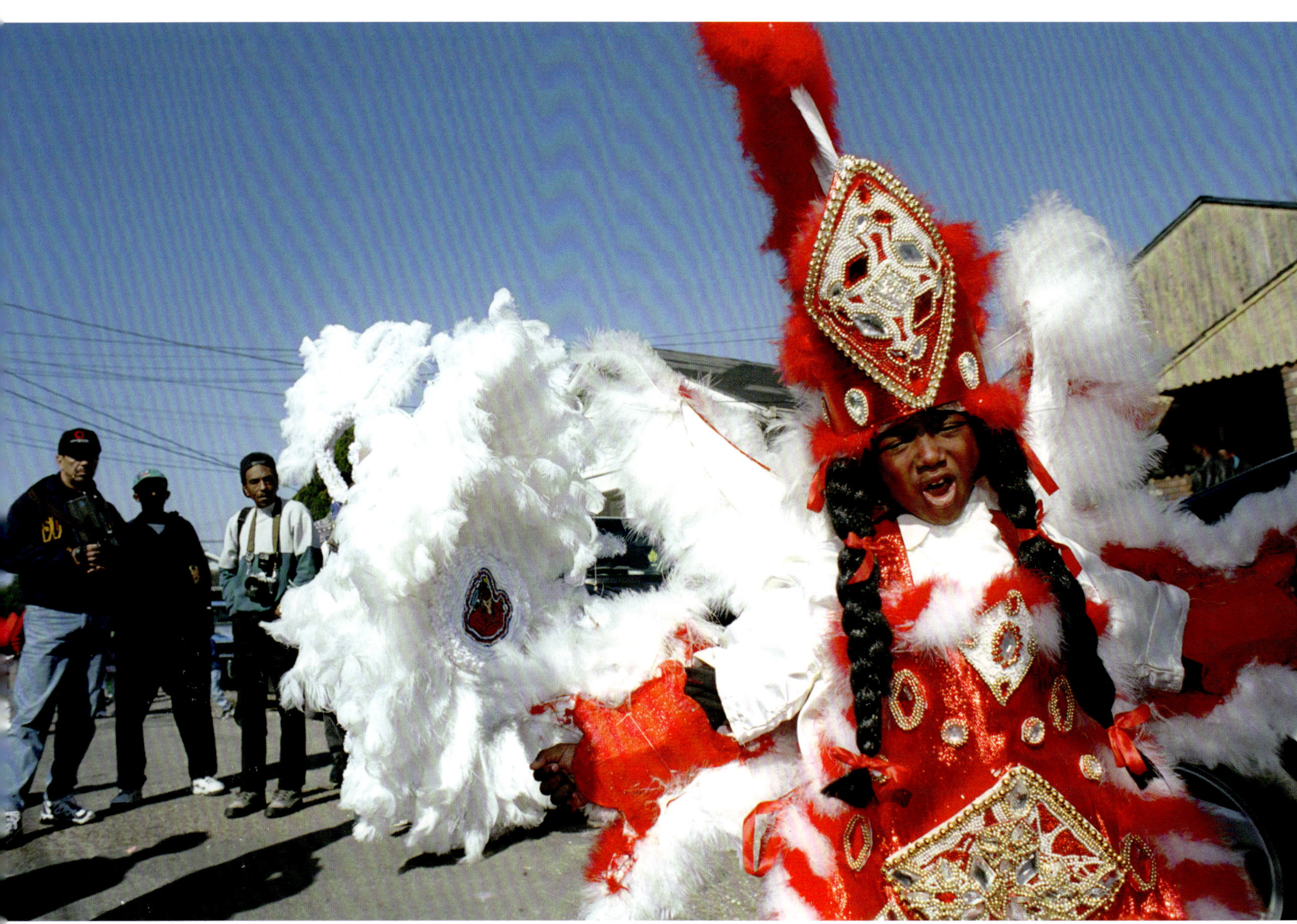

David Dejan, of the Flaming Arrows, lets out a cry of "Little Chief got boom, boom in the morning" on Mardi Gras 1997. Photo by John McCusker.

respective participants as they duel on the dance floor. But it is respectful, and the dance-off often ends with a hug. This display of language, dance, and music—in a spectacle African but not African, Indian but not Indian—contains elements both of improvisation and historical retentions of dance and collective black music making on Sundays, a tradition with antecedents in the city's colonial days. Yet vestiges of culture still older reside amid the cries of "Jockomo" against the drums pounding in syncopated cadence as the dancers stake their claim on the barroom floor.

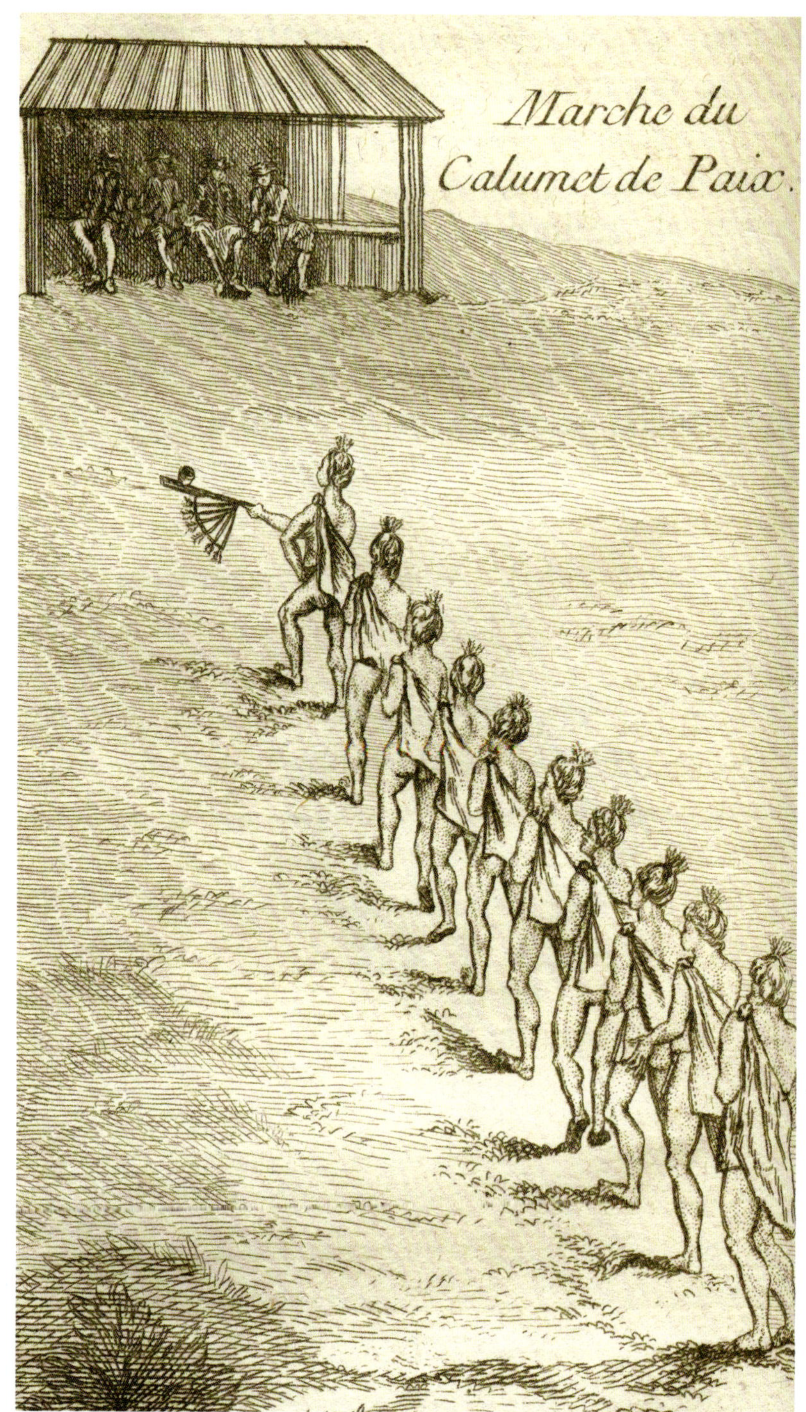

"Marche du Calumet de Paix" (woodcut) from Le Page Du Pratz, *Histoire de la Louisiane* (1758), depicting the peace pipe procession in New Orleans in 1718. This is the first known public musical procession in the city's history, concluding the war between the French and the Chitimacha. The Historic New Orleans Collection, Gift of Mrs. Henry C. Pitot in memory of Henry C. Pitot, 92-462-RL.

CHAPTER TWO

Balbancha

Long before the city, there was the river. Not only did it carry water, and thus life, across the continent, but with its myriad tributaries, this vast confluence also formed the main artery of long-distance transportation. Above all, the river gathered many groups of people together. Centuries ago, prior to Europeans and Africans arriving in North America, the "Mississippi"—an Algonquian name meaning "Great River"—was both a superhighway and a center of gravity for many families, bands, clans, tribes, and larger linguistic communities. The resulting nexus of cultures and tongues is reflected in other names that were given to the river by people who lived in the area that was to become lower Louisiana. At times, the local name was recorded as "Malabanchia," "Malbanchya," and "Barbancha," all of which are associated with the name "Balbancha," indicating a "place of foreign languages" (related to the Choctaw verb *balbaha*, "to speak a foreign language").[1] This was true both in the very remote past as well as in the early years of the United States. By the time of the Louisiana Purchase, the New Orleans region constituted the "most compactly multilingual part of the United States."[2] Over many decades, this name was applied by the Choctaw and other Native groups to the French colonial city that grew into the American metropolis near the mouth of the river. New Orleans, the recipient of all the flowing waters and population influxes, was indeed *Balbancha*, a remarkable place of many strange languages.

Just as the languages met and mingled along the river and the city, innumerable musical traditions flowed together. Balbancha—with an air of mystery and chaos, like a Babel of the New World, embodying a furious and continous recombination of sounds—became the city that is now known throughout the world for its distinctive musical idioms. But before delving into the complex mixtures of musical creation, before tracing the nuances of identity that have emerged from contact between many cultural groups over the past three hundred years, we should always keep in mind that the original populations in the lower Mississippi River valley were singing and dancing here long before the city existed. There is, in fact, a prehistory of New Orleans music. Those distinctive indigenous traditions continued after Louisiana had become part of the United States, while songs and styles were simultaneously being adapted and intertwined with African and European musical practices. As will become clear, drums and percussion instruments were especially widespread and shared among different groups, ritualized greetings proved critical, and a certain indigenous phrase has survived and shifted throughout the centuries, hidden within a vocalization that is both ancient and current—a lyric that sings the history of New Orleans.

When it comes to understanding the earliest music of the lower Missisipi River valley, besides extrapolating back from current native pratices and blended traditions, we have only fragmentary traces to go by—mostly in the form of material artifacts such as musical instruments. Much of our knowledge is inevitably derived from colonial archives. While reading the earliest accounts written during the colonial period, we must remember that all of the archival materials we have are heavily filtered by the experiences of European colonists and missionaries.[3] In a trenchant turn of phrase, Patricia Galloway suggests that producing narratives from such materials is tantamount to the effort to "wring blood from the stones of European incomprehension and representation of Native behavior and testimony."[4] Nonetheless, despite "discursive distortions," we can still try to restore as much of the context as possible by identifying the social, economic, and political circumstances of interaction, so we can "get closer to at least hearing echoes of Native words and seeing outlines of Native actions."[5] Moreover, while sifting through the colonial writings, we might listen more carefully to those non-Native witnesses who had more experiences living and interacting with indigenous groups, showing sympathetic feelings for the people they knew, and having a strong drive to understand the cultural traditions they encountered.

As we trace the specifically Native threads of tradition, we should also keep in mind that cultural blendings of disparate groups happened before European colonialism shifted the landscape. The peace pipe ceremony, which plays an important role in the history of New Orleans music, was given, borrowed, and spread first among different Native American groups in the middle of the continent, then later adopted by the French and carried to different regions by both indigenous people and French-speaking explorers, missionaries, and colonists. Each of these groups played a part in distributing calumet ceremonialism all the way down the Mississippi River valley. Throughout the process, different Native groups adopted the peace pipe and added their own specific traditions to what became a complex ritual of interaction, including singing and playing musical instruments. As will become clear later, different types of ceremonies also played a large part in fostering musical interactions, and among the Native American groups, the Acolapissa (also "Colapissas") and Choctaw communities stand out as having an especially strong and continuous impact on New Orleans music history.

Indeed, the sharing of musical practices stretches back to the earliest days of the French colony of Louisiana. For glimpses of these interactions, we are fortunate to have the narrative written by André Pénicaut, a carpenter who had traveled with Iberville to Louisiana in 1698–1699. In his famous and detailed account, he described many experiences living and working alongside Native Americans; besides the months he spent with the Natchez, he also made extended visits to several other groups during the more than twenty years he lived in Louisiana. In early May of 1706, Pénicaut volunteered to get food supplies from a nearby settlement of Acolapissa and Natchitoches since he "understood and spoke their language well and was even a friend of the chiefs of both these nations." With three days of rations and accompanied by eleven other Frenchmen, he set out from Fort Louis to the shore of Lake Pontchartrain, stayed a couple of days in the village, and participated in social events:

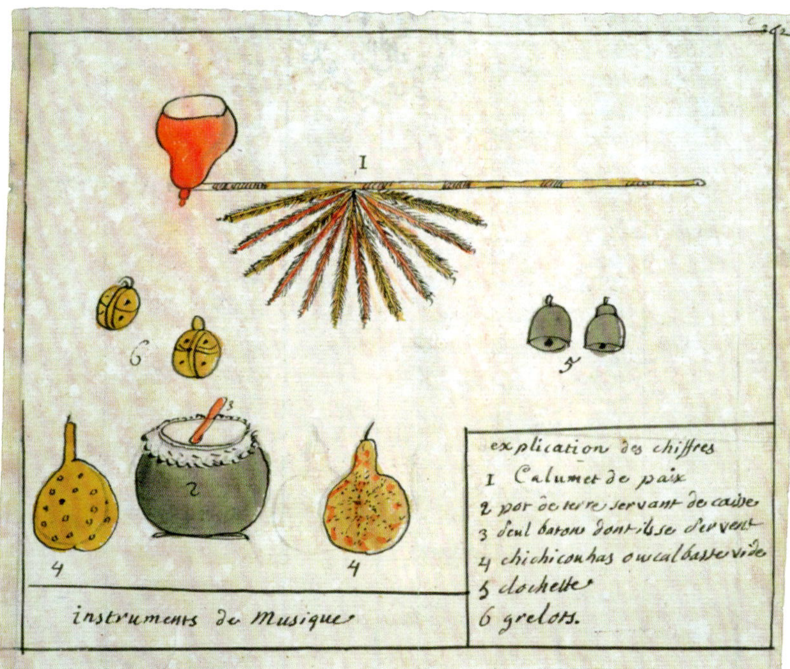

"Instruments de Musique" (watercolor) by Jean-François-Benjamin Dumont de Montigny, Mémoire de Lxx Dxx officier ingenieur (1747), Ayer MS 257. In addition to the calumet de paix, please note the drum and two "chichicouhas." Courtesy of the Ayer Collection, Newberry Library, Chicago, IL.

> We had in our group a companion named Picard, who had brought a violin with him. He could play it well enough to have these savages do some figure-dancing in step. They had us nearly dying of laughter, for the musical instrument had the whole village drawn up around Picard; it was the most comical sight in the world to see them open their eyes in amazement and every now and then cut the most comical capers ever seen. But it was quite another matter when they saw us dance a minuet—two boys dancing together. They would gladly have spent the whole night watching us and listening to the violin, had not the Chief of the Colapissas, fearing we were tired out, come to tell us that lodgings were assigned to us. All of them wanted to have us in their homes: the Chief of the Colapissas reserved the violin player to lodge with him.[6]

The next evening, the tables were turned as everyone laughed at Picard trying to keep up with the indigenous drummer and singers:

> When the sun had sunk low and all had eaten supper, we danced, as on the evening before, quite far into the night. Their dances . . . are conducted to the sound of a little drum. Our musician endeavored to keep time with the drum and the singers' voices. Although he made a most painful attempt that drew upon all his skill and caused us all to laugh out loud, he never was able to approximate their rhythm; and, as a matter of fact, their singing is more savage than the savages themselves. Although it is an incessant repetition, Picard could not get their pitch; but he made amends by teaching many of the girls in the village to dance the minuet and *la bourée.*

The first documented public event involving a musical procession in New Orleans is the "Marche du Calumet de Paix" (Peace Pipe March), which took place soon after Bienville founded the city in the spring of 1718.[7] Although the calumet ceremony was a relatively recent practice in the lower Mississippi River valley, it was linked to tightly structured, ritualized protocols of interaction that stretched back for centuries, including the "playing of a flute-like instrument," which had in earlier periods "served an analogous role" to the calumet throughout North America.[8] By the beginning of the eighteenth century, the French had learned how critical the calumet was in establishing good relations with indigenous groups. While it could be an ambiguous symbol that masked underlying hostility, the presentation of the calumet usually conferred the "ability to create peaceful interaction."[9] Bienville's older brother, Iberville, certainly understood its usefulness, having made "carvings on trees of his three ships, along with a depiction of a man carrying a calumet of peace" and presenting to the chief of the Bayogoula a "custom-made calumet made of iron" in the unusual shape of a ship and having a "white flag adorned with a fleur-de-lis" [and] "ornamented with glass beads."[10] In addition to smoking the pipe itself, the calumet ritual "involved elaborate processions, lengthy speeches, feasting, gift exchanges, and dancing," including "physical contact in the form of rubbing, the seating of participants on mats or skins, and the beating of posts coordinated with the recitation of war heroics."[11] Of course, it also involved singing and playing percussion instruments. Marc-Antoine Caillot, who worked in New Orleans as a clerk for the Company of the Indies from 1729 to 1731, wrote in his memoir about "how they perform the calumet ceremony when they come to the commander's house in New Orleans": "When they have finished making their speeches, four worthies get up, along with four Indians, and dance the calumet dance, all painted and ornamented with different types of feathers, to the sound of an earthen pot covered with a deerskin, ornamented with many bells and accompanied by their voices. This makes music as bizarre as their movements and dances."[12]

The musical procession in New Orleans in 1718 represented the culmination of the peace settlement after a ruthless war conducted by the French against the Chitimacha that had lasted several years and ended in the mass enslavement of the latter, who were the first group in the New Orleans area to suffer this particular kind of calamity on a large scale.[13] According to a letter sent from Arkansas Post in 1727 by Father Paul du Poisson, the Jesuit missionary (or "black robe," a term that is often used when a "man of the cloth" appears among Native Americans), Chief Framboise was the leader of the Chitimacha who "descended with his tribe to New Orleans to chant the calumet before the new Governor."[14] The colonist Antoine-Simon Le Page du Pratz was present at the ceremony and wrote a firsthand account of the proceedings in his *Histoire de la Louisiane* published in 1758.[15] It includes a description of the musical procession, how the singing dancers kept time with percussion instruments, after the Chitimacha emerged from their boats upon their arrival at the settlement of New Orleans. This particular passage, which was omitted from the earliest English translation and all subsequent reprints from the late eighteenth century, provides a unique glimpse of indigenous musical practices at the founding of the city:

> I was with Monsieur Bienville when they arrived on the river in several pirogues. They approached while singing the song of the Calumet, which they shook in the air, and in rhythm, to announce their delegation, which effectively consisted of the Spokesperson, as the people say, or Chancellor and a dozen other men. On these occasions they are adorned with the finest

> things, according to their taste, never failing to have a Chichicois in their hand, shaking it also in rhythm ["en cadence"].
>
> There were not more than a hundred paces from the place they disembarked to Monsieur Bienville's cabin. However, this little bit of land sufficed for them to keep their way nearly half an hour, always marching to the measure and cadence which regulated them.[16]

Le Page du Pratz added a note about the *chichicois*: "The Chichicois is a gourd pierced with two holes, for inserting a short stick, with the lower end serving as a handle. They put pebbles inside to make sound; in the absence of pebbles, they put in dry beans or kidney beans. It is with this instrument that they keep the beat while singing."[17] We thus have our first description of musical instruments being played at the beginning of New Orleans, the equivalent of shakers being used in a public parade. The word that Le Page du Pratz uses for the gourd rattle, <chichicois>, is the more common spelling from among a large variety of forms recorded in different accounts from the same historical period. The same term appears in Pénicaut's report of the ceremonies held by several indigenous groups in March 1699 at Fort Maurepas, which Iberville had just established, where they danced "'au son de leur chichicois' (to the sound of their chichicois)" and beat a water drum: "They have another instrument, too, made of an earthen pot in the shape of a kettle, containing a little water and covered with a deer skin stretched tight across the potmouth like a tambour; this they beat with two drumsticks, making as much noise as our drums."[18] Another spelling variant is mentioned by Jesuit father Mathurin Le Petit, in a letter sent from New Orleans in 1730, in his description of the Natchez using their "sicicouet."[19]

Most of the French colonists and missionaries would have been acquainted with this term, which was widespread among many different indigenous groups, through the medium of Mobilian Jargon, a trade language that was spoken by Native Americans, Europeans, and Africans throughout a large part of what is now the southeastern United States.[20] The spelling <šešekowa> represents the most likely reconstituted form in Mobilian Jargon, which could refer to a variety of percussion instruments,

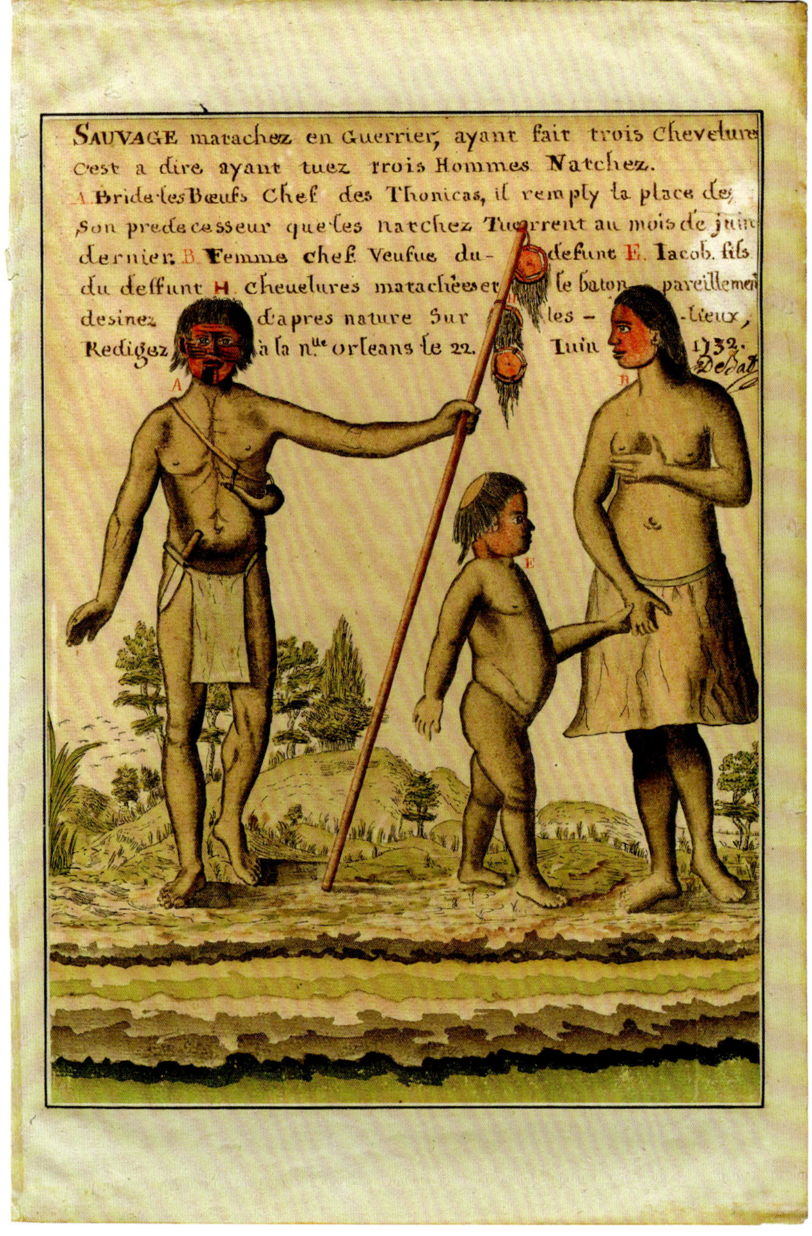

"Sauvage Matachez en Guerrier, Nouvelle Orleans, le 22 Juin, 1732" (watercolor). The Tunica Chief Bride les Boeufs, "painted as warrior," is wearing a breechcloth, knife, and powder horn, and holding a staff with scalps. He is accompanied by his wife and a boy named Jacob, the son of a deceased Tunica chief. Gift of the Estate of Belle J. Bushnell, 1941. Courtesy the Peabody Museum of Archaeology and Ethnology, Harvard University, PM# 41–72–10/18.

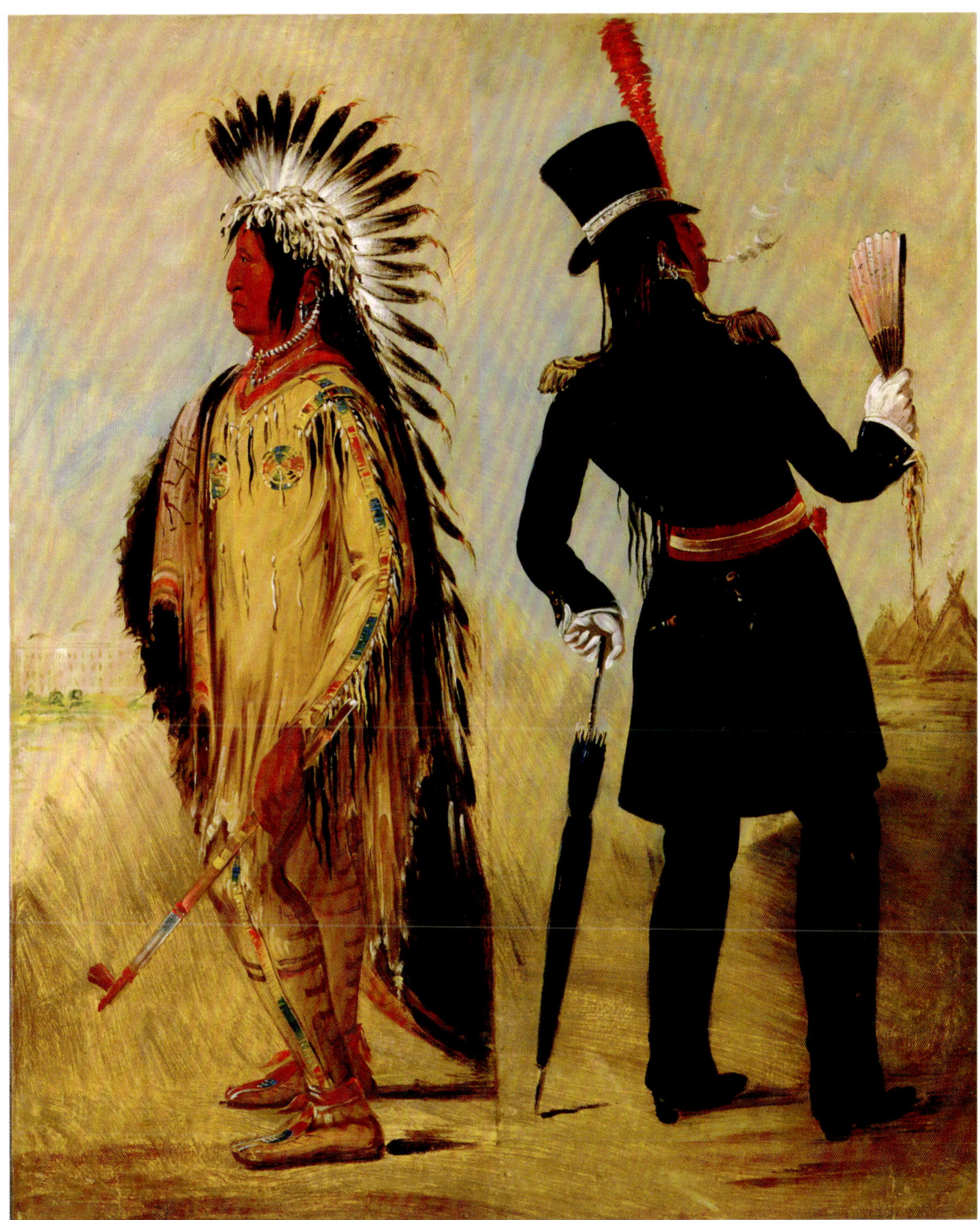

"Wi-jún-jon, Pigeon's Egg Head (The Light) Going To and Returning From Washington," 1837–1839, by George Catlin. Though he did not dress in the "French manner," this Assiniboine chief showed a deft adaptability not unlike that of the Tunica more than a century earlier. Smithsonian American Art Museum, Washington, DC / Art Resource, New York.

including gourd rattles and tambourine-like drums that were used in ceremonies throughout the Mississippi River valley.[21] In view of its likely origins, this term for the gourd rattle encapsulates its role in the vast network of trade and cultural exchange that existed throughout North America, as it appears to be one of the very few Algonquian-derived terms in Mobilian Jargon: "Because of the frequent occurrence of the variant forms of this Algonquian word in the literature, it may be supposed that, if any Algonquian word entered Mobilian [Jargon], the word for rattle did."[22] At the same time, the name likely has an onomatopoeic origin, as it mimics the sound that the *chichicois* makes. As it is picked up and given a good shake, the pebbles rattle within the hollow gourd: "shi-shi-kwa!"

Describing events that took place just a few years after the Chitimacha calumet ceremony in New Orleans, in late 1721 and early 1722, the Jesuit missionary Father Pierre F. X. de Charlevoix offers an important account of ongoing exchanges between European colonists and indigenous people. As he traveled down the Mississippi River, he met the chief of the Tunica and was impressed by the exhibition of French cultural traits: "[The chief] was dressed in the French fashion [and] carries on trade with the French, supplying them with horses and poultry, and is very expert at business . . . He has long since stopped wearing Indian clothes, and takes great pride in always appearing well-dressed."[23] Charlevoix assumes that a complete transformation has taken place, a seeming vindication of the deliberate "Frenchification" policies that were being carried out farther north, in the Illinois Country and other areas in the Great Lakes region, which had more than a century of French colonial presence.[24] In fact, Tunica chief Cahura-Joligo was described by another chronicler as "baptized and almost Frenchified."[25] Nonetheless, by triangulating the various written accounts, we catch a glimpse of what was likely an astute strategy on the part of the Tunica chief: "though he was observed as dressing in the French manner and owning a complete suit of French clothes, at least one chronicler described him as preferring to carry his breeches rather than wear them."[26] In effect, some indigenous groups and individuals were deploying cultural symbols they had gleaned from the French, creatively appropriating new resources to steer perceptions of themselves as potential allies or trade partners, or perhaps for other purposes that remain unclear.

An even more astonishing instance of transcultural exchange awaited Charlevoix as he approached settlements of the Acolapissa just upriver from New Orleans, on January 4, 1722: "As soon as we came in sight of the village, there was a drumbeat, and as soon as we disembarked, I was complimented on behalf of the chief. I was rather surprised, while approaching the village, to see the drummer dressed in a long robe which was part red and part white, with red-and-white sleeves. I asked about the origin of this custom, and was told that it was not very ancient, that a governor of Louisiana had made a present of this drum to these Indians, who have always been our faithful allies, [but] that this kind of official's uniform was of their own invention."[27] We have no other details about what kind of drum this was, which materials it was made from, or whether it was played with a stick.[28] In any case, the Acolapissa were highly attuned to protocols of interaction and had possibly considered that it would be "good form" to use this musical gift to greet other French colonists. This documentation of the Acolapissa drum is also an important reminder of how easily one can ascribe timelessness to an "exotic" cultural practice. Though "preoccupied with the question of Indian origins," Charlevoix was acutely aware of the possibility of change: "'New events . . . and a new arrangement of things give rise to new traditions, which efface the former, and are themselves effaced in their turn.'"[29] According to what we might call the "Charlevoix principle," we can never be too sure of how old or new a particular tradition might be, whether it has been handed down for generations within a specific cultural group or, instead, a relatively new phenomenon that has emerged from a recent encounter between groups.

In 1730, eight years after Charlevoix heard the Acolapissa drum, another musical encounter suggested how deeply blended European and indigenous cultural practices had become as the French continued to settle the lower reaches of the Mississippi River valley. During the summer of that year, a delegation of indigenous groups from the Illinois Country—the region between the Great Lakes and the upper Mississippi River that played "an important role in Louisiana's internal economy"—trav-

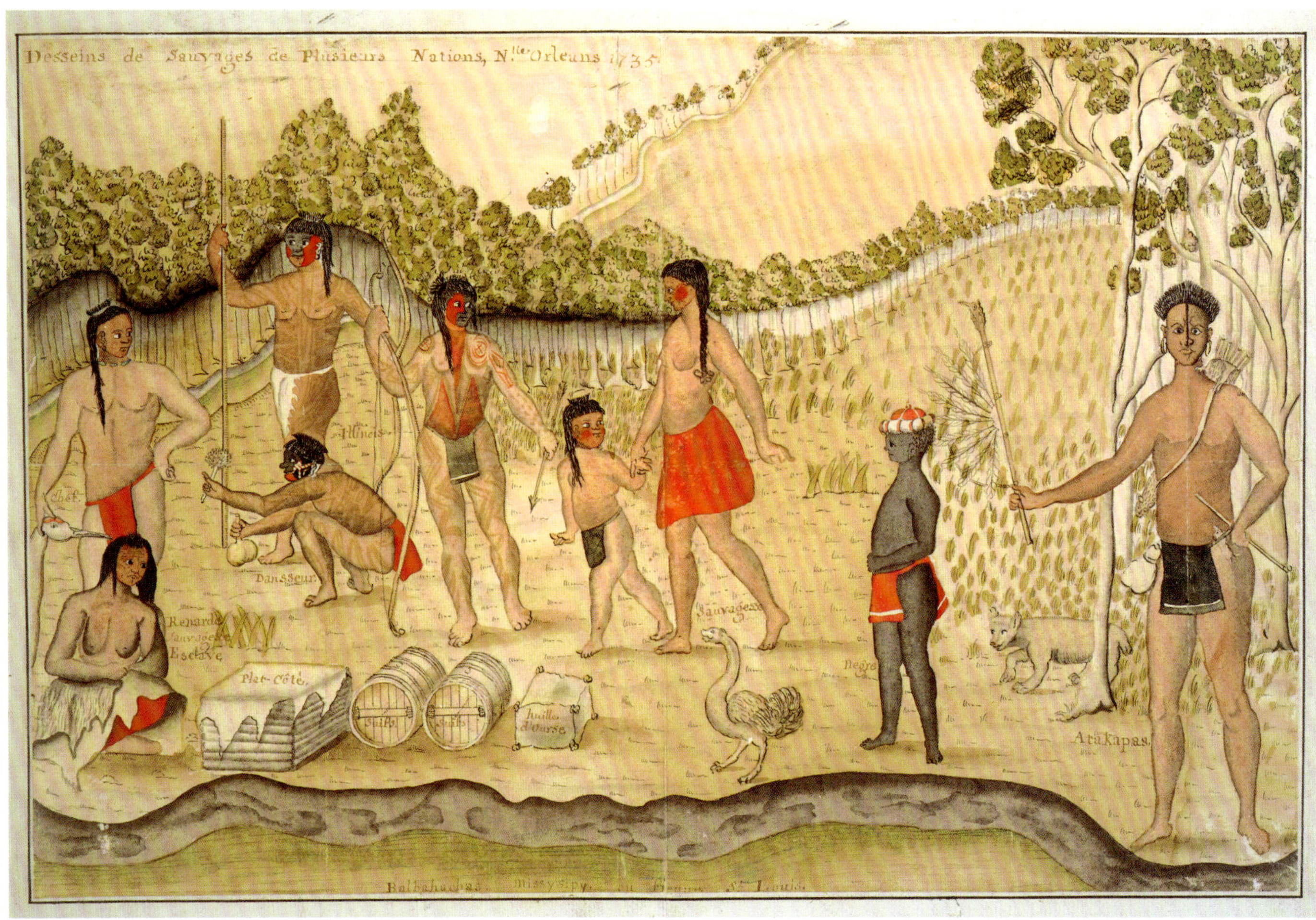

"Desseins de sauvages de plusieurs nations" (pen and ink with watercolor, 1735) by Alexandre De Batz. This image depicts individuals of different indigenous groups standing along the Mississippi River at New Orleans. At the bottom, part of the inscription reads "Balbahachas." Gift of the Estate of Belle J. Bushnell, 1941. Courtesy the Peabody Museum of Archaeology and Ethnology, Harvard University, PM# 41–72–10/20.

eled to New Orleans on a diplomatic mission.[30] On a more overtly political level, this was a gesture of solidarity with the French several months after the Natchez had annihilated Fort Rosalie, in late autumn of 1729, when wounded and dazed survivors straggled into the city to tell the news that "all was fire and blood" upriver.[31] The burgeoning population of New Orleans was excited by the arrival of the Illinois, led by Chief Chicagou and Chief Mamantouensa (leaders of the Michigamea and Kaskaskia, respectively): "People crowded into the church to witness the spectacle of 'savage' Indians worshiping and singing before the altar. The highlight for the audience was a responsive Gregorian chant in which Ursuline nuns 'chanted the first Latin couplet . . . and the Illinois continued the other couplets in their language in the same tone.'"[32] Of course, this was much more than a syncretic ceremony: it had become a combination of spiritual uplift and public entertainment. This performance of bilingual antiphony reflected the growing contact between Europeans and indigenous people, but more specifically the French and Kaskaskia, with the latter recognized as "the most Christianized of the Native peoples in the region [i.e., Pays des Illinois or Illinois Country]."[33] After singing their words to European melodies, the Illinois also "presented a calumet to the French governor," blending "traditional notions of Illinois reciprocity" into the ceremony.[34]

This complex event reveals how the pattern of French and Native interaction in the upper Mississippi River valley amounted to an "empire by collaboration."[35] Even if the social arrangements were far from idyllic, "the diverse inhabitants of Illinois lived together, spoke the same languages, and intermarried."[36] In effect, "French colonists and Illinois Indians [had] developed a flexible interracial order based on a huge network of kinship and fictive kinship linking together French and Native peoples."[37] Moreover, as in other areas in the middle of North America, elements of "native ground" existed in the Illinois Country; that is, places where "Indians were more often able to determine the form and content of inter-cultural relations than were their European would-be colonizers."[38]

This call and response between the Ursuline nuns and the Illinois in New Orleans also demonstrated how music could serve as a medium for interacting senses of spirituality. Several decades of contact with "black robes" had led to a considerable number of conversions to Christianity. One of the most well known of the indigenous Christians of the late seventeenth and early eighteenth centuries was Marie Rouensa, the daughter of a Kaskaskia chief.[39] After marrying the French colonist Michel Accault, she prevailed upon her parents to embrace Christianity, and likewise exerted a religious influence on her new husband: "According to [Jesuit missionary] Gravier, Accault acknowledged 'that he no longer recognizes himself, and can attribute his conversion solely to his wife's prayers and exhortations, and to the example that she gives him.'"[40] The intriguing circumstance of an indigenous person inspiring a European to return to Christian practices in the 1690s is similar to the role reversal that Father Le Petit noted in 1730 between the indigenous people visiting New Orleans and the French residents of that city. At the same time he celebrated the Christian practices of the Illinois in his letter to Father d'Avaugour, Procurator of the Missions in North America, he expressed his shock at the lack of religious practices among the French soldiers in New Orleans, as well as their poor taste in music:

> In the course of the day, and after supper, [the members of the Illinois delegation] often chant, either alone or together, different prayers of the Church, such as the *Dies irae*, etc., *Vexilla Regis*, etc., *Stabat Mater*, etc. To listen to them, you would easily perceive that they took more delight and pleasure in chanting these holy Canticles, than the generality of the Savages, and even more than the French receive from chanting their frivolous and often dissolute songs.
>
> You would be astonished, as I myself have been, on arriving at this Mission, to find that a great number of our French are not, by any means, so well instructed in Religion as are these Neophytes: they [i.e., the indigenous people] are scarcely unacquainted with any of the histories of the old and new Testament; the manner in which they hear the holy Mass and receive the Sacraments, is most excellent; their Catechism, which has fallen into my hands, with the literal translation made by Father Boullanger [*sic*], is a perfect model for those who have need of such works in their new Missions.[41]

In fact, "[u]nlike many other Indian groups, the Illinois were not hostile to missionaries and were open to prayer."[42] However, it is also important to keep in mind that, rather than a fixed fusion between European and indigenous ways, this wave of Christianization was part of an "ongoing set of adaptations."[43] If we take a look at the translation of the catechism mentioned by Le Petit, we can see that Native Christianity included many elements that were not completely synonymous with European spiritual concepts. Instead of the usual <Di8> ("Dieu" written with the grapheme "8," which could alternately represent certain vowels and "w"), the first line of Le Boullenger's version of the Apostle's Creed has <kichemanet8a>

"great spirit," which draws upon the Algonquian concept of *manitou*, which among other things could refer to "the spirit that gave a thing or a feature of the landscape, such as a rock or a waterfall, the power to influence human affairs."[44] It is interesting to note there was a wide range of differing insights and strategies among the Jesuit missionaries. While Le Boullenger saw fit to incorporate an indigenous spiritual concept into the Christian catechism as a reference to the Lord Almighty, other "black robes" would sometimes interpret *manitou* as "demon."[45] In fact, the term <manet8a>, identified as a "key word in the Illinois-Jesuit religious encounter," could be translated as "spirit," "God," or even "medicine" or "snow," revealing the challenges facing the missionaries as they tried to "graft French ideas onto Native terms."[46] Even the use of the calumet among the Illinois was a "recent adoption" in response to encounters with Siouan groups to the west, an "accommodation to the [ceremonial] language of their new territory," as the various Illinois groups moved in response to warfare with the Iroquois and widespread European incursions.[47]

In New Orleans, diplomatic ceremonies involving the calumet were common throughout the eighteenth century, and often involved many different indigenous groups:

> New Orleans hosted a series of ceremonial visits in the autumn of 1769, when Alexandro O'Reilly summoned lower Mississippi River tribes after completing the military occupation of Louisiana for Spain. On September 30, chiefs, interpreters, and other persons from the Tunicas, Taensas, Pacanas, Houmas, Bayogoulas, Ofogoulas, Chaouachas, and Ouachas approached the general's house with song and music. Inside he greeted them under a canopy in the company of prominent residents of New Orleans. Each chief placed his weapon at O'Reilly's feet and waved a feather fan over his head. O'Reilly accepted their fans, smoked their pipes, and clasped their hands.[48]

As various diplomatic missions came and went, there were Native Americans living in the city and its environs. "On the outskirts of New Orleans, groups of Houmas, Chitimachas, and Choctaws camped along Bayou St. John and Bayou Road [and in] the city's streets and in the marketplace,

Indian women peddled baskets, mats, sifters, plants, herbs, and firewood [while the men] sold venison, wildfowl, and cane blowguns and occasionally earned wages as day laborers and dockworkers."[49] Their involvement in city life was not restricted to economic activities: "Hundreds of Indians gathered in late winter to request gifts from officials and to join in the celebration of carnival."[50] While legal restrictions militated against the mixing of different groups, after several generations, "[m]any New Orleanians, identified as white, black, or free colored by the end of the eighteenth century, possessed various degrees of Indian ancestry."[51] Besides intermarriage, the intense social contact between groups promoted multilingualism, including various degrees of fluency in native languages. In the fall of 1826, a $200 reward was announced for anyone who could "apprehend and deliver" an escaped convict named John Simpson, known for his "florid complexion" and "red hair," describing him thus: "American by birth, but speaks the Spanish language well—he has lived some time among the Indians, and also speaks Choctaw."[52]

By the early 1800s, the New Orleans region was being swallowed by the growing political entity of the United States and adopting new categories of cultural identity in the process. The language of government was beginning to erase indigenous people from official records. In 1808, Governor William Claiborne remarked in a letter to James Madison that, in the region then known as the Orleans Territory, "there are now several hundred persons held as slaves, who are descended of Indian families," and only two years later, the Louisiana Supreme Court ruled that "persons of color may be descended from Indians on both sides."[53] Since the racial formation at the time had assumed tripartite division of whites, blacks, and *gens de couleur*, indigenous ancestry was effectively erased by fiat. The pervasive trope of the "vanishing Indian" that kept reappearing in public discourse throughout the following two centuries was thus facilitated by early bureaucratic maneuvers. This turned into a local variant of the "one-drop" rule: "Because of Anglo-American conceptions of race . . . anyone with visible or known African ancestry (one drop of African blood) was considered black for most purposes."[54] This prescription of racial categories persisted for many decades. Brian Klopotek explains further:

> People of mixed black, white, and Indian ancestry were classified as mulattoes by the 1910 census, undifferentiated from people of solely white and black ancestry. Surrounding populations in Louisiana acknowledged Indian ancestry in multiracial tribal communities by addressing them as Redbones, a derogatory term that denotes Indian, black, and white ancestry. The official census record, however, did not have a category to reflect that distinction, leading one to conclude that the record stated they were solely black and white instead of Indian . . .
>
> Similarly, in terms of previous federal acknowledgement of Indian communities, the BIA [Bureau of Indian Affairs] of the 1930s, because of the one-drop rule, extremely disinclined to treat communities with black ancestry as Indian tribes . . . Bureau records indicate that black ancestry among *some* Louisiana Indian groups made officials less inclined to serve *any* of the Louisiana tribes.[55]

There is evidence of many people in New Orleans of Native American and African descent in physical descriptions that appear in newspaper articles and advertisements through the middle of the nineteenth century. Sometimes in published criminal court proceedings but more often in personal ads that describe runaway slaves, there are phenotypical descriptions that often mention indigenous characteristics: "Louis is more Indian than Negro . . . wears long black hair parted in the centre, and has little or no beard."[56] Other advertisements focus on skin color and other facial features such as high cheekbones, which are attributed to Native American ancestry. Sometimes, an indigenous appearance is associated with being "Creole," which more often than not accompanies a remark that the person in question speaks French in addition to English. In fact, in keeping with the connotations of *Balbancha*, there are scores of runaway slaves described as knowing as many as two, three, or even four languages: "Harriet Tousaint . . . speaks French, English, and Spanish."[57] In 1859, there was a person who was being offered for sale as a "Body Servant," who would "suit any gentleman for traveling" and spoke "four languages—English, French, Spanish, and German."[58] The last language mentioned, incidentally, shows how the linguistic landscape of *Balban-*

cha was shifting by the second half of the nineteenth century. During the decade leading up to the Civil War and for several years after, a high tide of German speakers swept through the city, many continuing on their way to the Midwest, while some remained in the city long enough to purchase slaves, as suggested by this advertisement. Other cases of multilingualism help tell the story:

> TWENTY FIVE DOLLARS REWARD.—Ran away from David Lanaux's plantation, in St. Charles parish, HENRY, a bright mulatto, five feet six or seven inches high, strongly built, speaking English, French, and the Choctaw dialect. He formerly belonged to Mr. Beauregard, and was employed for some time in the office of the Bee. It is thought that he is in New Orleans, whence he will try to go to the other side of Lake Pontchartrain, or Westward. The above reward will be paid to whoever will lodge said runaway in any of the jails of this city or State.[59]

Besides encapsulating the harsh racial hierarchy prevailing in the middle of the century, this description offers a compressed account of what a runaway slave might experience and what options he or she might have. First of all, in Henry's case, since he could speak Choctaw, he likely had Native American ancestry or at least had close contact with Native Americans in and around New Orleans. He had already been sold at least once, and spent time in the city working in the office of the *Bee*, which was a well-established New Orleans newspaper—older than the *Picayune*—originally published only in French, but later adding English, and even Spanish, becoming a trilingual publication for a brief period. As many others in a similar predicament might do, Henry fled to the city, losing himself in the crowd, but clearly also seeking a way of traveling a longer distance in the shortest time possible. Another detail is significant: the idea that he might try to go to the north shore of Lake Pontchartrain suggests an awareness of that area being a safe haven for maroon slaves, especially those with Native ancestry, as Choctaws had lived on that side of Lake Pontchartrain during the entire colonial period, and stayed there as Louisiana became a part of the United States. In fact, even after Indian Removal and the

"Ball-play dance, Choctaw," 1834–35. Painter George Catlin was traveling through Indian Territory when he observed Choctaw stickball being played in the vicinity of present-day Oklahoma. "Choctaw men and women dance around their respective stakes, at intervals, during the night preceding the play. Four conjurors sit all night and smoke to the Great Spirit, at the point where the ball is to be started." Smithsonian American Art Museum, Washington, DC / Art Resource, New York.

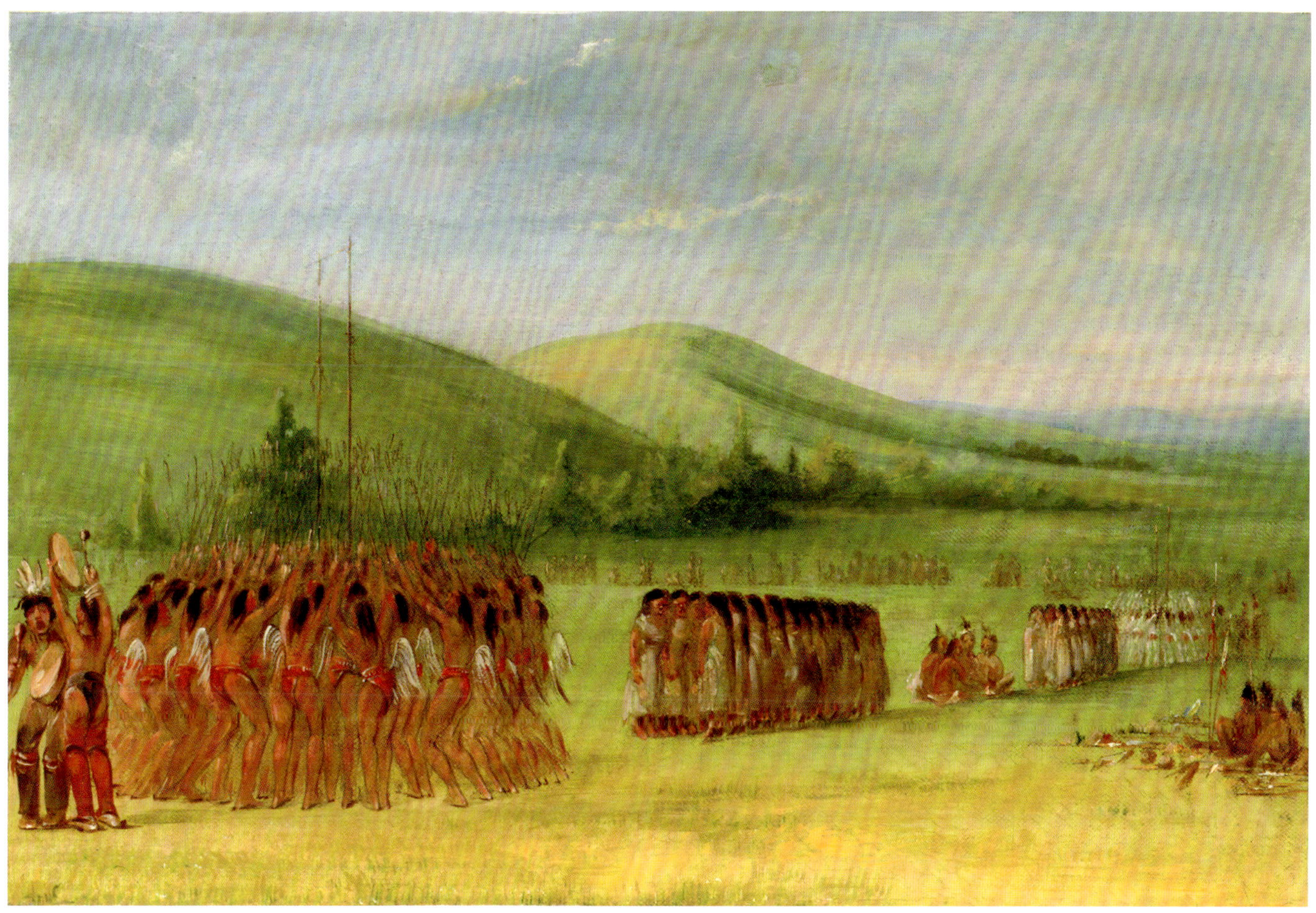

scourge of the Civil War and into the early twentieth century, there were still Choctaw communities living in that region, as described below.

Different indigenous groups continued to live in New Orleans and the surrounding region, often selling goods at public markets in the city. Another major realm of interaction between Native Americans and people of European and African ancestry was the sporting event called "Raquette" (variously named *ishtaboli, kapucha,* or *toli* in Choctaw), which was the "Crescent City's first popular, spectator sport," played throughout the 1800s and during the beginning years of the twentieth century.[60] "Racquette [*sic*] contests between Negro, white, and Indian teams, played then behind the city gates, were regular Sunday afternoon events by the time the United States acquired Louisiana," and in the early 1800s, "spectators assembled on the 'Communes de la Ville,' also known as Congo Plains, where players carrying short sticks in both hands tossed the small buckskin ball between two goal posts sometimes placed a half-mile apart."[61] Indeed, the playing field was where several cultural traditions overlapped in what sometimes became a violent frenzy, as Steward Culin reported to the Smithsonian Institution's Bureau of American Ethnology in 1901:

> The ball was put in play at the center flag, being tossed high in the air, and caught on the uplifted ball sticks. Then there was a wild rush across the field, the object being to secure and carry the ball and toss it against the tin plate, making a plat. The game was played with much vigor and no little violence. A blow across the shins with a racket is permissible, and broken heads are not uncommon. Play usually continues until dark, and, at the close, the winners sing Creole songs, reminding one of the custom at the close of the Choctaw game.[62]

Curiously enough, according to many newspaper reports throughout the late nineteenth century and early twentieth century, the initial toss of the ball up into the air was called the "bamboula," perhaps derived from Mobilian Jargon *babela*, but conflated with the famous dance associated with Congo Square and the musical composition by Louis Moreau Gottschalk. By comparing descriptions of the game and advertisements, we learn that it was likely pronounced in several different ways, reflected in various phonetic spellings, including "bambila" and even "bombeella."[63] In 1907, the Elks Lodge staged a massive three-day festival called "The Grand Bamboula." When queried about the meaning of the term "bamboula," Mayor Martin Behrman, who headed up the political organization known as the Choctaw Club, simply laughed and replied, "Oh, it means a little bit of everything."[64] Like an open space that can serve different social functions, such as a venue for musical performances or a setting for sporting events, the term "bamboula" apparently had taken on a variety of meanings in the public imagination, representing a convergence of different words as well as a convergence of cultures.

Native Americans would also occasionally sing and march through the streets of New Orleans. Choctaw musical processions in the 1820s were recounted in great detail by Father Adrien-Emmanuel Rouquette, a public figure widely known in the city during the last quarter of the nineteenth century. He spent many years not only acting as a missionary to the Choctaws of Louisiana but also living with them on the north shore of Lake Pontchartrain and gradually changing his life and even his physical appearance to match theirs—for example, by growing long hair—in a kind of embodied spiritual harmony. For this, he was called Chahta-Ima, "the one is like a Choctaw," and toward the end of his life he preferred to be known by this name, signing his various letters and essays accordingly. On the one hand, it is true that he had a distinctly romantic vision of life unsullied by so-called civilization, but as someone who was sympathetic to Native Americans at a time when many American citizens were not, and as someone who lived for a long time with the Choctaws, his voice is an important one to hear. In an interview conducted in the early 1880s, he recollects his childhood experiences in New Orleans during the early decades of the century, and in particular, shares details of Choctaws marching and singing in the streets of the city:

> When I was a child, in 1820, there were more Indians in the city than there were whites or negroes. Bayou St. John was lined with their encampments. A place was built on the Bayou Road to serve as a market, but the Indians took possession of it as a lodging place, and their claim to do so was not disputed. When they were intoxicated I heard their songs as they reeled through the streets, carrying bottles of whisky in their hands, and their faces painted blue and a bright red. As they approached doors and windows were always closed, and people ran to get out of their way, but I always mingled among them without being harmed. When there was a wedding the squaw bride was splendidly dressed. A little drum was beaten and a basket was carried around, in which all who were met were requested to drop in a contribution for the

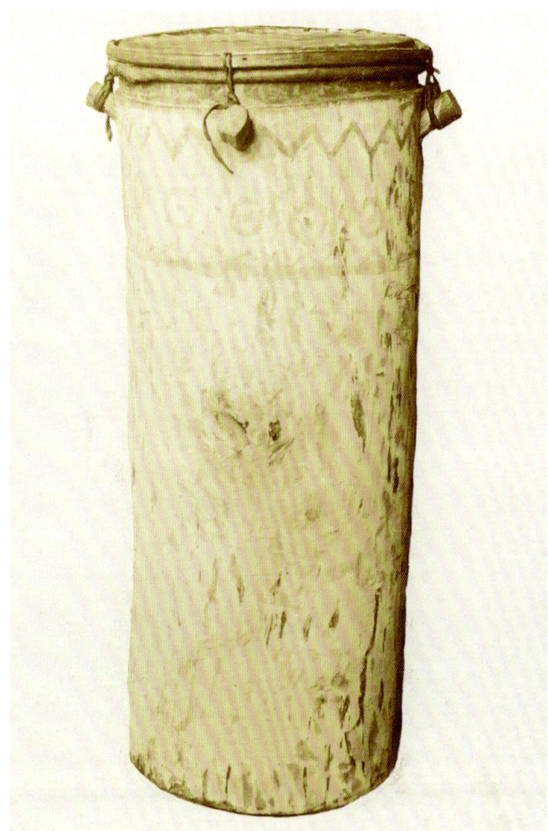

"Drum Made by Ahojeobe. THEY-BAH. Made by John at Bayou Lacombe, Louisiana" (1909). David I. Bushnell Jr. identified this drum as belonging to a Choctaw community living close to New Orleans on the north shore of Lake Pontchartrain. The size (thirty inches high) and construction of this drum are highly unusual for Native musical instruments in the region, suggesting a strong African cultural influence. In essence, this drum embodies the blending of musical traditions in the lower Mississippi River valley over the past three centuries. Gift of the Estate of Belle J. Bushnell, 1941. Courtesy the Peabody Museum of Archaeology and Ethnology, Harvard University, PM# 41-72-10/99968.563.

> benefit of the newly wedded twain. Men and women who performed this ceremony drank freely and made their rounds singing. The shrill voices of the squaws mingling with the warlike bass voices of the men would make you shudder. In 1835, very few of them remained in the city. They had returned to their old homes in Alabama. They had to go across St. Tammany and Washington parishes to get to Pearl River, which was the stream on which bordered the Choctaw country.[65]

Such Choctaw wedding parties, replete with musical accompaniment, were apparently not too unusual for New Orleans streets, as a similar band of singers and drummers was described marching through the city in 1839 with "a miniature kettle drum" played by a "single stick drummer," while singers "of both sexes and various ages, sounded every note on the gamut from D flat to X sharp," with all "dressed as gaudily as red paint, feathers and figured calicoes could make them."[66]

The prolonged cultural contact over the centuries had specific musical manifestations. By the beginning of the twentieth century, the Bayou Lacombe Choctaw "used a unique wooden or vine strip" around drum heads to tighten them, a feature "similar to African drum traditions" and potentially borrowed from drumming practices in Congo Square, in nearby New Orleans.[67] By the end of the War of 1812, the Choctaw had "borrowed the European snare drum, stretching a taut cord across the bottom of their cedar bucket drums to give them the 'snap' of European drums."[68] The use of European-style drums among the Choctaws probably began even earlier. In 1781, just as the American colonies were triumphing over the British in their bid for independence, the Choctaw chief Franchimastabé "led a war party to assist the British in Pensacola against Spanish attack," and even though this particular effort failed, the Choctaw warriors captured four Spanish drums.[69] It is likely that these drums were subsequently kept and played by the Choctaws or perhaps inspired the later manufacture of snare drums. Of course, invoking the Charlevoix principle, we cannot be too certain that any of these developments were necessarily wholesale adoptions from other cultural groups, but they certainly suggest that a significant amount of transcultural interaction had taken place over the past few centuries.[70] People did not share all of their life experiences across racial and socioeconomic lines, but music—like language—is a porous realm that allows the sharing of sounds.

Again we return to the story of Chahta-Ima, who acted as a key intermediary between different cultural groups. On May 11, 1858, close to the Choctaw village Buchuwa north of Lake Pontchartrain, Chahta-Ima was invited to attend the Choctaw Mourning Feast as *achuffa na hullo*, the only white person who was allowed to experience this sacred ritual. In the afternoon, as the final preparations for the feast were being made, Rouquette observed that his "Choctaw hosts 'were all tattooed' wearing robes of varying colors, 'trimmed with laces, pearls, and feathers, of dazzling gorgeousness.'"[71] The feast would be held under a "kind of shed covered with leaves."[72] Just at sunset, fires were lighted in the woods, and a single woman began to sing lamentations, gradually joined by other women who formed a circle, then men joined in this communal expression of grief. "From dark until midnight the chants and lamentations continued. First the low, stifled tones of lamentation followed by periods of piercing shrieks and thrilling notes of heartrending woe and anguish."[73] Just before midnight, silence fell among everyone present. The "bold and warlike" dance, *hihla*, began:

> Enacted and led on by their according voices, they described all sorts of rhythmical figures; and stopping all at once, with terrific whoops and yells, one of them would come to me and ask: "Is it good, *achukma*?" [Then Chahta-Ima replied,] "Yes, it is better than the white man's dance; *achukmafena*! It is good."[74]

Here we have the common Choctaw term *achukma*, meaning "good," and the phrase, *achukmafehna*, meaning "very good."[75] *Achukma* has also been described as a "word of salutation" and a "reply to the same."[76] Equivalents of this expression are found in Mobilian Jargon (often accompanied by *fehna*), but in a wide variety of forms throughout different records and manuscripts, including the following: *tchikamá*, *tchoucouma*, *chicamaw*, and *chikke-mau*.[77] From all these variants, we can make the basic observation that the initial vowel "a" of *achukma* is often dropped, a vowel can be inserted between the "k" and "m," and the vowels have a mutable quality. And in fact, this is exactly what we have with the following description of a Mardi Gras celebration in New Orleans in 1879:

> Every face looks like a mask, and every dress like a fantastic costume. "Huzza! Here's one of 'em. Chick-a-ma-feeno! Chick-a-ma-feeno!," they shout as an Indian makes his way through the crowd, jingling his bells and flourishing his tomahawk.

The term "chukma" (or some variant thereof) had already been used for centuries in the context of people greeting each other, and the Mobilian trade language had been spoken by people of many different backgrounds. Furthermore, the Mourning Feast of 1858 described above shows how the phrase *achukmafehna* was used to show appreciation for the Native American ceremony that was "better than the white man's dance." Just two decades later, accompanying the presentation of an Indian persona decked out in a dazzling costume during Mardi Gras, cutting through the general noise as the crowd of spectators parts to give the Indian right of way, "chick-a-ma-feeno" is indisputably derived from the Mobilian Jargon phrase—which could also be pronounced "chockomo feena"—here functioning as both a greeting and a show of splendor.

Songs are often movable meeting grounds of different cultural groups, and it makes sense that this phrase has been interpreted in various ways throughout time. New people bring new meanings to what they hear and sing. By the middle of the twentieth century, popular songs in New Orleans had incorporated permutations of this phrase, either as one of the main lyrics or as the title of the song itself: "Chocko Mo Feendo Hey" or "Chocko Mo Fendo Hando."[78] With the addition of the vocable "ne," the phrase becomes the well-known Mardi Gras chant and lyric in the song "Iko Iko": "Jockomo feena ne!"[79] Many attempts to provide a definitive meaning for this chant have fallen short, but this has less to do with interpretive abilities than with the fact that language changes over time. Furthermore, it is always possible for any given phrase or lyric to represent an amalgam of languages—like a miniature bayou of braided sounds. In any case, firmly embedded in a context of greeting, an indigenous phrase is certainly at the heart of this lyric associated with Mardi Gras Indian music.

As *Balbancha*, New Orleans is a linguistic and musical multiverse, where distinctive styles have emerged from interactions between different groups of people and overlapping language communities, but this rich soundscape did not germinate within a vacuum of silence. The juggernaut of the city's public musical performance traditions was set in motion by indigenous groups who danced, sang, and shook their chichicois, all moving in rhythm or "in time" ("en cadence"), expressing a different time-sense from their colonial audience. Chahta-Ima, the Louisiana priest who had devoted his life to the Choctaws, once stated that the "great error of modern science and societies . . . 'is to separate, to isolate men and things; to consider them incompatible, while instead of excluding each other, they should, on the contrary, embrace each other,' since the universe is 'a vast harmonious whole, a great coordinated system where all is graduated and scaled . . . where every part is adapted to the whole and the whole to each part.'"[80] With this proclamation, he expresses an idiosyncratic ideal of relationships between people and Nature, but also points toward that greater reality of a shared world. There is the perennial danger of people treating each other as mere things. Yet, despite the merciless hierarchies of power and the fiercest conflicts, there is also the possibility of a shared moment, a time and place where people can recognize their common experience of the natural realm, listen intently to each other, and create new ways of communicating and being together.

All of the previous musical practices flow into the living traditions of today, as indigenous people continue to sing and recreate their songs. Just as all of the words we use today have grown out of the speech of thousands of generations of human beings, with some sound combinations not changing much over centuries, these regional musical traditions include rhythms and strands of melody that have persisted since time out of mind. In a sense, while we recover the past, we also have to step out of a fixed idea of "history." We then realize that time itself is like the river, a moving presence that connects the ancient with the here-and-now in its constant current, giving life to the city of many voices.

CHAPTER THREE

Poor Lo

Lo! The Poor Indian.—A few—some dozen or two—of the once powerful tribe of Choctaw Indians, still hang about the purlieus of this city, in the neighborhood of the Bayou St. John. Near Clark's house, at the Bayou Road, where once blazed the council fire of their sachems, now burn their cooking fires, and the smoke of their miserable huts supplies the place of the smoke of the calumet—they wander about like ghosts of departed greatness. Periodically they serenade the citizens, when they turn out in all the remaining strength of the tribe—men, women and children.

—*Daily Picayune*, January 1, 1846

"Give me any color as long as it is red." They charge the visitor not to look upon the wine when it is red, but when the wheel is crimson, look at it, buy it, ride on it and be at peace with all the world. The crimson of the wheels, with the glow of the incandescents upon them and the crimson decorations, gives the booth a coloring that is attractive to the visitor upon entering the door . . . When a caller at the Syracuse booth is introduced to the man in charge, he is told that he is meeting with the chief of the Sycamores. All of the sellers, riders and persons connected with the Syracuse wheel are addressed and recognized as Sycamores, and that means Indian. All of the literature turned out in the interest of this wheel is done in war paint of the red man, with figures of Poor Lo, with feathers, pipe of peace and the other accompaniments that go with him in and out of battle.

—**"The Syracuse Exhibit"** (Bicycle Exposition), *Daily Picayune*, February 14, 1896

As New Orleans grew, the population changed with the times, but the Native presence in the city provides a stark illustration of one of the more peculiar metamorphoses: a face turning into a mask, a person turning into a persona. How can we begin to understand this development of the mutable image of the "Indian," from the ambivalent reactions during the antebellum period to the commer-

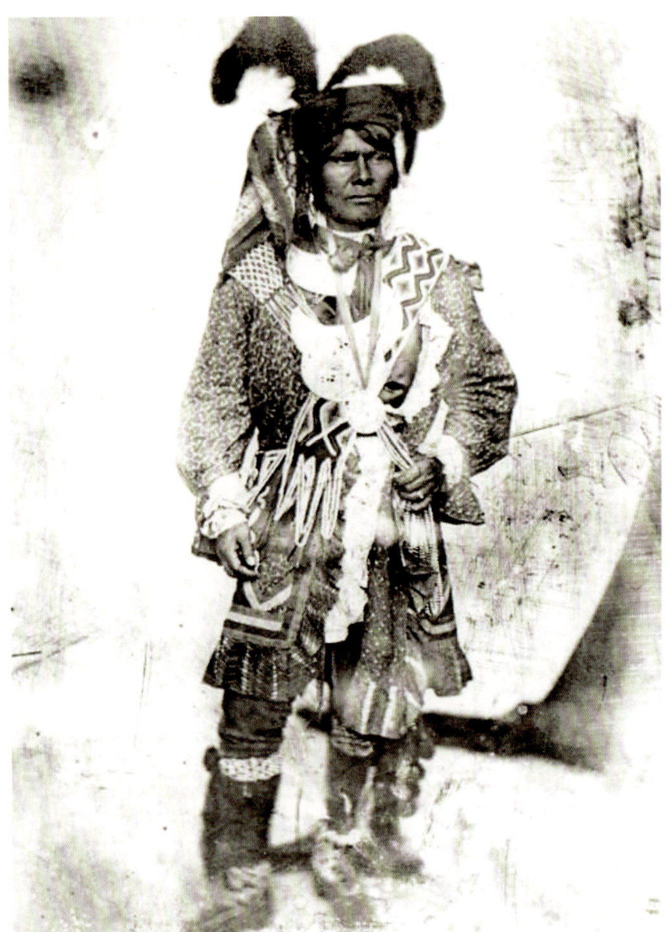

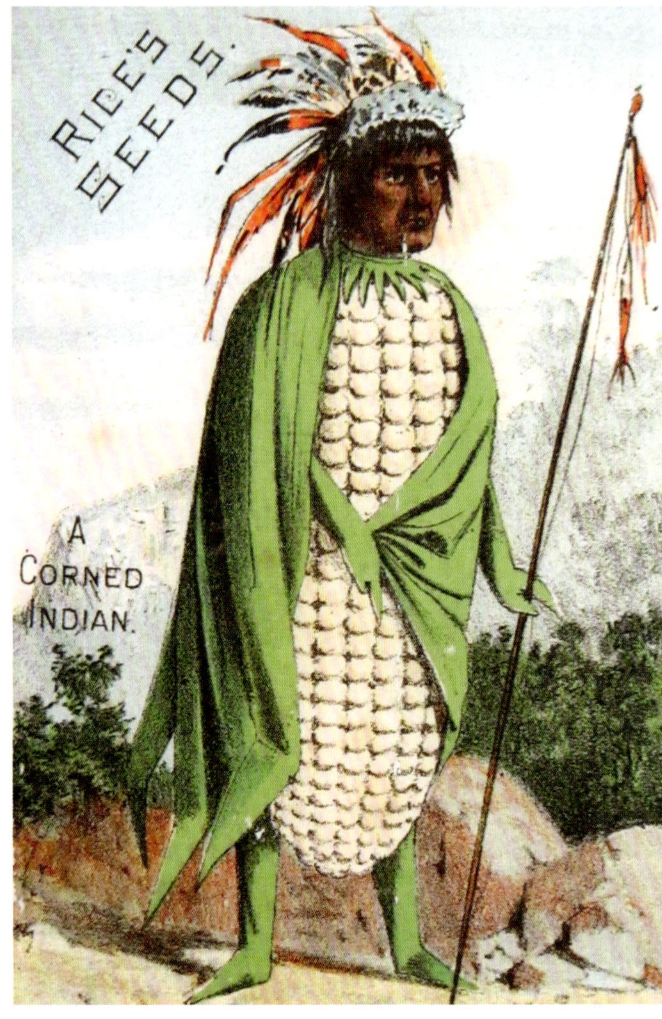

(Left) Billy Bowlegs, last Seminole warrior chief to surrender, 1852. Florida Memory Library, Image number: RC00958.

(Right) Indian in advertisement for seeds, 1883. This is a particularly grotesque caricature and stark instance of cultural appropriation, turning a sacred being into a commercial product.

cialized, industrialized caricatures of the late nineteenth century? By the mid-1800s, Indian Removal had sent tens of thousands of people on death marches toward an unknown fate west of the Mississippi. At this time, while Choctaws and other indigenous groups still lived in and around the city, the citizens of New Orleans expressed a variety of responses to Native Americans, ranging from disgust to fascination and sympathy. They saw Indians as living in a different world, yet were only dimly aware of how they and some of their European ancestors had forced that world upon them. They walked the same streets, inhabiting some of the same public spaces, but mostly moved and spoke past each other, as though living in separate but overlapping dimensions of existence. At least, this was the popular conception throughout the United States, broadcast by newspapers and various public institutions.

The deeper local reality was that many of the older families in New Orleans had some degree of Native ancestry, especially those who spoke French or Spanish, including enslaved African Americans as well as many free *gens de couleur*. These family ties reveal the cyclical nature of group interactions. One generation experiencing a greater degree of social intimacy might be followed by another steeped in a harsher climate of alienation and segregation. This pattern echoes earlier experiences in the British colonies, where marriages between people of European and African ancestry were not uncommon in the late 1600s, but then were banned in several colonies by 1700.[1] During the same time period, a few decades before the establishment of New Orleans, there were many incidences in the upper Mississippi River valley of marriages between French-speaking settlers and Native Americans. Even though colonial authorities tried to suppress this practice, it continued intermittently through the 1700s in Louisiana. By the time of the Louisiana Purchase, in the growing metropolis of New Orleans, many people in the city had an indigenous background as a result of these earlier intimacies.

Nonetheless, after the turbulent frontier clashes of the eighteenth and nineteenth centuries, when Native Americans were often perceived as an existential threat and an impediment to "civilization," Indians were increasingly experienced by English-speaking urban dwellers as a vanishing group eliciting more pity than terror. With the advent of the penny press in the 1830s—when printing newspapers became much more efficient and economical, and some dailies were sold for $0.01—a booming newspaper industry took root in New Orleans by the end of that decade, and a detailed record emerges of the shifting image of the Indian in the city. We are able to see how the more abstract experience of indigeneity, filtered through mass media, developed into a narrow, wizened stereotype by the beginning of the twentieth century, and how this in turn shaped the public persona of the "Indian" as it was incorporated into various forms of spectacle and entertainment in New Orleans.

Before New Orleans was engulfed by the United States as part of the Louisiana Purchase, the European settlers on the eastern seaboard already had a long history of interaction with Native Americans and, over time, they generated a collective image of the original inhabitants of the New World. Based partly on earlier colonial encounters throughout the Western Hemisphere, including the Caribbean, Mesoamerica, and South America, and partly on their own variegated experiences, the North American colonists, most of whom were from the British Isles, developed a bifurcated response. On the one hand, the colonists called the indigenous population "infidels" and "savages"—the latter term shifting from its etymological meaning "forest inhabitants" to the more pejorative sense of "barbarians"—but they also sometimes entertained a romantic, sanitized view of the proverbial Noble Savages, that is, human beings who were superior to the Europeans due to their natural purity.[2] At one end of the spectrum, the image of the Indian was the "Carib," a ravenous subhuman cannibal. According to this dark tunnel-vision view, the Indian embodied Nature in its most terrifying aspect, red in tooth and nail, a violent and uncontrollable destructive energy that negated the civilized legacy of Europe. The competing perspective, which is so distant as to seem at the vanishing point on the horizon, pictures the Indian as having perfect morality, a natural charity, as well as a superior intellect. The greater intelligence of the American Indian was supposed to have been proven by the complex, "polysynthetic" grammatical structures in various languages throughout the Western Hemisphere, as described by linguists in the early nineteenth century.[3] According to this more charitable yet no less distorted vision, Indians have been corrupted by Europeans, but are somehow still not quite human. They are portrayed as victims lacking free will and unable to adapt, as implied by the quote from the *Daily Picayune* in 1849, "like ghosts of departed greatness." Whether noble or nefarious, all of these cultural iterations of the imagined Indian obscure the nuances of actual experience, and instead of seeing people as they are, many of the assimilated English speakers in the United States projected their inner Other onto the public square, the theater stage, and the printed page.

Key events in American history, as celebrated in folktales, songs, as well as textbooks and primers, have long featured such strange, pale shadows of Indians. As part of the series of organized tax revolts during the late eighteenth century, the Boston Tea Party featured colonists who disguised themselves as Indians in a combination of camouflage and pantomime. Ostensibly dressed as "Mohawks"—although some contemporary accounts describe them as having the "shabbiest disguises . . . [including] 'old frocks, red woolen caps, gowns, and all manner of like devices'"—the Sons of Liberty wanted to hide their identities while flinging tea into the water in order to elude punishment from the British Crown.[4] It's possible that they were simultaneously expressing their Americanness and associating their bold act of defiance with the bravery of Indian warriors, but it's also likely that this was an "attempt to scapegoat actual American Indians," since "'the town of *Boston*, finding that it was generally condemned, said it was done by a Crew of Mohawk Indians.'"[5]

Simultaneously, there was a curiosity about indigenous people that translated into a mania for collecting images. There was a documentary impulse among painters like George Catlin, a self-taught artist who had trained for a career in law, but who then set out to "rescue from oblivion" a record of "surviving Indian life" during several years of travel in the West.[6] He roamed widely throughout the 1830s, committing portraits of Indians and scenes from their lives to canvas as he lived among them.[7] His paintings were exhibited in New Orleans and other cities throughout the United States, and by the early 1840s, he had traveled to London along with an Indian performance troupe that gave a command performance for Queen Victoria.[8] Meanwhile, in New Orleans, there was a thriving local market for selling various likenesses of Native Americans. In 1843, an advertisement in the *Daily Picayune* offered "a series of original designs, portraying events in the life of an Indian chief, drawn and etched on stone."[9] Later that year, a letter published in the same paper lamented the tragic death of a sculptor whose "greatest work" was "a fine statue of a North American Indian, six feet high."[10]

In addition, American authors during the first half of the nineteenth century, such as James Fenimore Cooper and Henry Wadsworth Longfellow, often drew upon romanticized images of Indians when it suited their dramatic purposes. Cooper's most popular work, *The Last of the Mohicans* (1826), underscored the increasingly widespread notion of the "vanishing Indian." In the epic poem *Evangeline*, which has had such a lasting impact on public perceptions of Acadians, Longfellow invoked the stereotype of Native Americans as selflessly virtuous:

> Once, as they sat by their evening fire, there silently entered
> Into the little camp an Indian woman, whose features
> Wore deep traces of sorrow, and patience as great as her sorrow.
> She was a Shawnee woman returning home to her people,
> From the far-off hunting-grounds of the cruel Comanches,
> Where her Canadian husband, a Coureur-des-Bois, had been murdered.
> Touched were their hearts at her story, and warmest and friendliest welcome
> Gave they, with words of cheer, and she sat and feasted among them
> On the buffalo meat and the venison cooked on the embers.[11]

This poem had been adapted for the stage and indeed became an "old favorite" with many performances in New Orleans theaters by the late nineteenth century, including a show at the Academy of Music on February 23, 1891, which featured Leon Parmet playing the character of "Lo, the Poor Indian."[12] It is interesting to note that the fragment of the poem quoted above contains the iniquitous alter-ego persona of the stereotyped Indian ("the cruel Comanches"), as if virtue and vice could never reside in the same group. This was one way of reconciling the collective experiences of different indigenous groups with the tendency to create a monolithic Indian persona. In this case, the vision split jaggedly along the lines of tribal affiliation, with a Shawnee Jekyll playing against a Comanche Hyde.

In his essay "A Tour on the Prairies" in *The Crayon Miscellany* (1835), Washington Irving describes his own personal encounters of Native Americans, including a quasi-anthropological sketch of musical practices:

> To add to the wildness of the scene, several Osage Indians, visitors from the village we had passed, were mingled among the men. Three of them came and seated themselves by our fire. They watched everything that was going on round them in silence, and looked like figures of monumental bronze. We gave them food, and, what they most relished, coffee; for the Indians partake in the universal fondness for this beverage, which pervades the West. When they had made their supper, they stretched themselves side by side before the fire, and began a low nasal chant, drumming with their hands upon their breasts by way of accompaniment. Their chant seemed to consist of regular staves, every one terminating, not in a melodious cadence, but in the abrupt interjection huh! Uttered almost like a hiccup. This chant, we were told by our interpreter, Beatte, related to ourselves, our appearance, our treatment of them, and all that they knew of our plans . . .
>
> . . . This mode of improvising is common throughout the savage tribes; and in this way, with a few simple inflections of the voice, they chant all their exploits in war and hunting, and occasionally indulge in a vein of comic humor and dry satire, to which the Indians appear to me much more prone than is generally imagined.[13]

Despite his generalizations, Irving at least begins to scratch at the surface of stereotypes by attempting a more nuanced view of Native Americans:

> In fact, the Indians that I have had an opportunity of seeing in real life are quite different from those described in poetry. They are by no means the stoics that they are represented; taciturn, unbending, without a tear or a smile. Taciturn they are, it is true, when in company with white men, whose good-will they distrust, and whose language they do not understand; but the white man is equally taciturn under like circumstances. When the Indians are among themselves, however, there cannot be greater gossips. Half their time is taken up in talking over their adventures in war and hunting, and in telling whimsical stories. They are great mimics and buffoons, also, and entertain themselves excessively at the expense of the whites with whom they have associated, and who have supposed them impressed with profound respect for their grandeur and dignity. They are curious observers, noting every-

> thing in silence, but with a keen and watchful eye; occasionally exchanging a glance or a grunt with each other, when anything particularly strikes them; but reserving all comments until they are alone. Then it is that they give full scope to criticism, satire, mimicry, and mirth.[14]

At other times, American authors used Native elements to illustrate the darker side of human nature. In Nathaniel Hawthorne's short story, "My Kinsman, Major Molineaux" (1832), the young protagonist is forced to watch the grim spectacle of his uncle, tarred and feathered, with a macabre procession taking place in the middle of the night:

> A mighty stream of people now emptied into the street and came rolling slowly towards the church. A single horseman wheeled the corner in the midst of them, and close behind him came a band of fearful wind-instruments, sending forth a fresher discord, now that no intervening buildings kept it from the ear. Then a redder light disturbed the moonbeams, and a dense multitude of torches shone along the street, concealing, by their glare, whatever object they illuminated. The single horseman, clad in a military dress, and bearing a drawn sword, rode onward as the leader, and, by his fierce and variegated countenance, appeared like war personified: the red of one cheek was an emblem of fire and sword; the blackness of the other betokened the mourning that attends them. In his train were wild figures in the Indian dress, and many fantastic shapes without a model, giving the whole march a visionary air, as if a dream had broken forth from some feverish brain, and were sweeping visibly through the midnight streets.[15]

In this violent and terrifying ceremony, mob rule is mixed with a carnival mood. The torches are flickering like flambeaux, musical instruments are blaring, and accompanying the horseman who "appeared like war personified" was a pageant of "wild figures" dressed as Indians. Hawthorne's story is like a porthole into a parallel world, where a nocturnal Mardi Gras parade serves the singular purpose of exacting physical retribution on a person hated by the public.

Whether angel or devil, the Indian played an important role in the political landscape of the growing United States. Again, like a ghost, or a dim memory of past life, this figure helped create the illusion of progress for an ambitious nation. "Northeastern audiences, in particular, were long since blind to the remnant Native people in their midst, preferring instead the romanticized and heroic Indians of the West of the past."[16] Historian Angela Pulley Hudson invokes the notion of "imperialist nostalgia": exalting a people and a culture even as your own civilization facilitates their destruction. But to make readers "pity truly the poor dying Indian, American authors and artists had to transform him from a bloodthirsty demon into a Noble Savage."[17] This "imperialist nostalgia" pervaded literary works, travelogues, paintings, and stage productions throughout the 1800s.

The caricature of the Indian in stage performances dovetailed with the long-standing entertainment practice of blackface minstrelsy. Considering all of its permutations, from the virtuosic emulation of African American musical ballads to the "dialect songs" that included caricatures of many different ethnicities and nationalities, and later embedded in various vaudeville acts, minstrelsy was the most popular and ubiquitous form of entertainment in the United States throughout the nineteenth century. "With burnt-cork make-up as the sole unifying link, the minstrel show grouped together short comic sketches, sentimental songs, instrumental solos, and speeches that mocked genteel oratory."[18] Taken at face value, many of these performances were grotesque portrayals, jarring to the ear and eye. Minstrelsy represented "comedy stripped down to instant identification of stock types and quick-fire repartee."[19] The musical accompaniment would not necessarily relate directly to the comic routines, which could be any number of buffoonish antics, including pseudoscientific lectures or Shakespearean soliloquies replete with malapropisms. The minstrel stage was a gawky, stimulating cauldron of entertainments, not unlike a funhouse mirror with grossly distorted images of the body politic, revealing the unconscious contents of an American public that was struggling to understand itself.

Why was this relentless mimicry so popular throughout the 1800s? A possible answer becomes clear when we step back and look at the most important changes happening in North America during that century. From the time of the Louisiana Purchase until the "closing of the Western frontier," the United States ballooned in size, swallowing up the continent, while massive waves of people from different parts of the earth rushed into the expanding nation. With the ensuing turbulence of languages, behaviors, beliefs, and skin colors, people grappled with the process of becoming American. In the middle of the century, the country convulsed, fought within itself, then became whole again through fire and blood, yet was still left seeking the elusive balance between liberty and equality. Even more people rushed in, adding to the chaotic and teetering harmony, reshaping communities through traditional customs and improvised practices. The minstrel stage became the place where this continuous and radical transformation of society was confronted, where individual and group identities split and merged, where confused feelings ran riot for all to see. In a sense, the nation had already become a vast variety show to itself and the world. Manifest Destiny was illustrated with Manifest Minstrelsy.

New Orleans was an especially prominent nexus of converging communities throughout the nineteenth century, and the growing population had a strong appetite for public entertainments. Although historical accounts have often emphasized the popularity of minstrel shows in northern cities, such performances were also, in fact, very popular in New Orleans. This trend was nonetheless fueled by established northern blackface troupes that included the city in their performance itineraries across the nation. In March of 1850, there are descriptions of the Campbell Minstrels, who offered "solo-violin and banjo performances," "extraordinary dancing," and "burlesques on Italian opera."[20] This group of minstrels was met with lavish praise for the next several years, as reported in late 1854, when they performed at Armory Hall. "As to solo banjo playing, we think it safe to say that Mr. Rumsey is far ahead of all the world, and Matt Peel, in his plantation banjo solo, shows that he is almost as clever in that line."[21] New Orleanians attended en masse to "welcome back these talented Minstrels to their old headquarters," indicating that the troupe had been popular in the city for some time.

After the Civil War, minstrel shows were increasingly performed by African Americans. "By the 1870s genuine blacks in blackface were a significant force in minstrelsy, and by the 1890s they had begun to dominate virtuoso dancing."[22] Billy Kersands was one of the most popular and successful African American minstrels of his generation, performing for both black and white audiences. In 1886, three weeks prior to Carnival, he performed with the Kersands Minstrels at the Avenue Theatre in New Orleans, then led a Mardi Gras parade.[23] The following year, he performed with the Richards and Pringle's Georgia Minstrels.[24] A few years later, in 1890, he was back in town performing with this troupe at the Avenue Theatre yet again, to receptive audiences: according to the *Daily Picayune*, Kersands was "quite popular here in New Orleans."[25] In 1900, he still had a substantial local following in New Orleans, as described in the following announcement of Rusco and Holland's Minstrels: "This is the organization that has annually played at the Crescent Theatre during the past several years. The topliner of the organization as usual is Billy Kersands, who has the largest following perhaps of any colored comedian in the country. During the engagement the entire balcony will be reserved for colored people."[26]

Another famous African American minstrel active during the same period was Bert Williams. After achieving fame and looking back on his career, Williams explained in an interview for *American Magazine* (1918) how he was "sensitive to prejudice" due to his own "mixed-race, British-Caribbean origins," but that the "segregation that separated the races gave him the opportunity to articulate the views of the forgotten man, unknown to most Americans, through the medium of the minstrel fool":

> I find material by knocking around in out of the way places and just listening. For among the American colored men and negroes there is the greatest source of simple amusement you can find anywhere in the world . . . But Americans for the most part know little about the unconscious humor of

> the colored people and negroes, because they do not come in contact with them . . .
>
> Many of the best lines I have used came to me by that sort of eavesdropping. For, as I have pointed out, eavesdropping on human nature is one of the most important parts of a comedian's work.[27]

Williams refers to his practice of "eavesdropping on human nature." This quality of listening carefully to others is not always evident in all minstrel productions, yet it is a crucial element for the possibility of emulating another cultural practice or enacting someone from another social group, including Native Americans.

The Indian as a stock character in both dramatic and comic theatrical productions, including minstrel shows, became more prevalent as the nineteenth century progressed. As early as the 1820s, while stories of Indian wars filled newspaper pages and Indian images decorated tobacco and medicine labels, there was a demand for Indian-themed entertainment nationally. "Thus many famous Indians of the past were revived as noble figures in the literature influenced by cultural nationalism during the first half of the nineteenth century."[28] Indian performers, authors, and lecturers like George Copway, Eleazer Williams, Peter Jones, and Maungwadaus, who had a performance and dance troupe, fed this appetite. Stage dramas, high and low, that tended to celebrate the Noble Savage theme could be found on both the grand theater stage and the sawdust floors of tent shows. The protagonist of John A. Stone's play *Metamora, Or the Last of the Wampanoags*, which was first performed in 1829, was none other than the famous actor Edwin Forrest, who built his career by playing the role of Indian chief for forty years, while "American audiences wept over the hopeless cause of the freedom-loving Philip as he tried in vain to defend his homeland against the hostile New Englanders."[29]

Toward the middle of the century, in the 1840s, the prospects for a professional Indian performer became so enticing that an escaped slave from Natchez named Warner McCary took on the Indian persona of "Okah Tubbee" and rode the Noble Savage wave, performing on a fife and telling tales of his fictitious Indian life. Under the name "Cary" or "Carey," he had been a popular performer in New Orleans during the previous decade. In fact, his local fame as a musician was such that, many years later in Philadelphia, despite his elaborate disguise and routine, he was recognized by a pair of New Orleanians visiting that city. They decided to attend his performance after spotting the following playbill:

IMMENSE ATTRACTION !
The Great Choctaw Chief, Okah Tubbee,
The Mighty Son of the Howling Forest !
WILL
Give a Grand Exhibition
THIS EVENING,
During which he will go through his wonderful performances on the Fife and other Instruments.

Besides presenting some of the characteristics of his countrymen, &c.

"His face was painted in fancy style, from his nose was suspended a huge silver ring, his head was surmounted by a wig and feathers, his body was encased in buckskin shirt and leggings trimmed Indian fashion with fringe, while his feet were stuck into a pair of gaudy moccasins. In addition to all, he was loaded down with little bells and tinkling gewgaws, and as he came upon the stage they rattled and jingled to the great delight of the more juvenile part of the audience. There was no mistake that he looked Choctaw, all over."[30] Nonetheless, once he began playing the fife so incredibly well, having "started off with a succession of trills and shakes which were truly astonishing," the two men in the audience realized that it was the performer they had known back home in New Orleans, one of them shouting, "Carey, by all the powers! Oh, I know you, Carey; you can't deceive me."[31] But this chameleon-like figure still had a long, illustrious career of further illusions ahead of him. After his turn as an Indian, he reinvented himself again as a Mormon prophet.[32]

A few years after *Evangeline*, Longfellow published another epic poem, *The Song of Hiawatha* (1855), which had a deep and enduring impact on the American public. "Although Longfellow's *Hiawatha* achieved great success during this decade, it was quickly ridiculed in one satirical imitation after another [. . .] The Indian now became mainly a literary staple of popular culture while serious men of letters searched elsewhere for inspiration and themes."[33] Thus the Noble Indian stereotype was diminished into minstrel caricatures. The very idea of an "authentic" Indian performance was lampooned in stage shows with titles like "Metamora: The Last of the Pollywogs."[34]

This national trend was reflected in a series of Indian characters that appeared in various forms of entertainment in the numerous theaters and public spaces in New Orleans. Sometimes this would take the form of simulated Indian dances.[35] The local newspapers published satirical poems that consigned the public's fascination with the Indian to the dustbin of history while simultaneously highlighting the burgeoning popularity of ragtime music, as in the following passage from "Ragtime Gives the Indian Song an Uppercut":

Sing me not of moons and maidens, or of feathered tribes galore,
Tell me not of Fiji troubles, for 'tis ragtime has the floor;
And along the troubled waters were stage managers cavort,
All the flags of rag are flying from the ramparts of the fort.

When the dulcet strains of wooing wake the echoes of the air,
You may bet that it's in rag-time, for the rag is surely there.
And throughout the lasting stretches of the way that glistens bright,
Rag will lift its dusky anthems 'neath the incandescent light.[36]

The sentimentality surrounding the vanishing Indian was banished by the joyful new strains of ragtime, and the moonlight and council fires were replaced by bright stage lights. At other times, there would be serious attempts at dialogue in indigenous languages, which could garner harsh

Native American women at the French Market in New Orleans are "at work on mosquito netting" and "Herbs &c. are spread upon blankets." The sketch encapsulates nuances of expression and a sense of activity and interaction. The writing notes, "The heads marked with crosses are Negro—All the others are Indian and look better." *French Market, Sketch No. 1*, by Alfred Rudolph Waud, 1871. Drawing in graphite and Chinese white (pigment). The Historic New Orleans Collection, 1965.16.

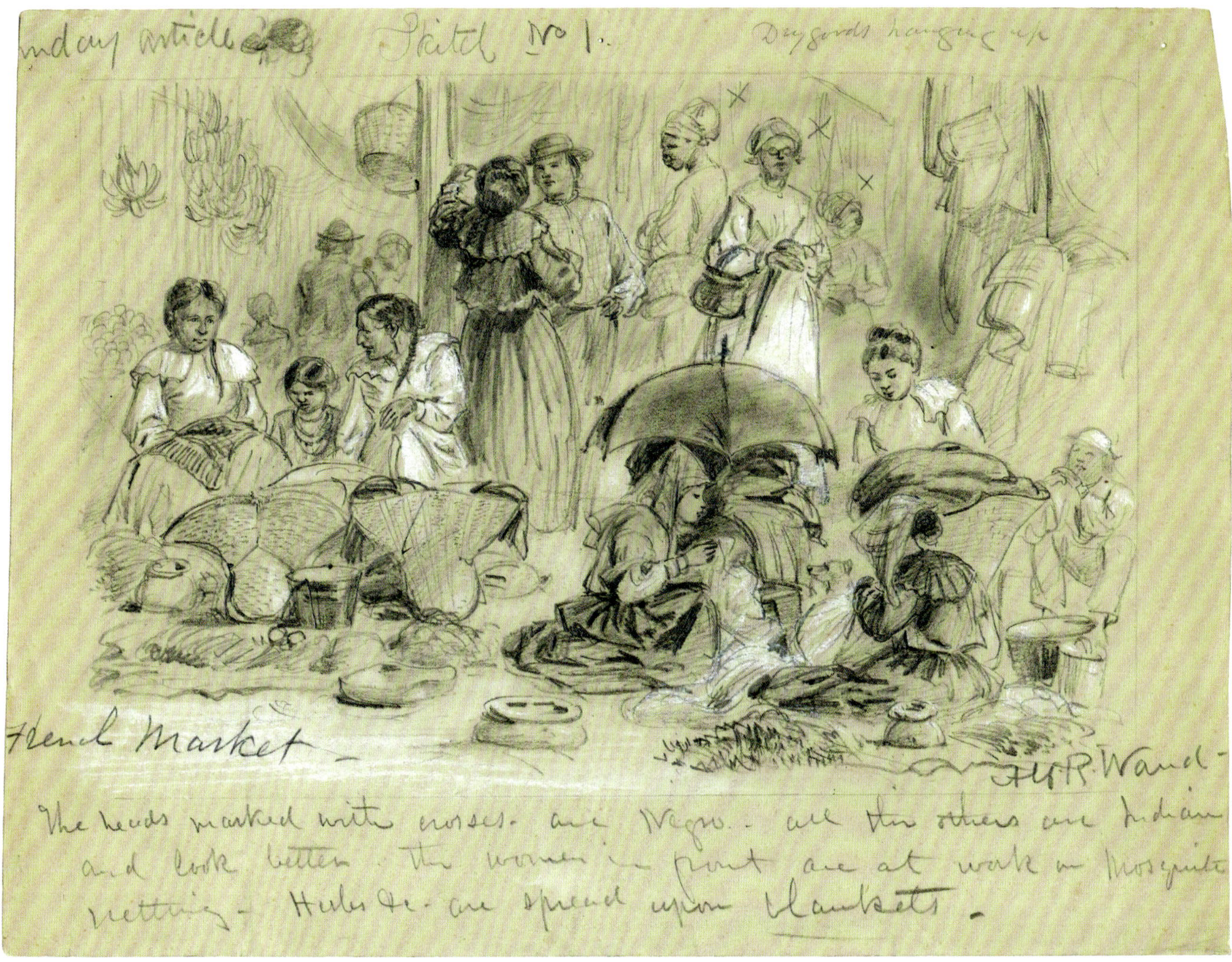

comments from critics. Here, the withering remarks are aimed at playwright Frank Dumont: "Where Mr. Dumont obtained his idea of the poetry and metaphor of the Indian language, we cannot imagine. It sounds very much like pigeon [*sic*] English. Seriously, Mr. Dumont should revise the text in this particular, for as the lines stand, they excite the laughter of ridicule."[37]

Near the end of the nineteenth century, the citizens of New Orleans would still sometimes encounter Native Americans in the public markets around town, but they were described more like living fossils than actual people, "strange beings, apparently half-civilized," offering for sale "dried sassafrass, from which gumbo, a noted Creole dish, is made, and varieties of herbs."[38] It seems that much of the English-speaking population of the city could only see the caricature that had been shaped by decades of stereotyping and which was now hermetically sealed with the tenets of Social Darwinism: "These patient, quiet women, with their swarthy skin and flowing hair, are Indians, descendants of the Chatas and Biloxians, the first possessors of the soil; yet in the great law of the survival of the fittest, rapidly dwindling before the march of progress, to give place to the superior and more cultured race."[39]

This vision of the vanishing Indian was relentlessly superimposed on living people, and even into the first few decades of the twentieth century, this took the form of elaborately choreographed installations of an "Indian village" in public spaces across the country. As mass production of luxury goods and massive department stores helped a consumer society come into full bloom, Native Americans were pressed into service to sell products. For the consuming public, this was a much more enticing alterative to the second-rate simulations, such as the fictive Sycamores selling bicycles at the Syracuse Exhibit in 1896. Twenty years later, in 1916, the people of New Orleans were treated to the "Hiawatha Indian Village," which was created downtown in the Maison Blanche building. On the third floor, advertisements promised that visitors would see "one of the most interesting and highly educational exhibits" with a "real Indian Tribe" within a "beautiful woodland setting," a "complete picture of real Indian life." All in all, it was designed as "a true reproduction, from the green grass of the forest floor, to the woodland bowers that screen the native Indian's sky."[40] In short, one of the most prominent department stores in New Orleans was offering a live-action diorama of Indians, where the "squaws and papooses and red-skinned warriors [could] be seen engaged in the pursuits of peace, the making of baskets and moccasins, the tanning of leather [. . .] as well as in the fashioning of arrows with their deadly poisoned tips."[41] Keeping true to one of the business imperatives of minstrelsy—the advertised promise of absolute verisimilitude—this exhibit invited the onlookers to witness

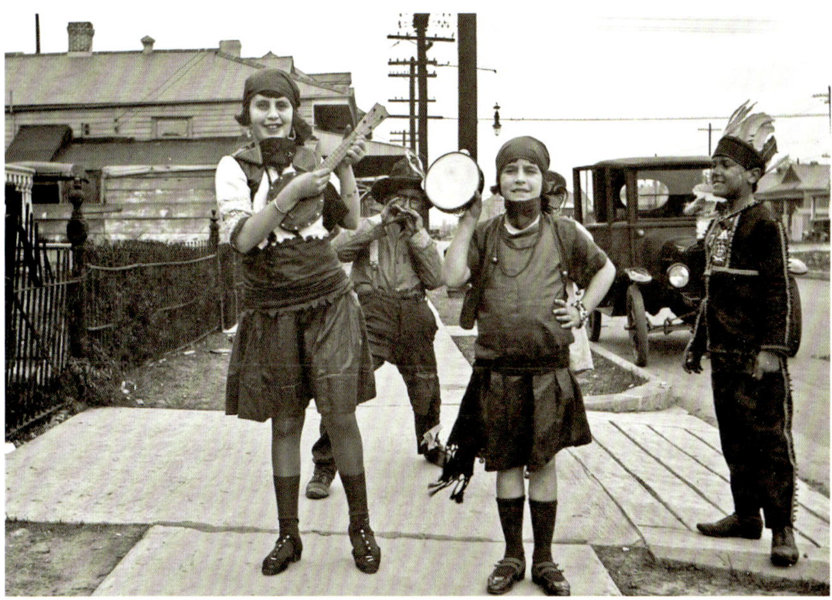

In a neighborhood near Bayou St. John on Mardi Gras 1924, four costumed children take to the streets to celebrate. Notice several have musical instruments and are dressed as various ethnicities. Dressing as an Indian was a popular children's costume choice throughout the twentieth century. "Two girls, small girl Bertha, 314 Hagan Ave," Mardi Gras, March 4, 1924. The Historic New Orleans Collection, Gift of Waldemar S. Nelson, 2003.0182.332.

the full range of Native artifacts in the safety of their favorite shopping place: "Bows and arrows, war clubs, shields, blankets, canoes and paddles, are all among the impedimentia of the band, and all are in the proper places around the campfire."[42] War and peace were contained within the rituals of consumerism, and this parallel universe "nativity scene" thrilled the visitors by re-feeding their primordial fears while ingratiating their sense of the progress of Western civilization.

In the waning days of the nineteenth century, with the so-called closing of the Western frontier, the perennial prurience of assimilated American citizens guaranteed that stage productions would incorporate greater numbers of Native Americans and their simulacra. Some early antecedents include P. T. Barnum's display of "several small groups of Indians in the museum Lecture Room as early as 1843."[43] It was not until the 1880s, however, that William Frederick Cody, aka Buffalo Bill, would offer a "fully fledged 'Wild West' show," which effectively "transformed history into myth."[44] This cultural production grew out of his experiences working as a Pony Express rider, a buffalo hunter, and a scout with the Fifth Cavalry.[45] Knowing how to ride and kill inspired him to focus on horse-

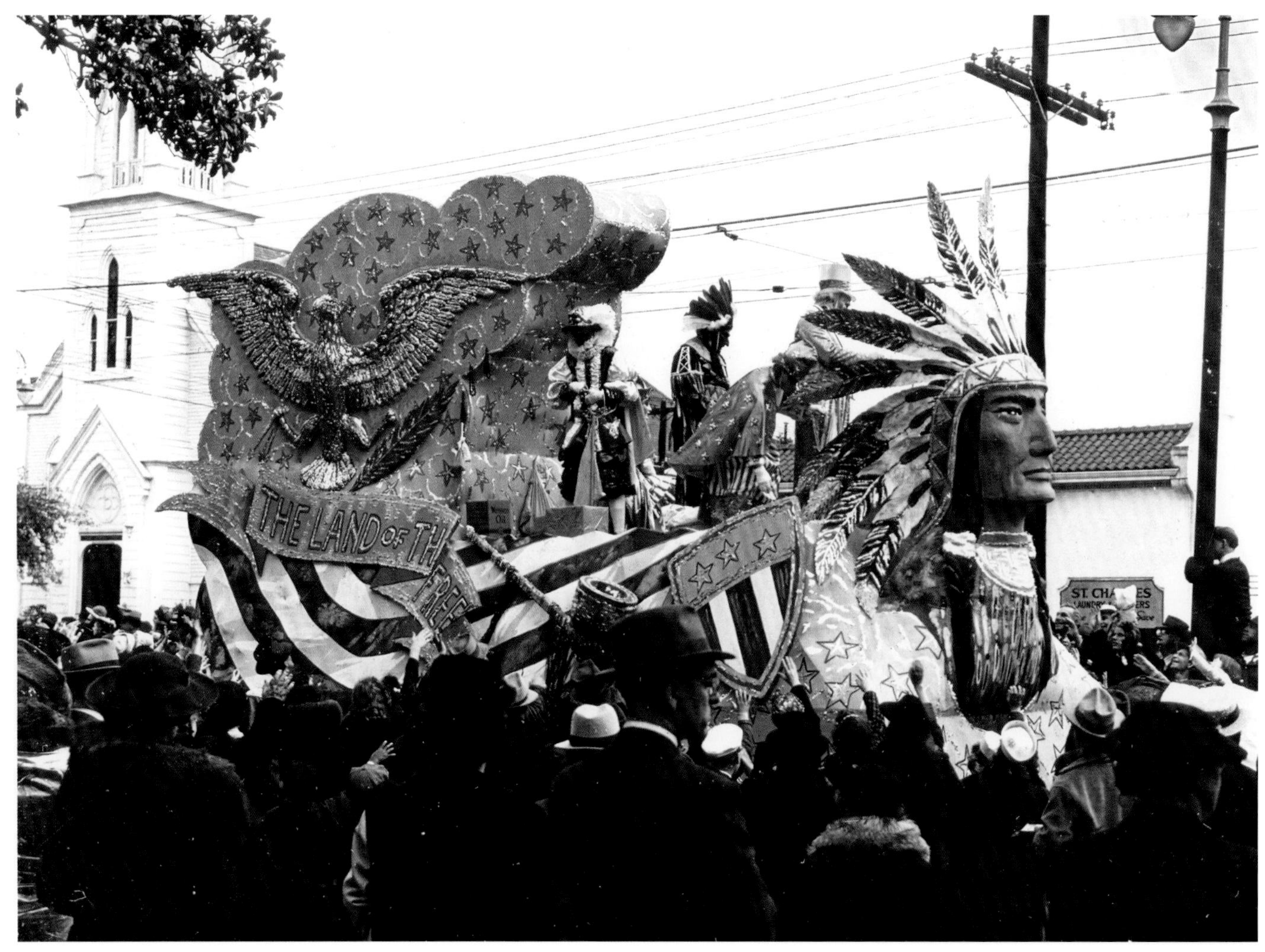

manship skills and "[s]hooting at all kinds of targets—glass balls, coins, cards—from every possible position" as part of his evolving entertainment complex, which included such macabre elements as exhibiting the hair of Yellow Hair, a Cheyenne warrior he killed in 1876.[46] He offered his "first large-scale 'exhibition' in Nebraska in 1883" featuring an "Indian Camp as 'a Living, Picturesque Reproduction of Savage Life,'" which anticipated the New Orleans department store display of 1916. Although it was billed as entertainment, Buffalo Bill's culminating production, the

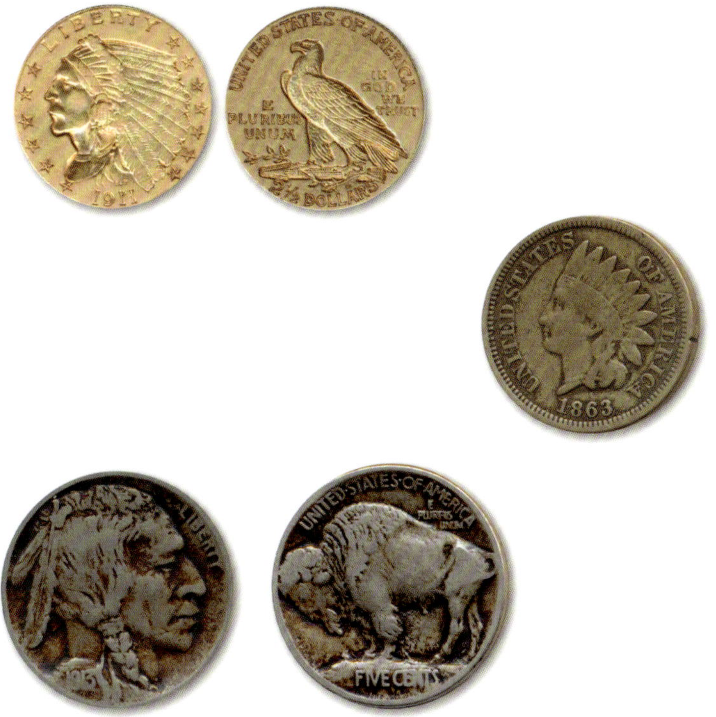

American coins: from Indian head penny, 1863, *right*; Golden Eagle $2.5, 1911, *top*; and Buffalo nickel, 1913, *bottom*. The Indian head on the Buffalo nickel was based on sketches drawn from life in contrast to the fanciful "Greco-Roman" image on the 1863 coin. Photo by John McCusker.

(Left) An Indian float, rolling down St. Charles Avenue passing St. Andrew Street, c. 1939. Indian imagery has been employed as a carnival theme in costuming and parades in New Orleans since the eighteenth century. The costumes of the riders on this float form a compressed narrative of Manifest Destiny, including a European explorer of the colonial period, a Native American, and what appears to be an Uncle Sam figure. A scroll on the side of the float proclaims, "The Land of the Free," accompanied by a giant pipe and an eagle above. The peace pipe has become a symbol of the new social order. The Historic New Orleans Collection, Gift of John and Priscilla Lawrence, 2001.16.12.

Wild West show, was intended to give the audience "the real thing" and broadcast an interpretive framework for the nation's history: "During its heyday, the Wild West was an action-packed, patriotic pageant. [After] the bitter squabbles over Civil War and Reconstruction and the scandals of the Gilded Age, the spectacle of the frontier tamed gave reassurance of the triumph of civilization and national reconciliation."[47] His alleged autobiography ("probably ghost-written by 'Arizona' John Burke, the Wild West's publicist"), first appearing in 1879 and sold at the show's ticket booths, gave the following starry-eyed rationale:

> I have sought to describe that great general movement westward—that irresistible wave of immigration which, arrested for a time by the Alleghenies, rose until at last it broke over and spread away across mountain, stream and plain, leaving States in its wake, until stopped by the shores of the Pacific.

> The evolution of government and of civilization, the adaptation of one to the other, are interesting to the student of history; but particularly fascinating is the story of the reclamation of the Great West and the supplanting of the wild savages that from primeval days were lords of the country but are now become wards of the Government, whose guardianship they were forced to recognize. This story is one well calculated to inspire a feeling of pride even in the breasts of those whose sentimentality impels to commiserate the hard lot of the poor Indian; for, rising above the formerly neglected prairies of the West are innumerable monuments of thrift, industry, intelligence, and all the contributory comforts and luxuries of a peaceful and God-fearing civilization; those evidences that proclaim to a wondering world the march of the Anglo-Saxon race towards the attainment of perfect citizenship and liberal, free, stable government.[48]

Considering its enormous success in captivating audiences, spawning dozens of imitators, and espousing a dystopian theory of Western progress, the Wild West show cast a spell of technicolor exceptionalism for America. For generations, people learned to stop weeping for "the poor Indian" and, instead, learned to love the gun as an instrument of xenophobic pride and cherish the symbol of the Indian head, stamped into coins, as the currency of a foreordained social order.

A few years later, during the winter of 1884–1885, the show rolled into New Orleans, where it enjoyed a four-month residency that overlapped with both the World's Industrial and Cotton Centennial Exposition and Mardi Gras, featuring "Plains Indian performers [who] attacked a stagecoach, high-stepped to a war dance, and hunted a buffalo."[49] The spectacles were doubtlessly impressive for the thousands of onlookers, including the African American citizens of New Orleans. Conventional historical wisdom has maintained that the Wild West show was, in fact, responsible for "creating one of the city's most fascinating and durable traditions" in the form of Mardi Gras Indian groups.[50] However, considering the numerous instances of black New Orleanians wearing Indian costumes before the mid-1880s, it might be more accurate to say that Buffalo Bill's Wild West Show influenced preexisting cultural traditions in New Orleans. In fact, the emergence of Mardi Gras Indians during the second half of the nineteenth century reflects several decades of synthesis between various ideas and images of the Indian as well as local family legacies.

By now, the tale of the United States devouring the continent while dehumanizing its original inhabitants has become so familiar that one can be anesthetized to the moral implications. The rich texture of family histories and local experience is buried under a national narrative of progress, or destruction masquerading as development. A statement of sympathy—"Lo! the poor Indian"—can be easily converted into the image of "Poor Lo" and back again. On the surface, both of these gestures involve looking and pointing outward at something outside ourselves. We might see this as a psychological gambit to avoid being haunted by historical truth, but even this is too simple.

"Every face looks like a mask," someone once said about Mardi Gras back in 1879—the same year that Buffalo Bill's autobiography showed how "Western progress" had gone wild. New Orleans is now within the United States, and sometimes acts as its cultural mask to the world, but we should ask whether people are always hiding when they adopt a persona, or if they're actually exposing what's inside. While reconnecting with ancestors and reenvisioning themselves, the Mardi Gras Indians are turning the "White Man's Indian" inside out.

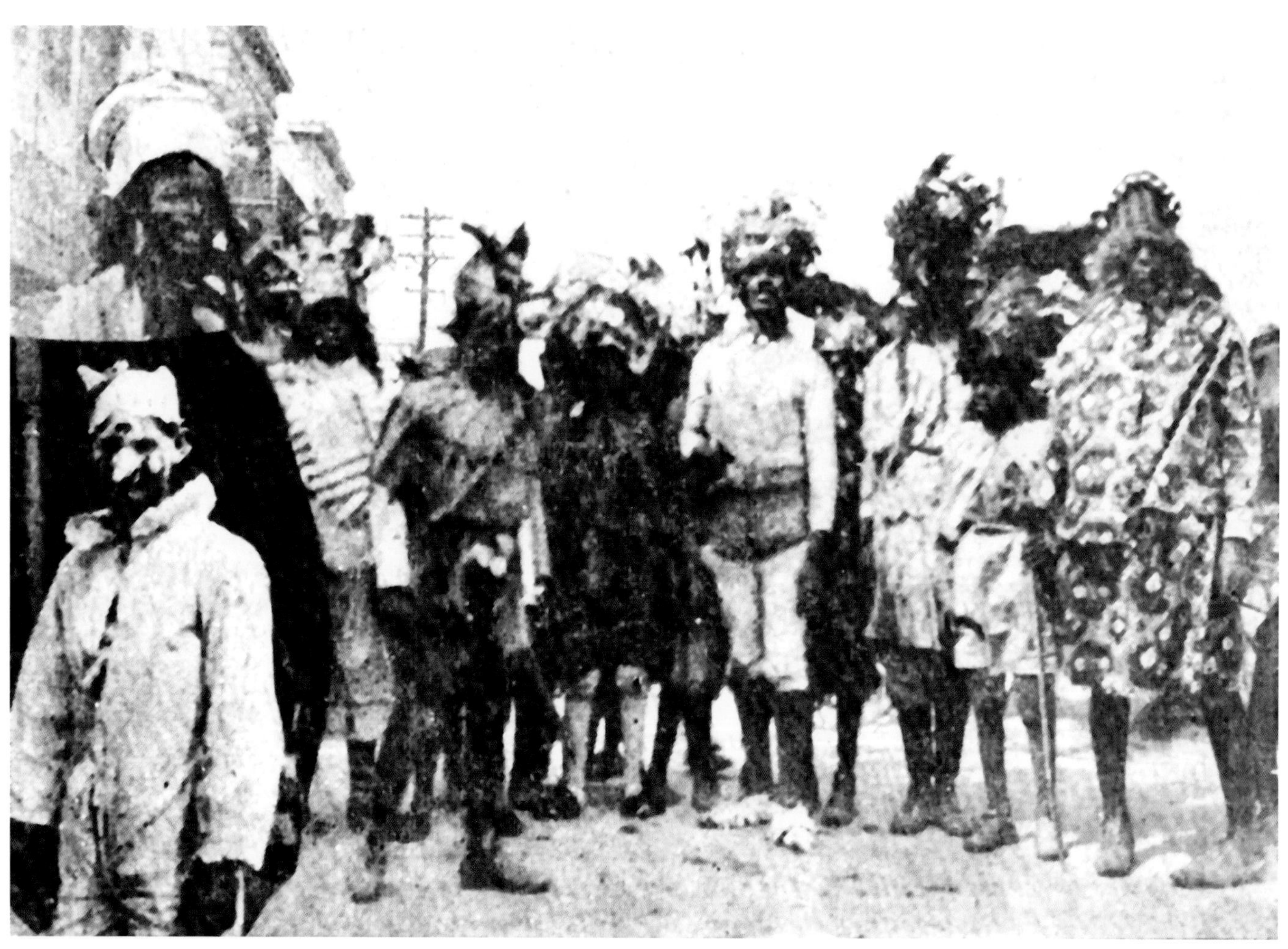

A group of Mardi Gras Indians, February 26, 1903. This is the earliest known photograph of Mardi Gras Indians. Times-Democrat. Louisiana State Museum Special Collections.

CHAPTER FOUR

Chick-a-ma-feeno

An Identity Emerges

On Mardi Gras 1895, there was a newsworthy altercation in Algiers, the New Orleans neighborhood that sits across the Mississippi River from the city's downtown. A group of black carnival revelers had gotten into a scuffle that afternoon with some local white youth.

> Maskers Visit Algiers, and a Free fight lands them in jail. At 3 p.m. yesterday Algiers was imperiled by what appeared to be a band of hostile Indians. Much consternation was caused when this intrepid band of red men made their debut, but soon the pulses of the spectators resumed their normal beat. Ere many minutes elapsed, and while making their rounds, the band became entangled with some white maskers, and a fight ensued, which resulted in the arrest of the whilom Indians, and their confinement in the dark recesses of a special cell in the Eighth precinct station. On closer examination the Indians were discovered to be colored men, who gave their names as follows: Joe Horton, Hy. Jerry, Harry Conners, Henry Lean, Eddie McKinley, John Smith, R.J. Jones, and Walter Brown. They feel very much aggrieved, and claim that they were out for fun, and that they have for the past four or five seasons made visits to Algiers and have always enjoyed themselves, and never before have been molested. They are all workingmen and showed no signs of drunkenness when seen by a reporter. (*Daily Picayune*, February 27, 1895)[1]

The report of this incident, or "humbug," is perhaps the earliest definitive news citation of a group of black men dressed as Indians in New

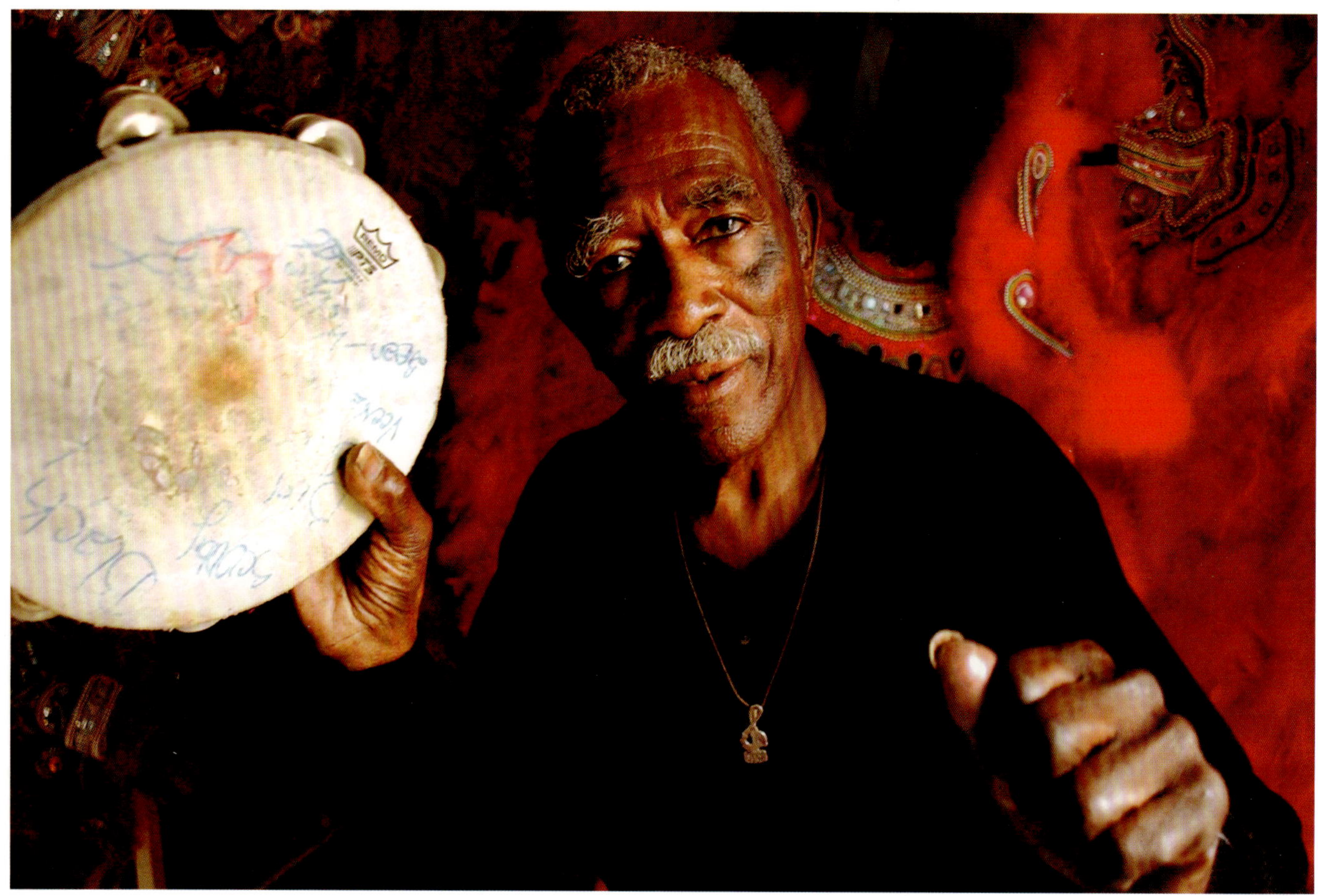

Longtime Big Chief Allison "Tootie" Montana, eighty-one, made his last suit for Mardi Gras 2004. He died the following year. Photo by John McCusker/The Times-Picayune.

Orleans on Mardi Gras.[2] How did this practice come to be and how long had it been going on? Contemporaneous accounts from newspapers and other sources of Indian sightings in the city during the nineteenth century offer some clues. In addition, there are the tales from oral histories of the current participants themselves. By gathering these various strands of written history and living memory, we can illuminate the cultural system of the Mardi Gras Indians in a way that goes beyond conventional narratives. Most importantly, by listening to a certain phrase sung by the Indians, in all its permutations and rhythmical accompaniments, we can discover the deeper roots of their practices.

The story of Mardi Gras Indian origins, as represented in the collective memory of the participants themselves, rests as much on individually held beliefs as it does on a specific narrative. The history, as it is often told, stakes out two vaguely defined periods: their emergence as a carnival practice "after the Civil War" and their derivation from an earlier time when the indigenous people of Louisiana offered assistance and protection to Africans and their descendants suffering under institutionalized slavery. In fact, during "the colonial period, slaves had perceived Indian country as a potential refuge from bondage, and the increasing presence there of blacks owned by tribal members during territorial years may have even encouraged some runaways to take advantage of the confusion accompanying the movement of slaves to and from Indian jurisdictions."[3] However, there are some who firmly believe there were Africans in the Americas before Europeans arrived on the North American continent.[4] In any case, there is a wide spectrum of beliefs, grounded in a variety of experiences.

Big Chief Allison "Tootie" Montana (1922–2005) said that the Creole Wild West, often credited as the first tribe, started back in the 1880s. According to his account, his great-uncle Becate Baptiste was present at the founding of the tribe, which took place at his family's home at 1313–15 St. Anthony Street.[5] Elements of Montana's creation story are buttressed by genealogy and public records: his great-uncle "Becate Baptiste" was likely Baptiste Eugene, the older brother of his grandmother Jeanne Eugene Herara.[6] In 1884, when Baptiste was eleven years old, the extended family (including the Heraras) moved to St. Anthony Street, according to the City Directory.[7]

Other insider perspectives on Indian origins include those of Golden Blades Big Chief Paul Longpré (1913–2014), who ran in the 1930s with the legendary "Brother" Cornelius Tillman. He said that Tillman's father, Robert Sam Tillman, founded the Yellow Pocahontas uptown with a man named Sam Tweed. Longpré claimed that these two had a split, and Tweed brought the Yellow Pocahontas tribe downtown, while Tillman stayed uptown and founded the Creole Wild West, having taken the name from the Hagenbeck and Wallace Wild West Show.[8] Longpré also said the first year Tillman masked as an Indian chief was 1897.[9] A year later Tillman was murdered.[10]

However, Longpré's version is problematic. The Hagenbeck and Wallace partnership did not exist before 1907, and it was primarily a circus, though it added a Wild West component by 1917.[11] Indian-themed shows and exhibitions had been staged in New Orleans throughout the late 1800s and early 1900s. Over the course of three decades, Dr. W. F. Carver's Wild West (1884), Buffalo Bill's Wild West Show (1884–1885), and the 101 Ranch Show (1908) all made stops in the city.[12] Moreover, thus far, no record has emerged of Sam Tweed, leading to speculation that this may have been a nickname. Robert Sam Tillman, born 1871, was "Brother" Cornelius Tillman's uncle, not his father.[13] According to Longpré's version of events, the Yellow Pocahontas would be the first founded tribe, with the Creole Wild West second, which goes against the grain of widely held belief. Furthermore, the date given by Longpré is well after Indians were first sighted at Mardi Gras by news reporters and others.

While rich in detail, these narratives contain contradictions and raise other questions. The presumption in Montana's story is that the Indians were founded at St. Anthony Street because it was "Becate" Baptiste's home, as he is the protagonist in the story. However, Baptiste was only eleven in 1884 when the family moved to St. Anthony Street. Longpré's perspective also offers a founding Indian, Tillman, born 1871, who would have been thirteen that year. Putting the pieces of this puzzle together requires contextualization. Namely, we must consider the general history of masking at Mardi Gras, the many ways the holiday has been celebrated in the city, the emergence of the Indian character as a Mardi Gras costume choice in the 1800s, and the biographies and backgrounds of identified nineteenth-century Mardi Gras Indians.

From the earliest days of the city, the colonial citizens of New Orleans dressed up in a wide variety of costumes during Carnival season. "Eighteenth century Paris, from which many New Orleanians came, had a vigorous tradition of popular entertainment that probably influenced New Orleans Carnival, particularly its range of costumes and characters."[14] In fact, Marc-Antoine Caillot included in his memoir a very early account of a Carnival parade in New Orleans, which took place only just over a decade after the city was established. In 1730, he participated in a Lundi Gras celebration, accompanied by music and flambeaux, in the vicinity of Bayou St. John. As a young man, Caillot was eager to use the occasion as an excuse to have fun:

> We were already quite far along in the Carnival season without having had the least bit of fun or entertainment, which made me miss France a great deal. The Sunday before Mardi Gras, upon returning from hunting, where I had gone to try and dissipate my boredom, I found a friend waiting for me in order to invite me to a supper he was giving for a few people. He told me that I would have all the diversions there that one could partake of in the city. Indeed, that very evening, I began to savor the first pleasures in the colony, where I had already been for a few months. We spent not only an evening but the whole night, too, singing and dancing. When I returned home, I was certain that those would be the last pleasures I would partake of during the Carnival season, since it was already quite near the end, but, no matter the sadness one feels, it seems that those days are dedicated to pleasures and to having fun. The next day, which was Lundi Gras, I went to the office, where I found my associates, who were bored to death. I proposed to them that we form a party of maskers and go to Bayou Saint John, where I knew that a lady friend of my friends was marrying off one of her daughters. They accepted, but the difficulty of finding appropriate clothes made us just talk about it. However, since I myself was desirous of finding out how people would have fun at this wedding party, I proposed this excursion for a second time, that evening at supper. But, upon seeing that no one wanted to come along, I got up from the table and said that I was going to find some others who would go, and I left.
>
> I was, in fact, in a house where I did not delay in assembling a party, composed of my landlord and his wife, who gave me something to wear. When we were ready and just about to leave, we saw someone with a violin come in, and I engaged him to come with us. I was beginning to feel very pleased about my party, when, by another stroke of luck, someone with an oboe, who was looking for the violin, came in where we were, to take the violin player

> away with him, but it happened the other way around, for, instead of both of them leaving, they stayed. I had them play while waiting for us to get ready to leave. The gentlemen I had left at the table, and who had not left the house, came quickly upon hearing the instruments. But, since we had our faces masked, it was impossible for them to recognize us until we took them off. This made them want to mask, too, so that we ended up with eleven in our party.[15]

Caillot then described their costume choices, which included indigenous characters:

> Some were in red clothing, as Amazons, others in clothes trimmed with a braid, others as women. As for myself, I was dressed as a shepherdess in white. I had a corset of white dimity, a muslin skirt, a large pannier, right down to the chemise, along with plenty of beauty marks, too. I had my husband, who was the Marquis de Carnival; he had a suit trimmed with gold braid on all the seams. Our postilion went in front, accompanied by eight actual Negro slaves, who each carried a flambeau to light our way. It was nine in the evening when we left.

It is significant that he uses the phrase "accompanied by eight actual Negro slaves" ("acompagné de huit veritables Esclaves negres") to indicate that these were not other revelers in disguise.

There was at least one unplanned excitement lying in wait for this merry band. While marching through the woods toward Bayou St. John, the maskers ran into a few bears. They instantaneously scattered in all directions, and so did the bears. They regrouped and later formed a musical parade as they approached their destination:

> When we had gone a distance of two musket shots into the woods, our company was soon separated at the sight of four bears of a frightful size, which our postilion, passing close by them without even seeing them, had woken by snapping his whip. These animals, at the light of the flambeaux, went running, just like we did from the fear we felt, without knowing where we were

going or what we were doing. Nonetheless, after our first movements, they went away, and we continued on our way, laughing about the little comedy we had just seen, which had really given us a fright.

When we got to the bayou, we sent a slave to go find out what was going on, namely, if people were dancing and what they were doing. During this time, we prepared ourselves, and upon returning the slave told us that they had just gotten up from the table and they were dancing. Right away, our instruments began playing, the postilion started cracking his whip, and we walked toward the house where the wedding celebration was taking place.[16]

They could be forgiven for being a little skittish, as the French colonists were in the middle of their existential struggle with the Natchez at that time, and there was a prevalent concern that, after the destruction of Fort Rosalie upriver during the previous autumn, New Orleans would also be attacked, casting a paranoid mood over the city. Certainly not all indigenous groups were hostile; after all, it was later in 1730 that the city received the diplomatic delegation from Illinois Country pledging solidarity against the Natchez. Indeed, over several decades, there had been numerous spiritual and musical encounters between the French and indigenous groups, signaling the possibility of rapprochement. Nonetheless, one can suppose that dressing in "red clothing" was likely the extent of any Frenchman's Indian costume at that particular time, as certain dangers attended sartorial verisimilitude during the Carnival season of 1730.

A little before the 1781 Mardi Gras, when New Orleans was part of Spain's New World empire, a colonial official at the Cabildo warned of "a great number of free negroes and slaves who, with the pretext of the Carnival season, mask and mix in bands passing through the streets looking for dance halls." Colonial documents also mention feathers being used as a disguise, suggesting that they should be banned. Ultimately, during their rule of the former French colony, the Spanish commissioners directed the militia to prohibit all kinds of masking as well as the nightly dancing by negroes.[17] Whether this was the first example, or merely one of the earliest, of governing authorities attempting to regulate or even ban Carnival celebrations in New Orleans, it was certainly not the last.

The decision of the Spanish authority in this case underscores the persistent fear that Carnival would provide cover for slave intrigue, and there was always an unease over the enslaved being able to shift their identity unnoticed against the backdrop of the Carnival. Indeed, the largest slave uprising in American history would later take place upriver from New Orleans in 1811, as white masters were busy preparing for the Carnival season.[18] Whatever effect this decree may have had in 1781, or the many other regulatory attempts that would come in the American period the following century, accounts of Carnival masking throughout demonstrates a spirit that was innovative, resilient, and adaptive.

While white Carnival activities were, on the whole, legally permitted between Spanish rule and the Louisiana Purchase, Carnival celebrations by people of African ancestry were driven underground. Furthermore, many Americans, including Governor W. C. C. Claiborne, alternated between concern and disgust with the frequent Creole balls and the obsession that Creoles had with dancing. "They occupy much of the public mind," he wrote back to Washington. Claiborne was publicly mocked for not speaking French and—perhaps less forgivably—not being able to do French dances. In 1806, when word of a political and military coup plot led by Aaron Burr reached the city, it gave Claiborne an excuse to suspend Carnival. These seasonal celebrations were put aside and did not fully rebound for years.[19]

> It was not revived the next year, or the next, or for many more. The authorities explained that ill-feeling between Creoles and Americans was high and that, also, there was a racial situation. Who could predict what might happen if masked men walked the streets again. Besides, the Americans never approved of Mardi Gras. They considered it a part of the wickedness of New Orleans.[20]

But the festival did not die. In 1823, under petition from the citizens, the balls were again permitted, and soon they were more "numerous" and "brilliant" than before.[21] By 1827, street masking was again legal. "The negroes have two or three holidays" in New Orleans which are like a "Saturnalia," wrote a Protestant minister visiting from New England during the 1823 Carnival season. He described a celebratory procession at Congo Square where a group of black maskers followed behind a king who wore a series of "oblong, gilt-paper boxes on his head, tapering upwards, like a pyramid. From the ends of these boxes hang two huge tassels, like those on epaulets. He wags his head and makes grimaces . . . All the characters that follow him, of leading estimation, have their own peculiar dress and their own contortions. . . I have seen groups of these moody and silent sons of the forest [native Indians] following these merry bacchanalians in their dance, through the streets, scarcely relaxing their grim visages to a smile, in the view of the antics that convulsed even the masters of the negroes with laughter."[22]

Real Indians following eclectically costumed black maskers in a procession originating at Congo Square is a snapshot moment worth noting. This early glimpse of Carnival, when seen in light of later accounts, suggests group masking processions were already an institutional practice. The exotic costumes as described are unique and, notably, not representative of any typical character the writer was familiar with, like a clown or a Harlequin. It underscores the role of Congo Square, with its processions, music, and "contorted" dance, as both an Afro-Creole cultural gathering point and a crossroads where a French-speaking slave "king," a New England minister, and indigenous "sons of the forest" could find themselves on Mardi Gras. While music is not mentioned in this retelling, the description of participants dancing makes it clear it was present. That indigenous Indians were on the scene "following these merry Bacchanalians in their dance" underscores the continued Native American presence in New Orleans and the apparent ease they felt joining in with dance "contortions" of the black procession.

This cultural overlap was not an occurrence unique to Carnival or Congo Square. Visiting writer George J. Joyaux wrote about a scene he witnessed in 1831 on Lake Pontchartrain:

> Every Sunday the negroes of the city and surroundings meet in a place called the Camp. It is a huge green field on the bank of a lake about three leagues from New Orleans. . . . [and they] are gathered in a large number of distinct

> groups; each has its own flag floating atop a very tall mast, used as a rallying point for the group. [They] dance with extraordinary speed and agility [and make] their music by beating and rolling their sticks on their drums; a sharp sound is produced, repeated two or three times by the surrounding echoes. Several Indian families—settled not far from the lake—also come to the camp to share these ludicrous pleasures.[23]

The ongoing presence of Indians on the periphery of urban New Orleans in the antebellum era and their continued cultural overlaps with people of African descent into the 1830s offers validation for the Mardi Gras Indian retention and connection belief so present in its oral history. Before 1838, Mardi Gras maskers had "formed lines and chains and walked and run through the streets on Mardi Gars to the amusement or disgust of spectators, but without real organization or plan."[24] That changed in 1838 when the *Commercial Bulletin* reported the following:

> The European custom of celebrating the last day of the Carnival by a procession of masqued figures through the public streets was introduced here yesterday, very much to the amusement of our citizens. The principal streets were traversed by a masquerade company on horseback and in carriages, from the fantastic Harlequin to the somber Turk and wild Indian. A delightful throng followed on the heels of the cavalcade as it marched through our city suburbs, and wherever it went the procession raised a perfect hubbub and jubilee. The exhibition surpassed anything of the kind ever witnessed here.[25]

The *Picayune* also noted the pageantry that year: "A large number of Creole gentlemen of the first respectability, went to no little expense with their preparations. In the procession were several carriages superbly ornamented—bands of music, horses richly caparisoned—personations of knights, cavaliers, heroes, demigods, chanticleers, punchinellos, &c, &c, all mounted."[26]

The next year the French language newspaper *L'Abeille* announced places where maskers would gather the day before Mardi Gras, adding there were one thousand balls being held over the course of that season.

Regulatory action, while still present, was largely ceremonial. In 1846, the city council's last act of their last meeting before Mardi Gras was to grant "permission to wear masks in the streets on Mardi Gras day."[27] The main threat to Carnival in this period was public outcry from the seasonal tradition of throwing flour on passers-by.[28] There were numerous well-publicized instances when this prank veered into criminality when sawdust or some other unpleasant substance was thrown, annoying and sometimes injuring the public. In 1848, a local newspaper denounced this practice as a "diabolical abomination," but also noted the holiday had passed without any major incident that year: "No accidents, however, thanks be to Providence, occurred."[29]

Despite its comeback, there was an ongoing concern among Carnival enthusiasts that the old celebration might die out. In 1842, the *Picayune* questioned whether there would be a Mardi Gras that year, pointing out that they had heard "not a word about it." The article also took on Carnival critics, almost certainly the white Protestant elite, poking back at their controlling "utilitarian spirit of the age" and demands for a rational purpose to justify "a harmless revel": "It originates with and gives existence to humor. Then why should it be abandoned?"[30] A few days later, it was clear that Mardi Gras had not been forsaken:

> Ourselves, and a great many others, if we are not mistaken, were not a little surprised yesterday at witnessing a jolly turnout of masqueraders. An impression had gone forth that the old custom was to be abandoned, and so secret had the movers kept their operations, that they completely succeeded in creating sensation by surprise. Horse, foot, cab, coach, omnibus and cart passed our office about 5, P.M., and such a panorama of ludicrous objects it would be hard to conceive, without the aid of actual observation.[31]

Starting with the Mistick Krewe of Comus in 1856—followed by the Twelfth Night Revelers, Rex, Momus, and others—wealthy, uptown, Anglo-American society began their own Carnival organizations, practices, and rituals. It was these krewes that ultimately shifted carnival away from the entertaining chaos of masking, balls, often rowdy behavior in dance halls, pranks, and impromptu or loosely constructed processions, toward another type of festival built around scheduled, organized parades along established routes (publicized in advance), led by military bands, marching units, flambeaux for night parades, and most important, artfully decorated floats carrying riders. Unlike the often necessarily secretive antebellum Creole Carnival celebrations, which sometimes faced unkind media attention as well as government regulation and harassment, Rex's annual Carnival proclamation was carried on page 1 of the *Daily Picayune*, and he was toasted by the mayor and dignitaries along the route. This full civic embrace of a holiday that many had tried to regulate and even abolish as late as 1859 turned on the fact that the city's political and cultural elite were now Mardi Gras's new self-appointed masters. They even persuaded Reconstruction-era governor Henry Warmouth to make Mardi Gras a state holiday despite the fact that he had been lampooned in the Momus parade. By 1885, the seeds of modern Mardi Gras had taken root following Comus's lead and "the lords of misrule" would boast that they had civilized the Creole Saturnalia. In any event, they had changed it forever.

> It was they (the Americans) who gave Mardi Gras its present pattern. It was they who at least to some extent took it away from the people and changed what had been an unorganized and informal street revel into an entire social season, a highly stylized program of balls and pageants, related to debutants and a caste system as rigid, although in a different way, as that of the creoles.[32]

There was another important change. Earlier celebrations were marked by newspaper notices inviting all maskers to meeting places and providing routes for the planned processions. In contrast, Comus was a members-only organization, so individual maskers had now become spectators instead of participants.[33]

Certainly, to the Americans, what they had done with Mardi Gras was yet another example of the civic improvements they had undertaken in transforming a filthy and corrupt colonial city into a gleaming metropolis. In their eyes, the new Mardi Gras was a sign of progress. Nonetheless, while the old line's high-minded selection of grand themes rooted in mythology and their use of artfully crafted floats carrying riders were innovations, those lovely decorative floats often carried messages of racial animus and Confederate sympathies taking aim at the Reconstruction government and federal authorities. The "old-Line" krewe ascendency happened against the backdrop of mob violence. James Hogue reminds us that, between 1866 and 1877, while New Orleans was the capital city of Louisiana, the city became a battleground for five major armed conflicts instigated by organized white supremacist militia groups.[34] These violent events included the massacre at the Mechanics' Institute in 1866—with an official count of 38 dead, 184 wounded in the fighting, though the actual numbers were likely much higher—and actions of the White League against the Reconstruction-era police force at Liberty Place in 1874.[35] This "uncivil war" culminated in the final collapse of Reconstruction on April 24, 1877, when "newly inaugurated president Rutherford B. Hayes ordered the federal troops who had been guarding the Louisiana state capitol in New Orleans to return to their barracks."[36] All the while, black citizens of New Orleans faced the systematic reversal of political and social gains won since Emancipation.

In the meantime, the public culture of New Orleans reflected an atavistic attitude toward the federal government, as illustrated by the themes of various Mardi Gras krewes. Comus rolled with the theme "Missing Links to Darwin's Origin of the Species" in 1873 and portrayed President Grant as a tobacco grub and General Benjamin Butler as a hyena.[37] Comus's embrace of the budding "science" of race was on display in 1877, the year federal troops left, choosing the theme "The Aryan Race."[38] In 1884, Robert E. Lee's daughter Mildred Lee, as well as daughters of Stonewall Jackson, H. D. Hill, and Jefferson Davis, were fêted at the Comus ball. Lee's daughter danced the first quadrille with the monarch while former Confederate president Jefferson Davis watched from a box seat with his daughters. That was the first year the courts of Rex and Comus met.[39] Though not called so at the time, she was the *de facto* "first queen" of Comus, and the other Confederate daughters served as the maids. Within the gilded pageantry, the tableau was a definitive affirmation of the sentiments of unre-

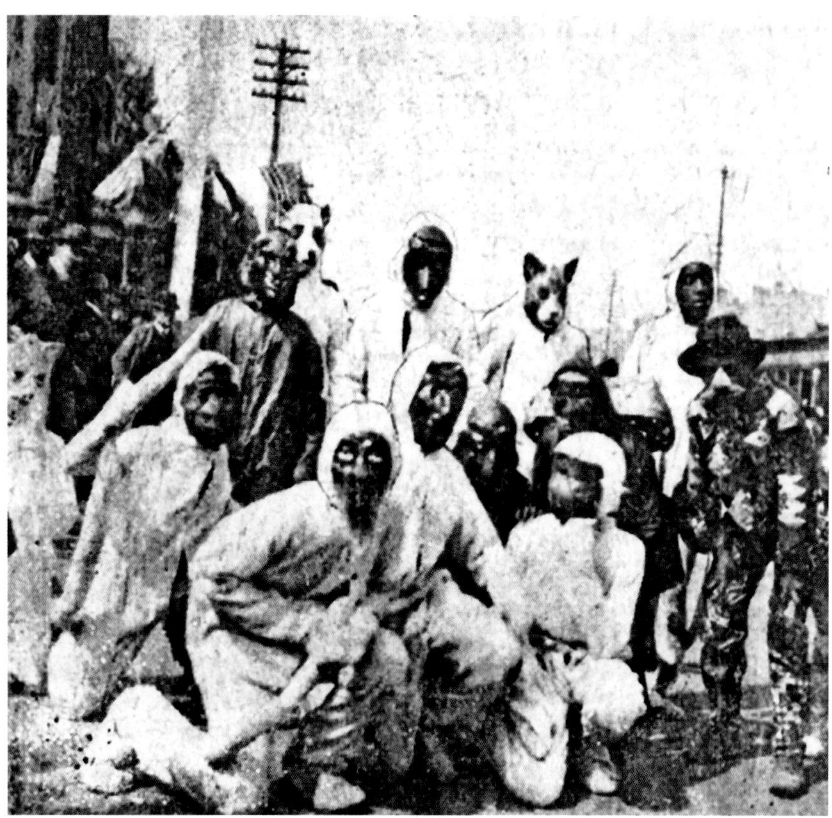

A group of white monkeys at 1903 Mardi Gras. Louisiana State Museum, Special Collections, Times-Democrat, February 26, 1903.

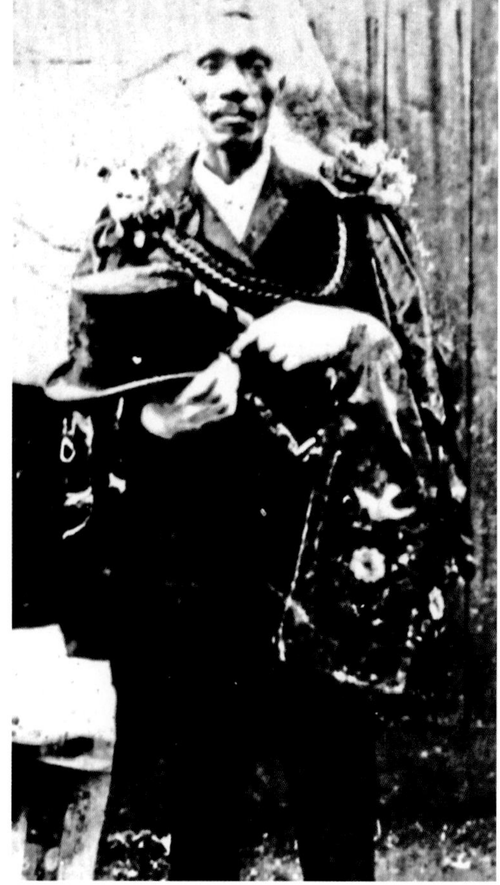

William "Willie" Armstrong, the father of Louis Armstrong, dressed as the Grand Marshall of the Order of the Oddfellows in New Orleans. According to Louis, Willie masked as a white monkey on Mardi Gras. Photo from the author's (McCusker) collection.

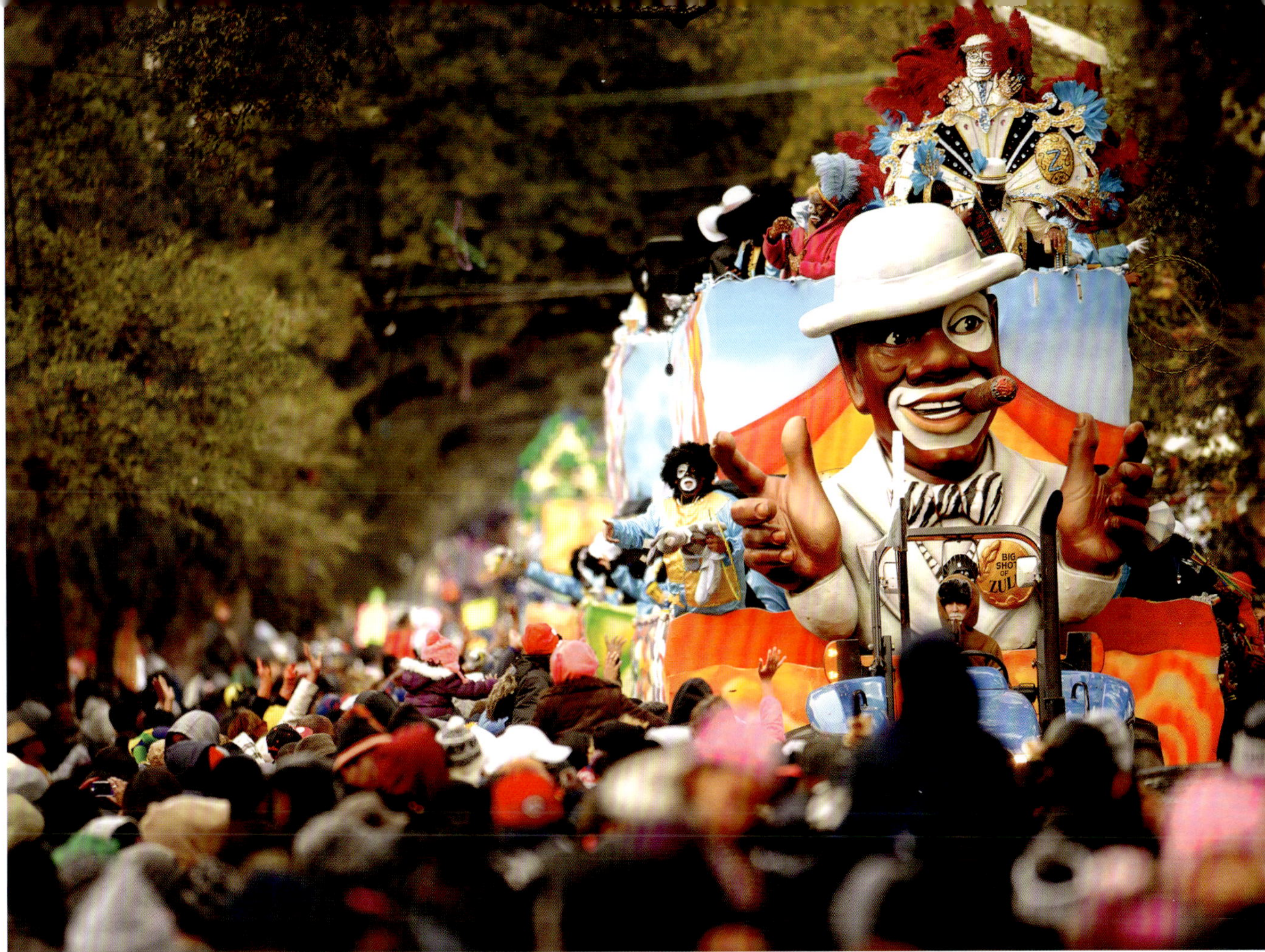

The Zulu Social Aid and Pleasure Club parades down Jackson Avenue in 2015. Originally formed as "The Tramps" in a club house on Perdido Street, near South Rampart in 1909, the founders were inspired by a vaudeville performance at the Pythian Temple featuring a skit set in Africa called "There Has Never Been and Will Never Be a King Like Me." Photo by John McCusker/New Orleans Advocate.

constructed Confederates of the antebellum gentry. Mildred Lee's visit to New Orleans coincided with the unveiling of the giant General Robert E. Lee statue at what became Lee Circle (Tivoli Circle). In the course of a few decades, the same elite class that had once criticized Creole Carnival celebrations as a threat to public order and authority was using Mardi Gras to openly challenge and mock the legitimacy of the national government while fostering nostalgia for the Lost Cause.

To people of color, whatever reforming Carnival needed, it would not have included them being marginalized in the celebration of what had also been their holiday. The "old line" krewes appropriated what had been an organic, admittedly but gloriously chaotic, grassroots, multicultural holiday, and set themselves up as the main event instead. With attention now placed on white American Carnival balls and parades, the Mardi Gras celebrations of other groups faded into shadows and background noise. *Pro Bono Publico*, indeed. Still, wistful glimpses of that other side of Carnival occasionally made it to the pages of the newspapers:

> Not many years back there was a rivalry between different wards as to the number of "Mardi Gras" each would put upon the streets. There were bands of masqueraders, twenty, thirty and fifty strong, parading the streets and performing all manner of queer feats. They were looked upon as a part of Mardi Gras Day, and their presence would have been sadly missed. (*Times-Democrat*, February 25, 1903)[40]

By the early twentieth century, there were numerous established group masking themes within the black community. These included groups of Skeletons (who took to the streets before dawn), white monkeys (groups of black maskers in white body suits and monkey masks), and Baby Dolls (prostitutes who dressed in baby doll outfits with dollar bills poking out of their garters) and the Zulu Social Aid and Pleasure Club.[41]

Louis Armstrong, who reigned as King Zulu in 1949, remembered his father, Willie, masking when he was a boy.

> My father was a guy who masked every year . . . He used to mask in a big white monkey suit . . . The trouble with a guy who'll pass you in a monkey suit, he's liable to hit you in the chops with their tails . . . Because their tails have marbles in them . . . A lick in the chops with those tails would make them swell up, just like, two beef hearts.[42]

Like the Indians, these maskers traversed the city in roving groups on Mardi Gras.

In nineteenth-century accounts—both antebellum and postwar—it is clear there were well-established "characters" or "typical" costumes that were popular, even ubiquitous, for decades, even as Carnival practices and attitudes changed. Many years, there were doubts expressed about the vitality of Mardi Gras when fewer maskers were seen, only to have another

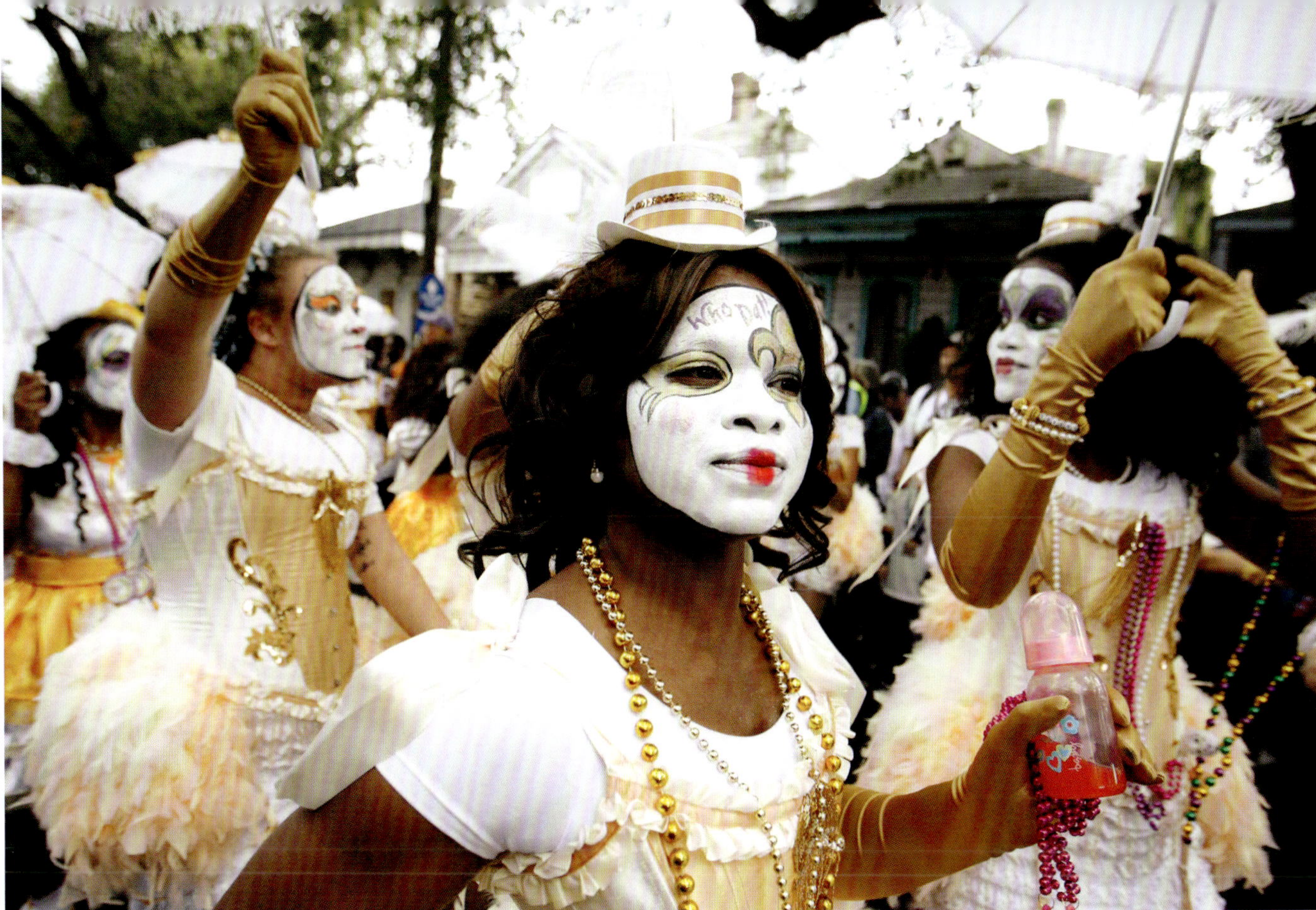

A group of latter-day Baby Dolls strut down Jackson Avenue in the Zulu parade on Mardi Gras 2012. Black prostitutes began masking as sexualized "Baby Dolls" around 1912. In recent decades, new groups calling themselves "Baby Dolls" have emerged in homage to the demimonde maskers of a century ago. Photo by John McCusker.

year's report say the opposite. Through it all, masking persisted. Harlequins, clowns, Arabs, Turks, peasants, nobles, Hindus, boys dressed as girls, and girls dressed as boys are mentioned time and again. One of the most enduring and popular costume selections was noted during Carnival in 1838:

> The principal streets were traversed by a masquerade company on horseback and in carriages, from the fantastic Harlequin to the somber Turk and wild Indian. A delightful throng followed on the heels of the cavalcade as it marched through our city suburbs, and wherever it went the procession raised a perfect hubbub and jubilee. The exhibition surpassed anything of the kind ever witnessed here.[43]

When he visited New Orleans during the 1846 Mardi Gras, Englishman Charles Lyell witnessed a lively and thriving festival and "a variety of costumes—some as Indians with feathers in their heads, and one, a jolly fat man, as Mardi Gras himself."[44] In 1854, Indians were witnessed as a theme for collective masking as well: "We saw, here and there, groups of maskers attired in fancy dresses, but there was no large procession as has sometimes been the case. A party of Indians, in full costume, was the most notable thing of the kind we saw."[45] The next year a man was hit in the head by a club wielded by a "wild Indian."[46]

The consistent presence of Indian maskers at Mardi Gras against the national embrace of Indianness—both authentic and in stereotype—marks the universality the Indian character had achieved as an American icon. Costumed Indian sightings at Carnival were so common that one writer called seeing them "inevitable": "An inevitable Indian queen strutted before us, in all her gorgeousness of aboriginal paint and feathers. That she is pretty, we are assured from some pleasant, stolen glimpses we had of her face."[47] News accounts find masked Indians traveling both alone and in groups, and in this 1870 case, caught up in the judicial system:

> The Relics of Mardi Gras
>
> There was never a rose without its thorn, nor a pleasure without its pain. The truth was found ample illustration in the municipal courts on (Ash) Wednesday morning . . . . The parti-colored costumes of an Indian warrior hung in shreds and patches from a form bruised and battered in a struggle with the police.[48]

The following year, someone relishing the sight of Mardi Gras costumes was disappointed by someone who did not behave in accordance with his assumed persona:

> Among the revelers we observed a tall and graceful Indian, his hirsute adornment trading [*sic*] the ground after the manner of the chief described in Catlin's painting. We saluted him with a few familiar Choctaw words, and as "ye gentle savage," it was his duty to have replied as becomes the denizen of the woody wilds. But he spake never a word, not comprehending the meaning

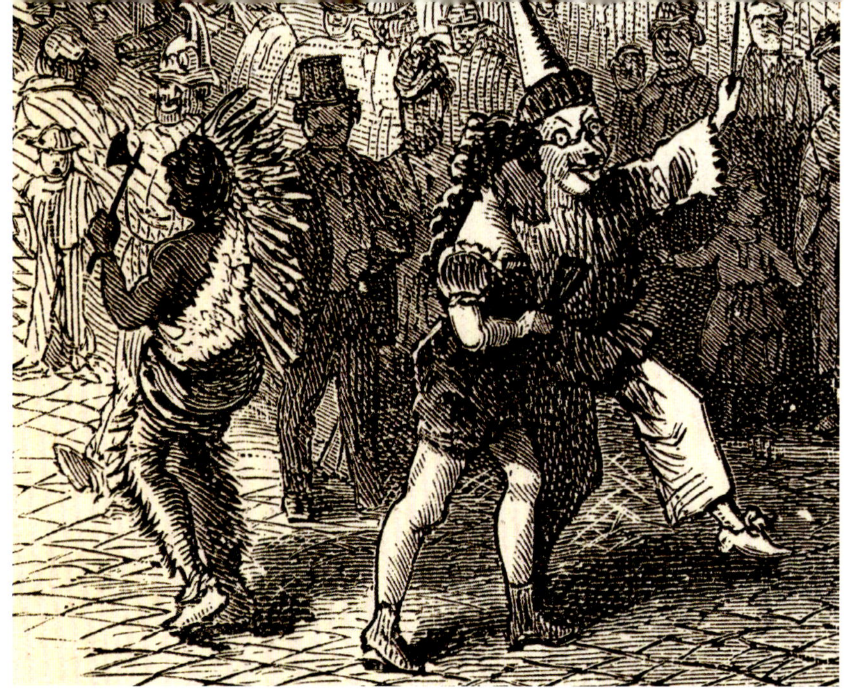

Mardi Gras in black and white: Detail from an 1875-era Mardi Gras drawing showing an Indian among the maskers at Mardi Gras. From the book *The Great South; A Record of Journeys in Louisiana, Texas, the Indian Territory, Missouri, Arkansas, Mississippi, Alabama, Georgia, Florida, South Carolina, North Carolina, Kentucky, Tennessee, Virginia, West Virginia, and Maryland by Edward King*. Documenting the American South collection, The University Library of the University of North Carolina at Chapel Hill.

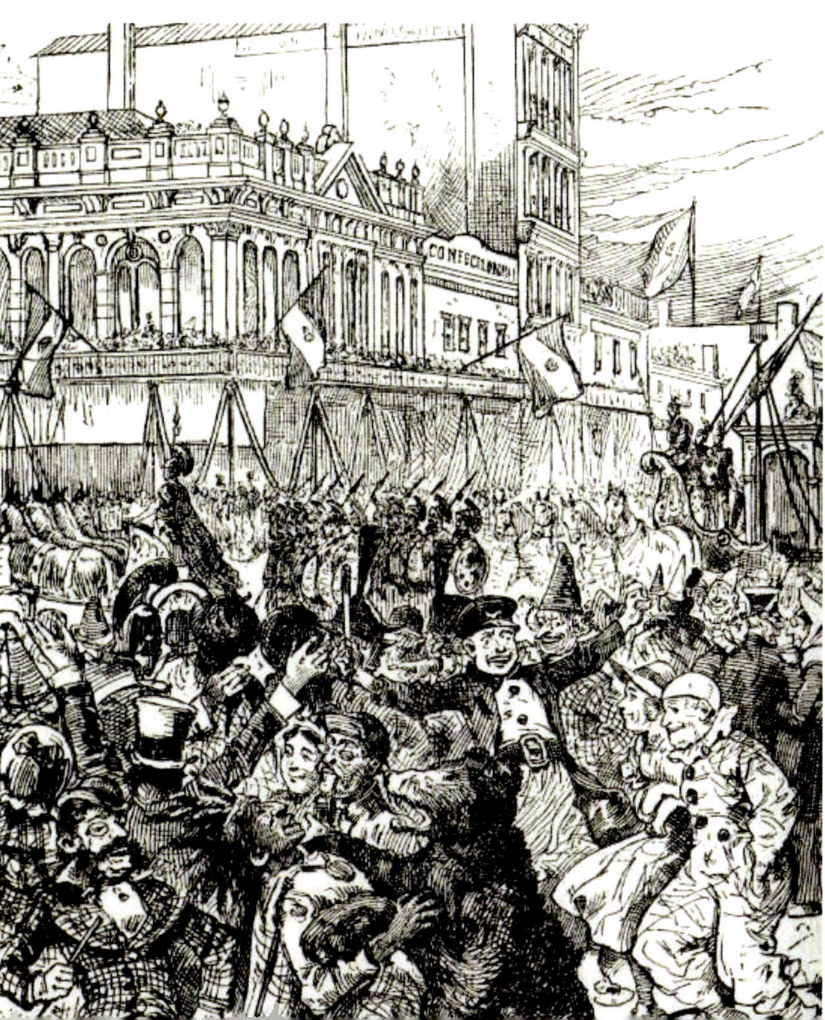

Illustration from Mark Twain's *Life on the Mississippi* (1883) showing an Indian among Mardi Gras maskers. Documenting the American South collection, The University Library of the University of North Carolina at Chapel Hill.

> of our words of recognition or salutation. What business had he dressing a character he could not play?[49]

Not only does this vignette reveal how Catlin's exhibits continued to affect the collective imagination when it came to how Indians are supposed to appear, but the mock-disdain incidentally shows that the Indian was a Carnival character familiar to New Orleanians by the 1870s.

A year later, a journalist observed as "An Indian chief, in war paint, with an immense plume of eagle feathers, passed along, but his war whoop was not as good as his disguise, and he failed to create terror in the hearts of hearers."[50] By Carnival 1885, a *Picayune* writer noted that costumed Indian "tribes" (*plural*) had taken over the scene: "As usual the maskers assumed all classes and nationalities as characters, but the Indian predominated, and whole tribes of red men were to be seen marching up and down the streets."[51] Another writer also spotted groups of Indians during the 1885 Carnival season: "Now and then a masker drifted by: a string of feathered Indians, far more agreeable to the eye than the occasional real brave who pushed his way stolidly through the crowd."[52] One wonders what one of those Native Americans thought of all the make-believe Indians around them? Were some of them in town with the Buffalo Bill Wild West Show, which was visiting that Carnival, or were they native to the New Orleans area? Costumed Indian groups were spotted again in 1891 when the *Picayune* writer noted "Indian warriors in paint and feathers."[53] The consistent newspaper references to Indian costuming and group masking, over seven decades, demonstrates that both were established, collective practices and therefore expected components of the festival.

At some point in the years preceding the appearance of the 1895 Algiers story, Indian masking became, to some members of the African American community, something more than just a costume. The possibility that this process was already under way decades earlier is raised by the observations of a *Picayune* reporter on Mardi Gras in 1879.

> The effect of the procession is queer. It makes everybody look at his neighbor twice to see that he is not a Mardi Gras. Every face looks like a mask, and

> every dress like a fantastic costume. "Huzza! Here's one of 'em. Chick-a-ma-feeno! Chick-a-ma-feeno!" they shout as an Indian makes his way through the crowd, jingling his bells and flourishing his tomahawk. "Isn't he bully?" cries one, "Sitting Bully!" yells back another; and the crowd laugh and cheer.[54]

In her memoir, Elise Kirsch (1876–1966) wrote about her early childhood in New Orleans, where she lived in the Seventh Ward. On Mardi Gras Day in 1883, she witnessed this scene:

> At about 10 a.m., that day there was a band of men (about 60) disguised as Indians who wore the real Indian costumes and their chiefs had turkey feathers running down from around their heads way down in the back. They came along from St. Bernard avenue on Robertson Street, shouting and screaming war whoops and carried tomahawks—on their way back would stop and perform war dances, etc., and would run for a block and begin again. Though frightened when very young, we always waited for the passing of the Indians.[55]

Though lacking the racial specifics of the 1895 Algiers story, it would be a strain to argue these observations, made over a decade earlier, were not of black Indians, given the detailed annual observations described by Kirsch and the quotation of the Mardi Gras Indian phrase "Chick-a-ma-feeno" in the 1879 *Picayune* account. First of all, the location provided in Kirsch's memoir, Robertson and St. Bernard in the Seventh Ward, is an area noted as a hot bed of Indian activity. But more significantly, "Chick-a-ma-feeno," with its Mobilian Jargon roots detailed previously (chapter 2), is hardly just an impromptu expression that a casual Indian masker, or those around him, would have uttered. In fact, this is exactly the phrase that signals a connection to a much deeper history preceding the Wild West shows of the 1880s. After all, many Native Americans and African Americans in the New Orleans area shared a legacy of blended traditions.

The 1895 Algiers story in the *Picayune* identified several practicing Indians in its report, possibly the first bit of journalism to do so. This one, from 1900, names more:

> Every Mardi Gras bunches of negroes get together masked as Indians and a hundred-strong race through the streets playing fool antics and at the same time have their eyes open for trouble. They always find it when they clash with another organization of their kind and usually there is a free for all fight when they meet.
>
> It was so yesterday when the Red, White and Blue and the Chickasaws met in the afternoon at the corner of Perdido and Franklin streets and as a result two blacks are wounded and three of the Indians are in custody. All negroes take Franklin Street as their St. Charles Avenue and of course they cut up all their monkey shines to win laughs and comment. The two parades were turning side by side and some outsiders began talking of the better appearance of the Chickasaws. The Red, White and Blues were jealous and some black buck cracked one of the Chickasaws on the head. That started the fight and in a few seconds, everybody was clubbing around, and it looked as though the street would be flooded with coon blood. The negroes got out their pistols and the big blacks were bolting into houses and through windows and falling into the quarters.
>
> John Henry Lewis, who is about 30 years old, had it out with Lawrence Clementine, and as Lewis was getting the worst of the affair he pulled his pistol and began firing. His shot caught Clementine in the left side of the stomach, making a dangerous wound. After that Lewis ran down Franklin street and someone fired at him, the bullet hitting him in the left hip and making an ugly wound . . . . The police went around grabbing the hoodlum coons and got Willie Williams, the one who fired at Lewis.[56]

An aggregation of names from the 1895 Algiers story, this one from 1900 as well as those mentioned in oral history, raises the veil of anonymity on individual nineteenth-century Indians. These men include a Creole plasterer, "Becate" Baptiste Eugene (1873–c.1926?); a teamster, Joseph Horton (1866–1910); two carpenters, Henry Jerry (1869–1940) and John Henry Lewis (c. 1884–1933); a fireman and army veteran, Henry Lean (c. 1841–?); a truck driver, Henry Marigny (1878–1960); a mason, Robert Sam Tillman (1871–1898); a race track worker, Milton Sparks (1869–1928); and a laborer, Willie Williams (1870–?).[57] (See Appendix I for biographies.)

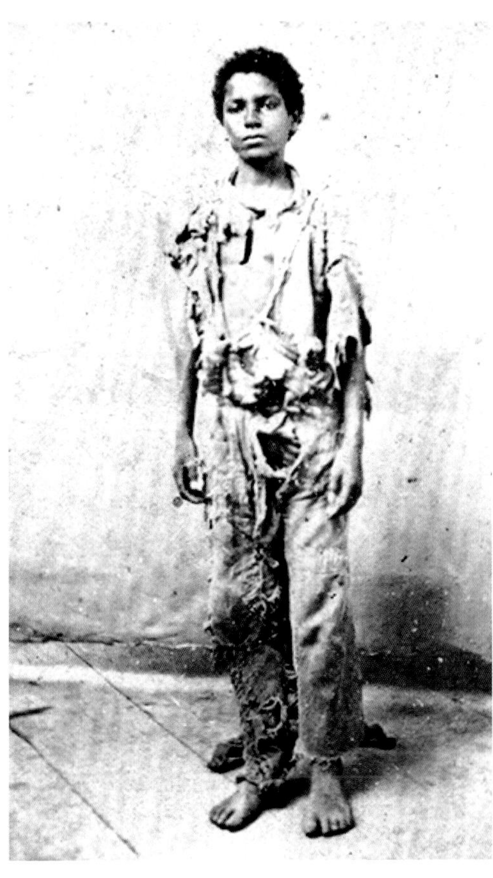

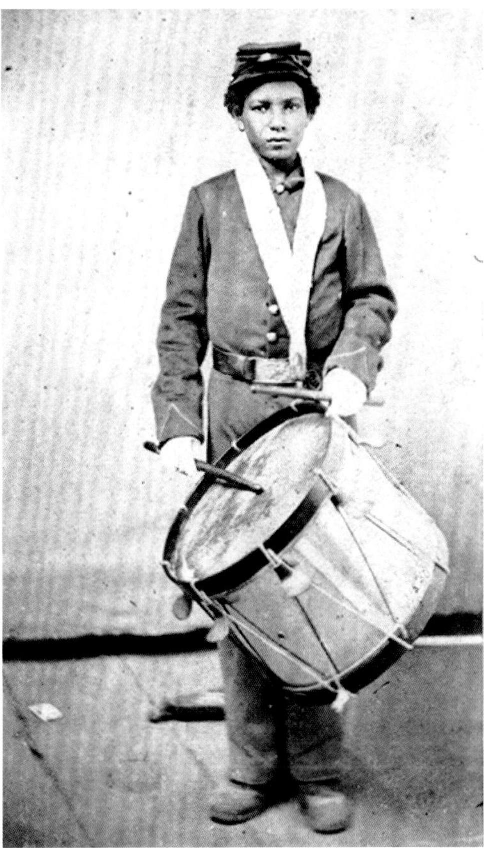

(Left) 1863. An enslaved boy named Taylor ran away from a Louisiana plantation and made his way to the Union lines. Library of Congress, Prints & Photographs Division, LC-DIG-ppmsca-52168.

(Right) Taylor after enlisting in the Corps d'Afrique as a drummer boy. Library of Congress, Prints & Photographs Division, LC-DIG-ppmsca-52169.

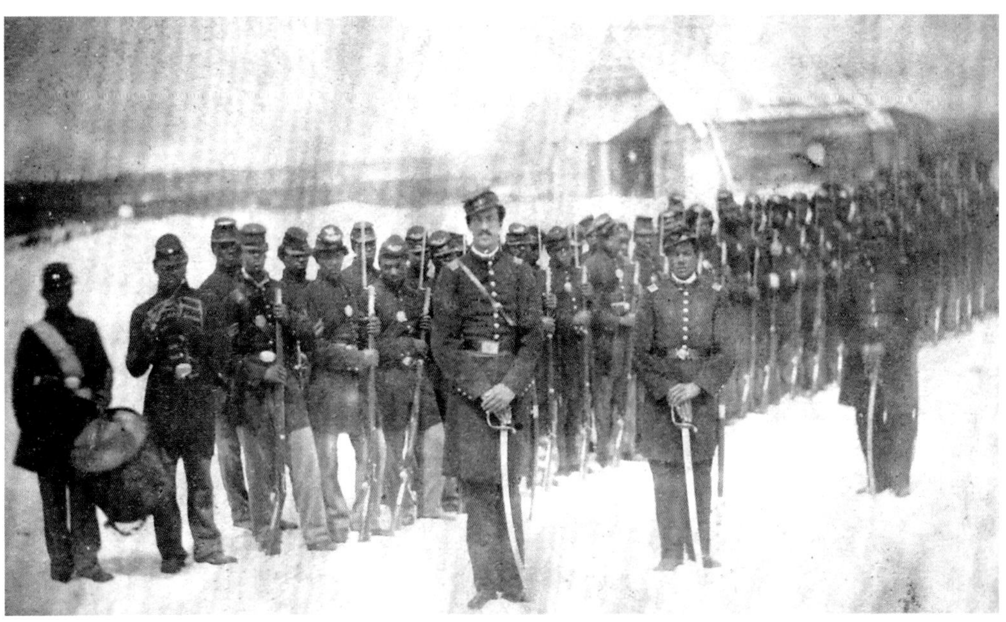

The Corps d'Afrique, 1863. "Once let the black man get upon his person the brass letters U.S.; let him get an eagle on his button, and a musket on his shoulder, and bullets in his pocket, and there is no power on the earth or under the earth which can deny that he has earned the right of citizenship in the United States" (Frederick Douglass). Union veterans played a role in Reconstruction politics and benevolent, social, and secret social organizing as Reconstruction ended. Image Courtesy Nathan W. Daniels Diary; Vol. I, 1861, Dec. 1864, Library of Congress.

These Indians—some teenagers, one in his fifties—found themselves celebrating Mardi Gras within the same tradition emerging from neighborhoods throughout the city. What was the common thread among these identified Indians, if not vocation, neighborhood, or age? Part of the answer may be the service records of many of their fathers from the Civil War. After all, many African Americans living in and around New Orleans had a leading role in achieving their own liberty: "Louisiana contributed more black soldiers and more black officers to the Union cause than any other state, North or South."[58]

"Becate" Baptiste's father, Jean Baptiste Eugene, served in the Corps d'Afrique, which had been established by General Major Nathaniel Banks of the Union army on May 1, 1863.[59] Jean Baptiste Eugene then served in the Seventy-Third Regiment, United States Colored Infantry. Joseph Horton's father, Henry, also served in the Corps d'Afrique and then the Colored Infantry. Milton Sparks's father, Milton Sr., was a sergeant in the 117th Regiment, United States Colored Infantry. Henry Jerry's dad, Samuel, 1840–1870, was a sergeant in the Corps d'Afrique and later in the Eighty-Seventh Regiment, United States Colored Infantry. Henry Marigny's father, Henry, was a first sergeant in the Forty-Seventh Colored Infantry. Henry Lean, one of the men arrested in Algiers in 1895, was a veteran of the Seventh Colored Louisiana Infantry.

Many of the soldiers in these units, notably the Corps d'Afrique, participated in the capture of the Confederate fort at Port Hudson in 1863, taking heavy losses after three ill-advised frontal assaults, but they garnered fame and admiration up North for engaging in the first large-scale military action by black soldiers for the cause of the Union.[60] The Corps-sponsored parades led by brass bands and members of the unit also performed in New Orleans theaters singing camp songs and dancing.[61] The Corps d'Afrique was later reorganized and given standard US Army unit numbers.[62]

In the years during wartime occupation and later Reconstruction, African Americans eagerly took part in the freedoms their newfound citizenship promised. Their participation in the military was especially important, according to Frederick Douglass:

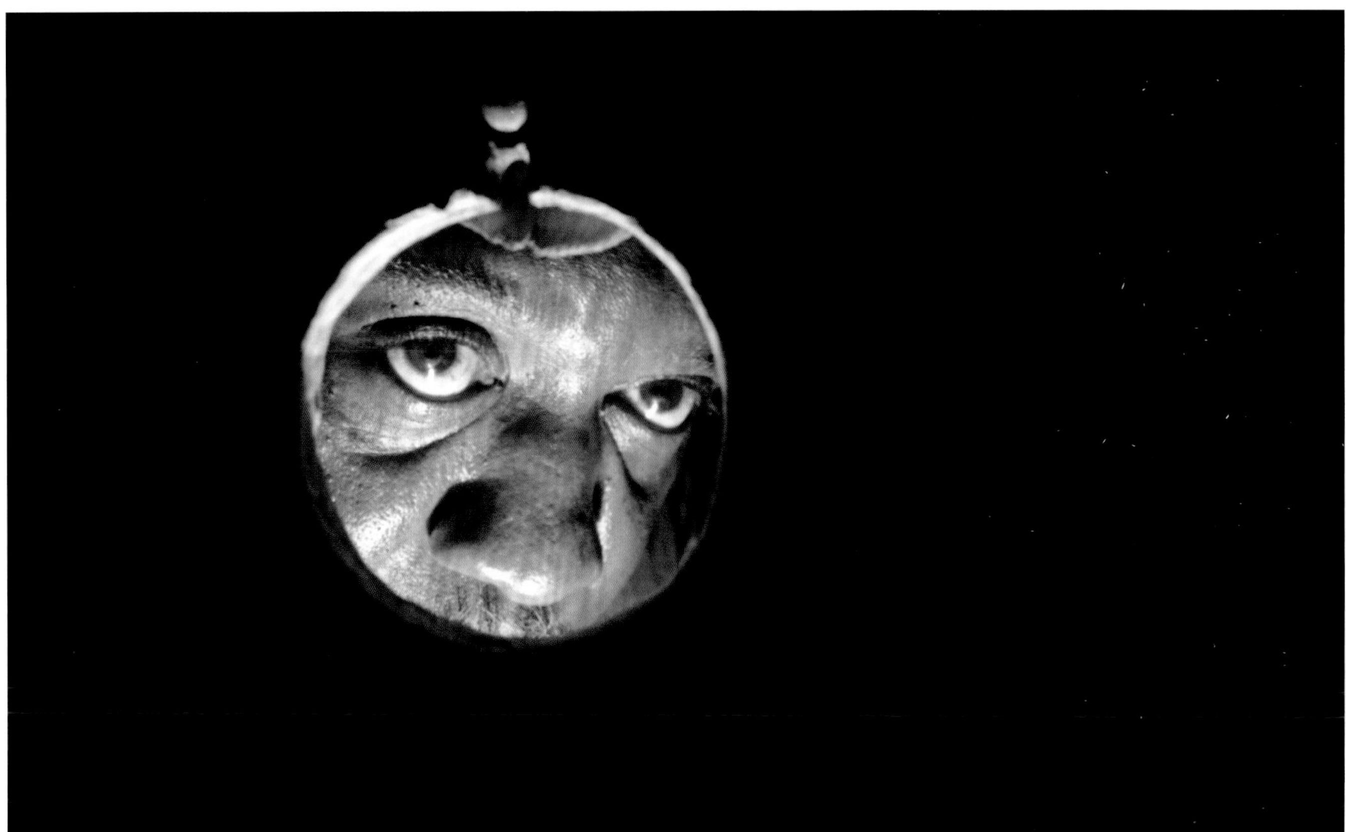

Inside Looking Out and Outside Looking In. Hammond Jones mans the peephole at a meeting of the Young Men Olympian Junior Benevolent Association in 1997. The YMO Jr. BA is the last of New Orleans's once-ubiquitous fraternal and burial associations still operating. It was founded in Central City in 1878. African Americans formed societies after hard-won rights were lost when Reconstruction ended and they again found themselves as the Other. Photo by John McCusker.

> Never since the world began was a better chance offered to a long enslaved and oppressed people. The opportunity is given us to be men. With one courageous resolution we may blot out the hand-writing of the ages against us. Once let the black man get upon his person the brass letters U.S.; let him get an eagle on his button, and a musket on his shoulder, and bullets in his pocket, and there is no power on the earth or under the earth which can deny that he has earned the right of citizenship in the United States.[63]

During Reconstruction, African Americans registered to vote and were elected to public office. Corps d'Afrique veterans were particularly active in political organizing.[64] Political meetings were held on the old dancing ground at Congo Square, and Freedmens Banks opened, along with inte-

Arthur Batiste and Herbert "Wizard" Gettridge Sr. at a meeting of the Young Men Olympian Junior Benevolent Association at Bulls Hall in 1996. The Olympians are the last functioning benevolent society in New Orleans that still buries its members with music and holds Sunday brass band parades. The group was one of dozens founded in New Orleans after the end of Reconstruction in 1877. These groups funded brass band music in the years before the dawn of jazz. Photo by John McCusker.

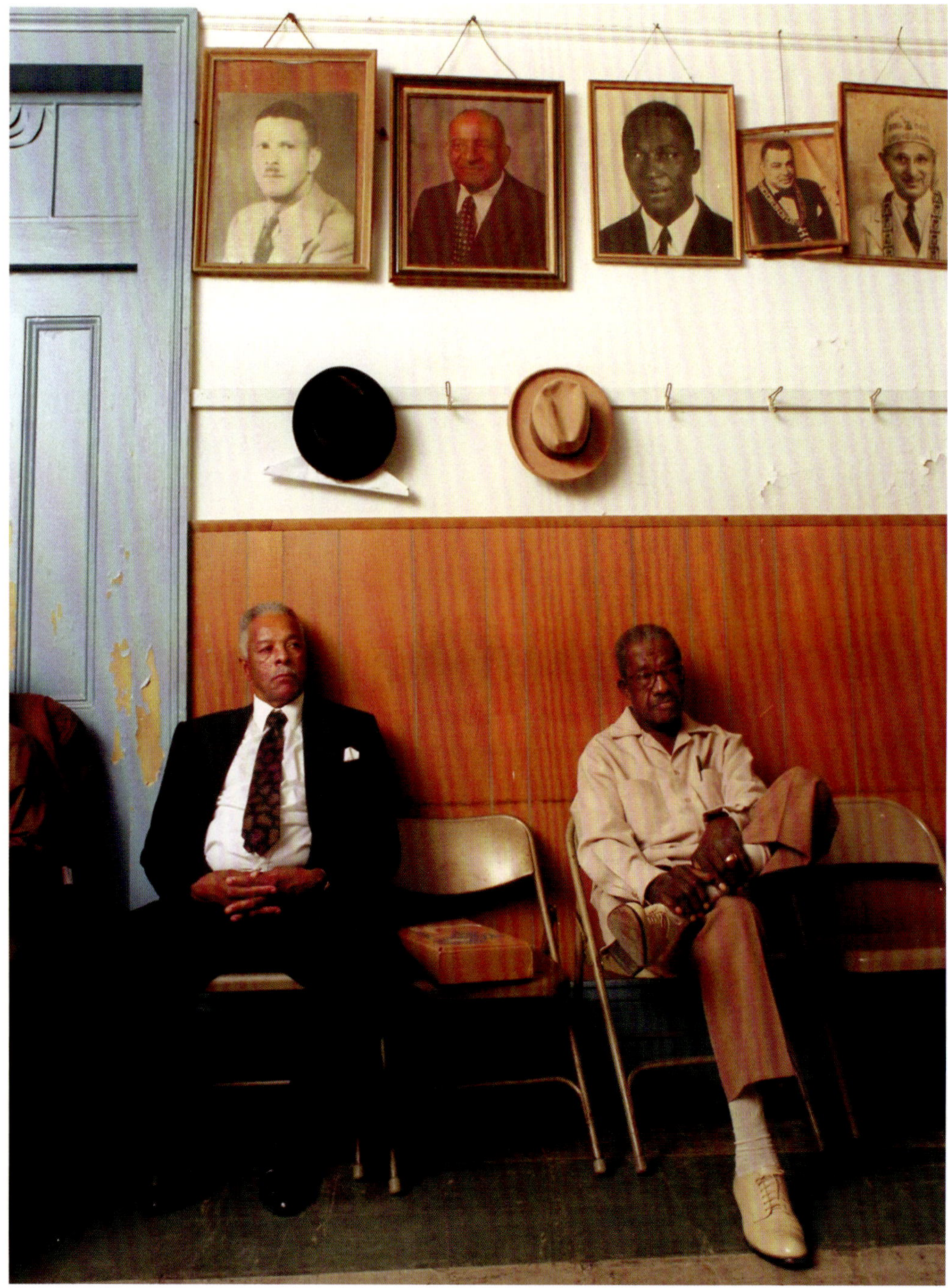

(Right) Harold Dudley leads a funeral parade for a Zulu Social Aid and Pleasure Club member in 1993. Zulu was founded in 1909 and was originally known as the Tramps. They bury their members with full honors and a brass band. Photo by John McCusker/The Times-Picayune.

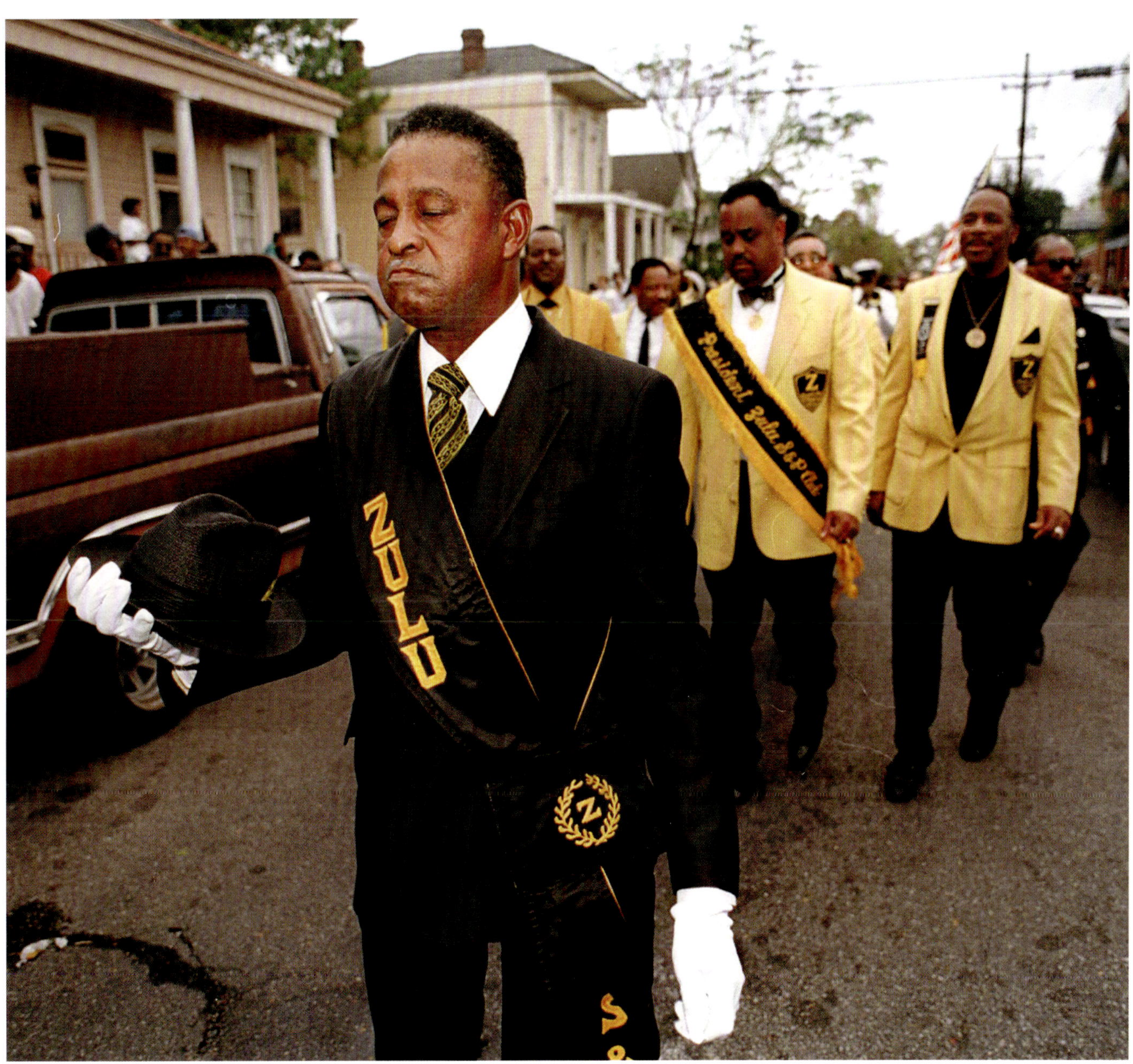
ZULU

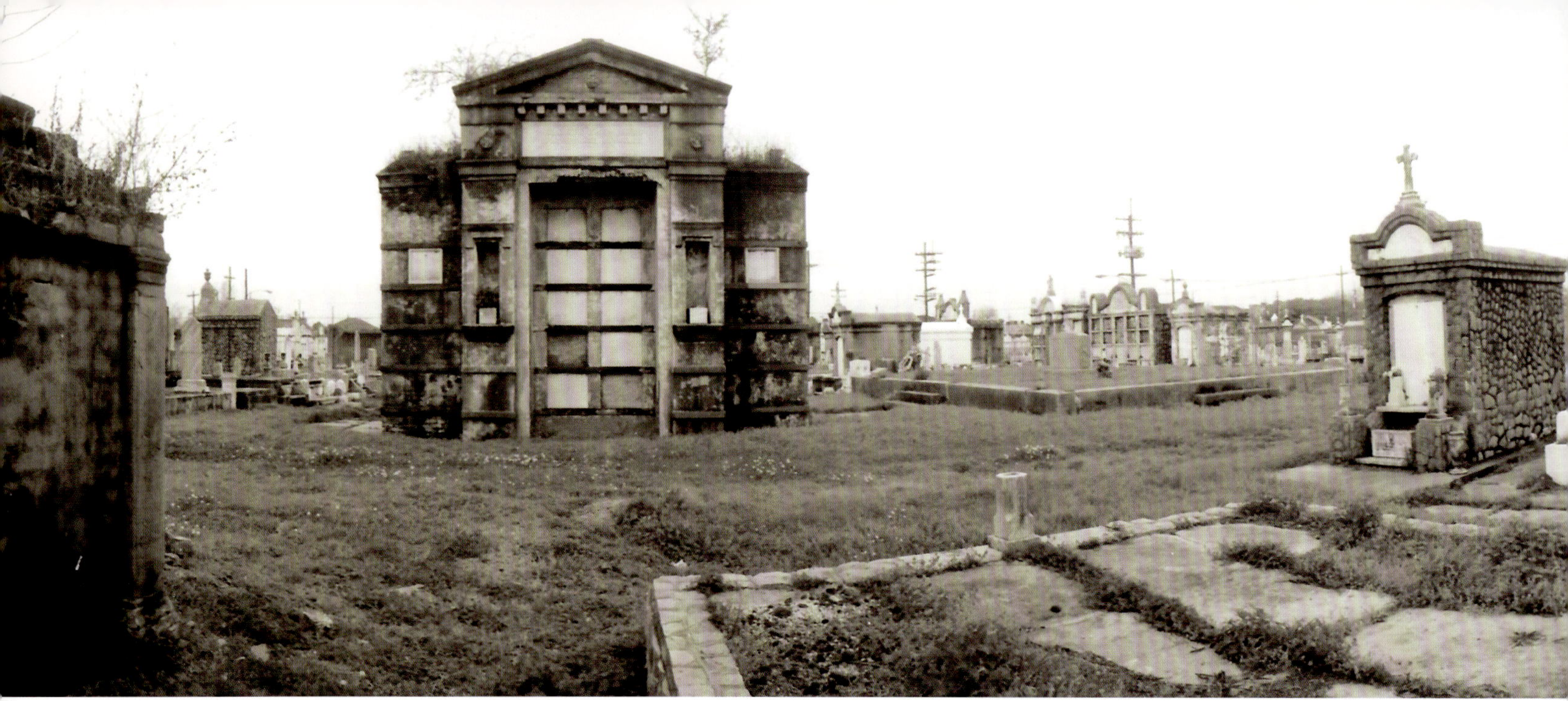

Société Française de Bienfaisance et d'Assistance Mutuelle, Lafayette #2 Cemetery in Central City, one of over a dozen benevolent society tombs there. Photo by John McCusker.

grated schools. This was possible due to the protection of federal troops (which included many African Americans), and the metropolitan police, which was also manned with black veterans.

But the hard-won political and social gains slipped away violently as the federal troops departed in 1877. The state's interim governor, P. B. S. Pinchback, a former officer in the Corps d'Afrique, recommended that the Freedmen form mutual aid and benevolent societies to create a social safety net in times of need and to create a forum to discuss the issues of the day and inform others. Governor Pinchback had ample reason to believe that the black citizens of New Orleans needed additional means to support each other as much as possible; after all, like all the governors of Louisiana who served between 1865 and 1877—but as the only African American governor of a southern state—he faced attempts at replacement or impeachment, death threats, assassination attempts, and an armed attempt to overthrow his government while he was in office.[65] It was a prescient repurposing of an existing institutional model that had been ubiquitous in New Orleans since the 1840s.[66] Post-Reconstruction black mutual aid societies were founded throughout the city, from the center of the metropolis to the outskirts, channeling concerns of a com-

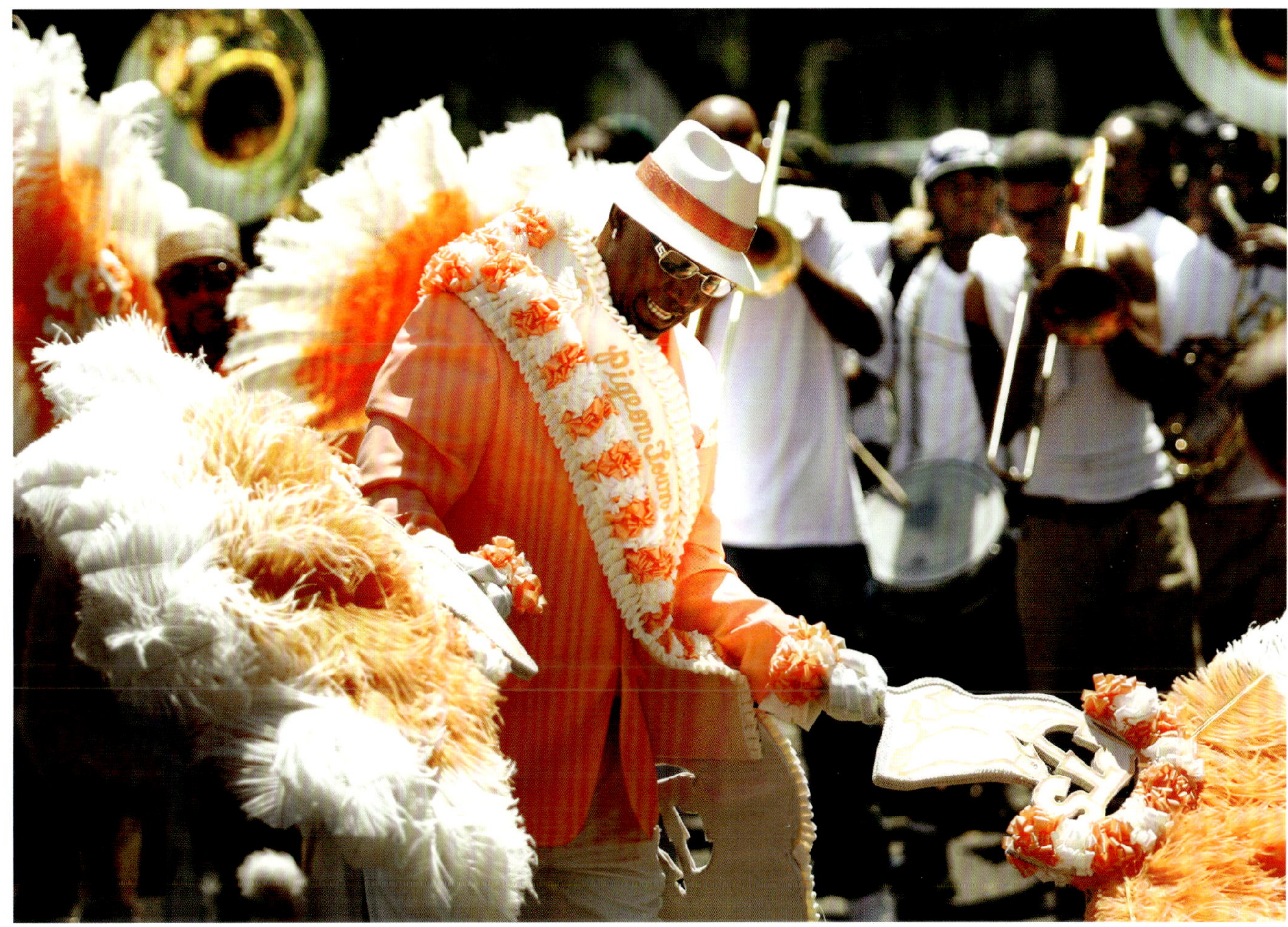

The Original Pigeontown Steppers take to the streets uptown in 2012, dancing with the music of the Stooges Brass Band. Photo by John McCusker/The Times-Picayune.

munity that had gone from enslavement to tasting freedom, only to be cut off by the rise of Jim Crow. That message resonated with Milton Sparks's father. Union army veteran Milton Sparks Sr. worked as an organizer in Reconstruction politics.[67] He also founded benevolent societies and social and pleasure clubs in keeping with Pinchback's advice.[68] As a dividend, this organizing activity ensured employment of African American brass bands at funerals and parades and transported an established practice to a new level of popularity among black participants. This wind band tradition would play a major role in the development of New Orleans jazz.[69]

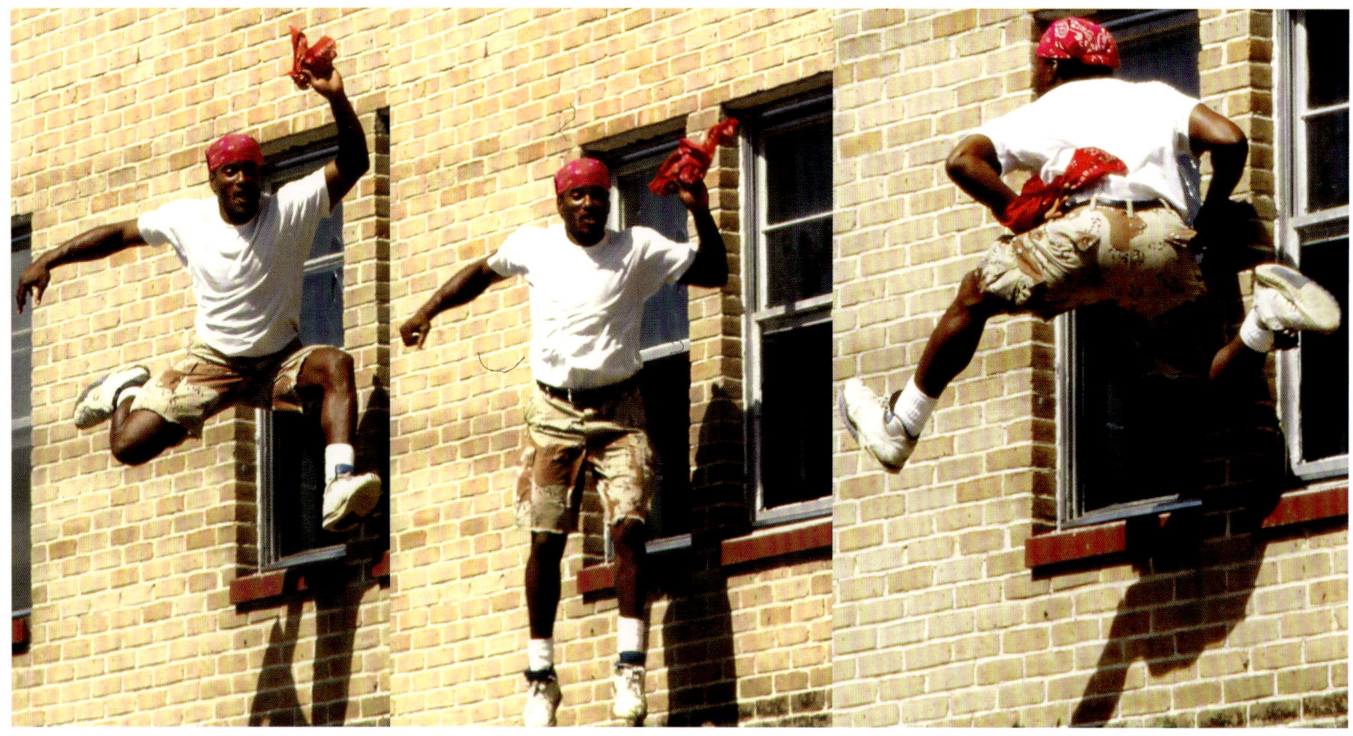

A sequence of a man dancing atop a ledge at the now-demolished Melpomene Projects in New Orleans in 1992. Photo by John McCusker.

Just as important, mutual aid and benevolent societies created a forum for now marginalized community leaders like Milton Sparks Sr. to pass information to the public and care for their own.

Men like Jean Baptiste Eugene, Samuel Jerry, and Henry Horton, who had served in the Corps d'Afrique, had shared wartime experiences. A question worth asking is whether it was these veterans, who had fought and bled together, that first brought forth the Indian tribes, by rechanneling their shared experiences as actual warriors into a Carnival identity. As Reconstruction collapsed, and black community organizing expanded underground in the late 1870s, did Mardi Gras Indians emerge as an expression of pride and resistance in a movement driven by black veterans?

To identify as American Indians, who at that time were in open armed conflict with the American military, was to identify with fearless fellow travelers who symbolized pride and resistance to persecution, aggression, and genocide. It was an identity both subversive and fundamental in its

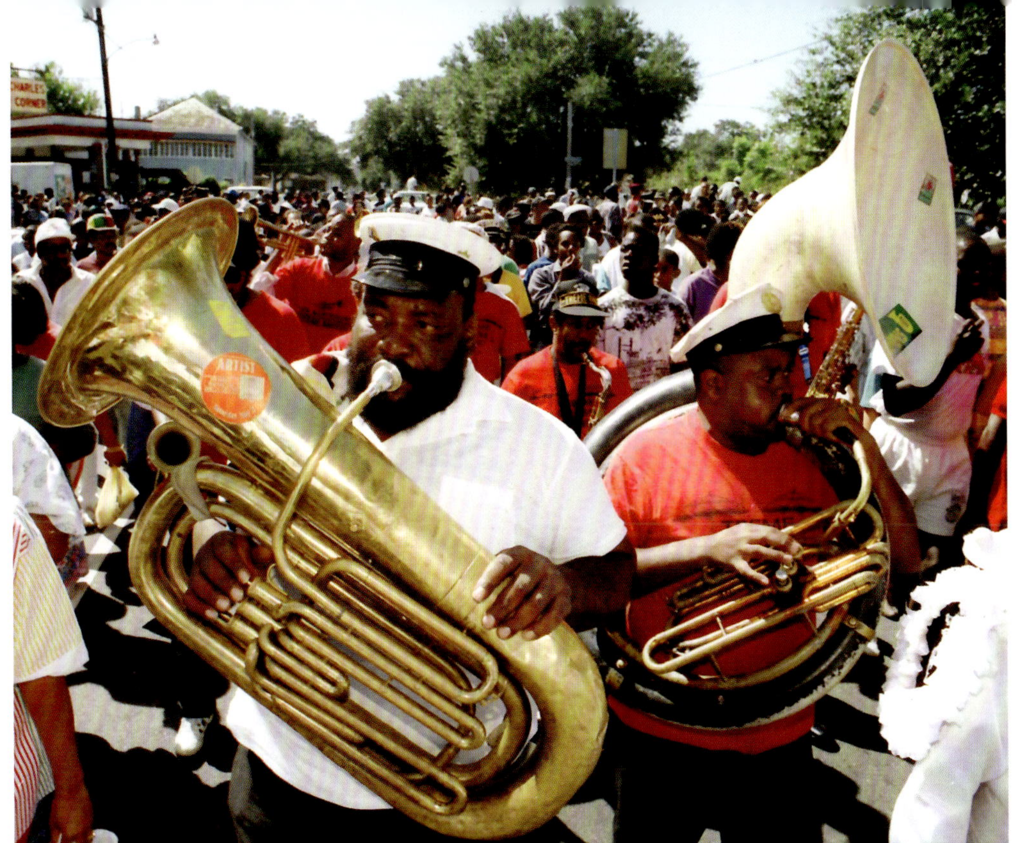

Anthony "Tuba Fats" Lacen playing a Sunday brass band parade or "second-line" in 1992. The fraternal orders, benevolent societies, and masonic groups that paid for parades a century ago have been replaced by social aid and pleasure clubs. Photo by John McCusker.

Lil Rascals Brass Band, James Durant, sax; Kerwin Dewan Scott and Ezell Quinn on trumpets; Kerwin James, tuba; Corey Henry, trombone, marching through Treme in celebration of the Rebirth Brass Band's tenth anniversary in 1993. Photo by John McCusker.

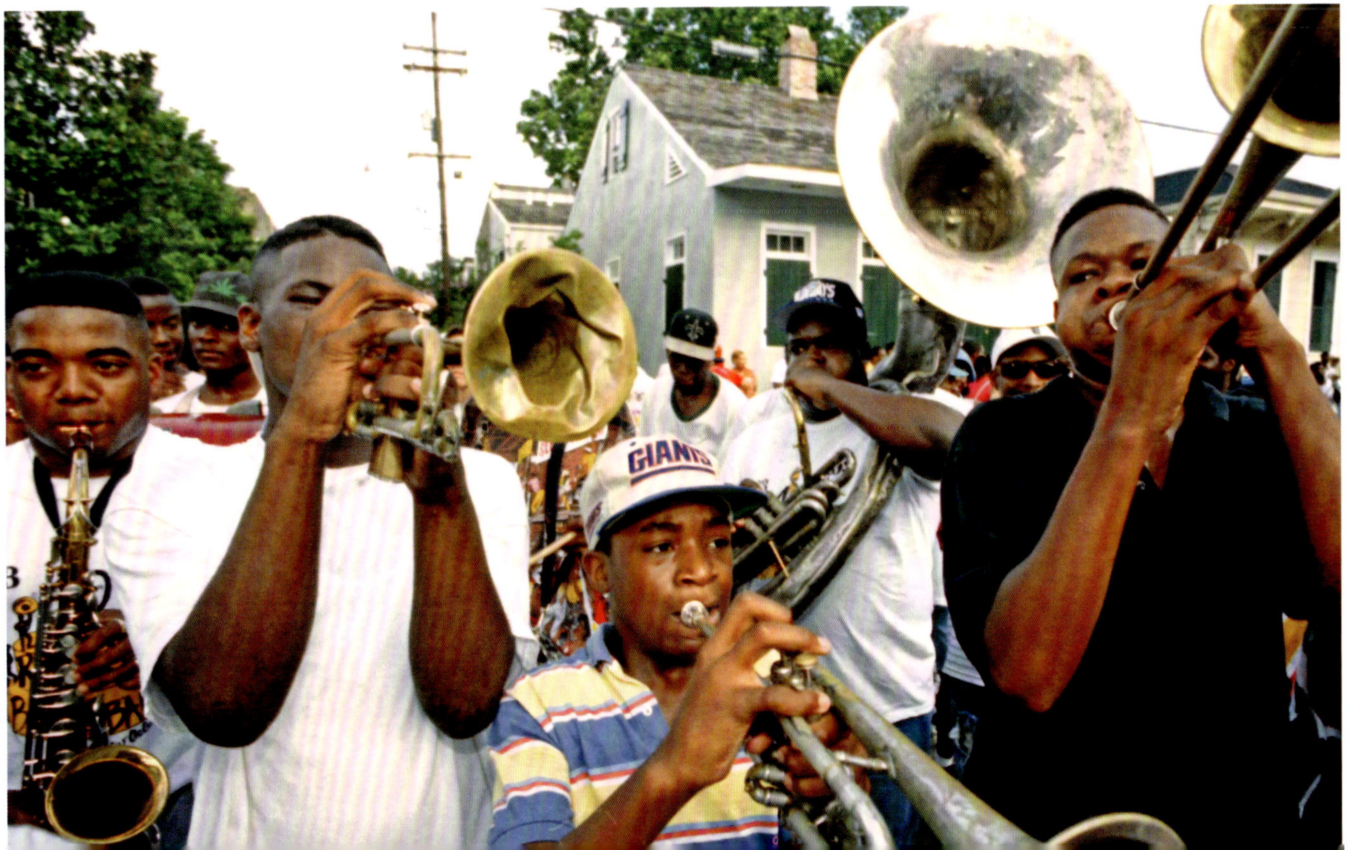

declaration of humanity. The desire to escape a debasing reality is one that must have burned deeper among the Indians' founders than that of even the most earnest Carnival masker. On Mardi Gras, a teamster, a chauffeur, a laborer, a porter, or a plasterer is an "Indian of the Nation," part of a collective city-wide community existing on the margins, apart from what Carnival had become. A projection of the pride, cocksureness, virility, strength, and ultimately, the beauty and creativity kept hidden the rest of the year. On Mardi Gras, a man, via Indianness, could be a man. Not unlike the former slaves who transformed into the soldiers of the Corps d'Afrique, many of those soldiers, and those in other black units, served as the enforcement agents for federal occupying and later Reconstruction governments. Reconstruction's end left them abandoned. Their faith in full citizenship eroded as political and social gains were systematically driven back by some of the same men who fought to keep them enslaved. Indians traveling the city at will was a reconquering of that ground.

> Coming out of slavery, being African American wasn't socially acceptable. By masking like Native Americans, it created an identity of strength. Native Americans under all the pressure and duress, would not concede. These people were almost driven into extinction, and the same kind of feeling came out of slavery, "You're not going to give us a place here in society, we'll create our own." In masking, they paid respect and homage to the Native American by using their identity and making a social statement that despite the odds, they're not going to stop.[70]

Certainly, Henry Lean, a Seventh Colored Louisiana Infantry veteran of the Civil War, had a vision for the battles he would dance that day as he donned his suit and departed the Third Ward with his tribe on Mardi Gras morning in 1895. At fifty-five, Lean was the oldest in his party by far. He boarded the ferry to Algiers with his gang that afternoon to seek out other Indians. Though the day ended badly for him with his arrest, the news record of that unfortunate encounter in Algiers pulls Henry Lean from anonymity and recognizes him as the oldest known Mardi Gras Indian (born c. 1840). Moreover, this raises the possibility that it was the generation born *before* the Civil War, including individuals like Henry Lean, that was masking Indian when "founders" like Tillman and "Becate" Baptiste Eugene were still children. Being a man twenty-five years older than the other men in his tribe surely indicates Lean was a leader, or at the very least, an elder among his gang. It is quite likely that the younger men were following the rituals learned from an elder, not the other way around. How else to explain the observations of the *Picayune* writer, who in 1879 quoted others surrounding a costumed Indian at Carnival, who were crying out the oldest known Mardi Gras Indian expression "Chick-a-ma-feeno"? If that writer *was* in the presence of a Mardi Gras Indian, perhaps Henry Lean was there.

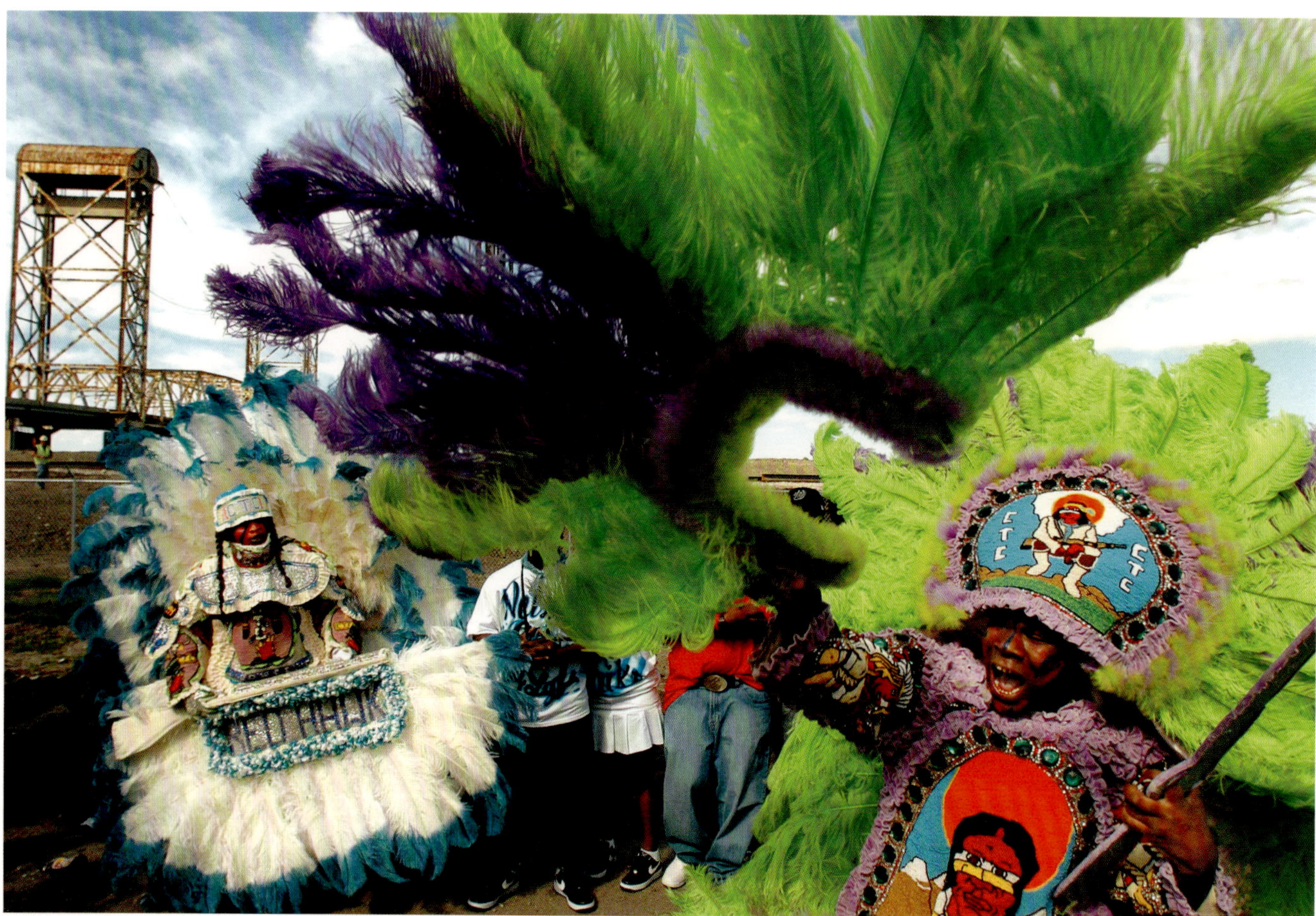

Alphonse "Dowee" Robair and Darrell Lee Preston sing "Indian Red" at the Industrial Canal breech in the lower Ninth Ward on Mardi Gras 2006 with their tribe the Red Hawk Hunters. The spot is where a 150-foot barge crashed through the failing floodwall during Hurricane Katrina. Over one thousand New Orleanians died in the flood. Photo by John McCusker/The Times-Picayune.

CHAPTER FIVE

Rebirth

Outlier as Icon

The twentieth century was a dynamic one for the Mardi Gras Indian tradition. It saw suit making go from a simple costume to the elaborate creations of today, the more conspicuous presence of women through a greater degree of public participation, the "discovery" of the tradition by new audiences, and ultimately the commercialization and commodification of Indian music and images. Through these changes, the Indians also worked to shed a persistent cloud of ignominy that had hung over them since the previous century.

In media accounts as early as 1895, Indians became associated in the public mind with weapons and violence against each other as well as menacing the general public. Jelly Roll Morton, in 1938, notes the inter-tribe fighting in his turn-of-the-century remembrances: "They would be armed with fictitious spears and Tommy-hawks and so forth and incidentally sometimes some of them would break the rules and have some real material to fight with. With steel and so forth and some even had pistols. And I have known many cases where there have been killings in the city of New Orleans with the Indian bands."[1]

The *Picayune* affirms Morton's recollections in this account from 1900: "Although not as numerous as usual, yet there were several squads of Indians seen yesterday. These were principally negroes as was evident when the perspiration washed the paint from their faces, giving them a much more ferocious appearance than the wildest red man of the plains could give himself. Some of these Indians were armed with real guns and rifles."[2]

Violence within the Indian culture between tribes was an undeniable reality. Three people were shot and one killed in an Indian shootout in 1900.[3] Big Chief "Robbe" Robert Lee recalled an incident at the 1923 Carnival when a little girl on the parade route was hit by an errant pistol round fired by Cornelius "Brother" Tillman.[4] Tillman was arrested and spent time in jail as he had over a dozen times in 1922–1923. He became so familiar to the police they often booked him as "Brother Tillman." Police shot him in the leg in 1923 on suspicion of armed robbery.[5] "In the past, if a fellow wasn't rough, he didn't mask," "Robbe," who once ran with Tillman, told Al Kennedy.[6] Big Chief Donald Harrison's father certainly knew this. He forbade his son to run with the Indians fearing for his safety, such was their reputation.[7] So great was the fear of Indian violence that merchants on North Claiborne Avenue between Esplanade and St. Peter streets called upon the police to break up Indian dancing near their stores on Mardi Gras 1911: "Patrolman Ernest Wenck and Henry Helmers not allowing rival 'Indian' maskers to give a war dance is said to be in measure largely responsible for the few arrests, as there is usually a fight between the Indians before the dance is over."[8]

What is less talked about in the discussion of violence and the Indian tradition is the violence that was directed *at* them throughout their existence. The *Picayune* observed in 1898 there was a time when "Squads of youths, armed with sticks [would] attack the pseudo-Indians."[9] Among youth in the Irish Channel uptown by the river, fighting with blacks and going after them with bats was a regular part of carnival.

> The whites, of a rough order and from that riverfront section known as the Irish Channel, took advantage of the day and their masks to make open war upon the Negroes, whom they hated with all the racial animosity of the ignorant and because the Negroes were competing with these poor and hard-working immigrants for work as longshoremen and wharf laborers.[10]

Organizing into tribes in the 1870s served as a bulwark against threats both within and without. But while this fostered an esprit de corps within tribes, it also solidified the Indians' place as an outlier. This is something the Indians were much aware of throughout their history.

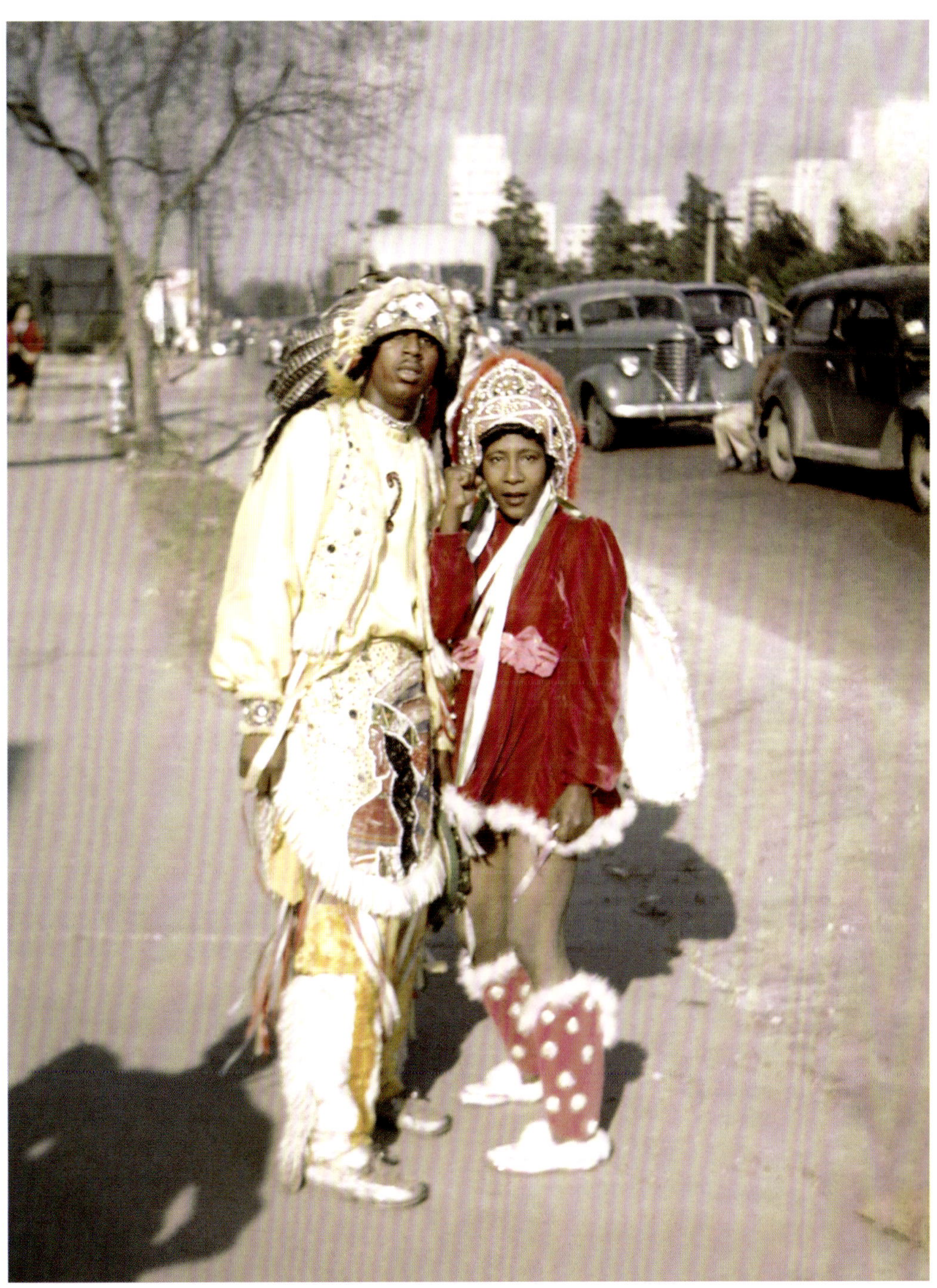

"Two Mardi Gras Indians." Two Indians on Mardi Gras c. 1950. Note the man's red face paint. The Historic New Orleans Collection, Gift of Ms. Beverly T. Lynds, 2002.84.7.

"Whoop! Here we come! boys and girls! I'm Swiftfoot and he's Bull Head. We are Cherokees and we are out on the warpath! Whoopee! whoopee! Clear the way!"

"Oh girls!" exclaimed Julia, catching hold of Lucy as a band of eight dusky and fearful-looking warrior Indians turned the corner and bore down toward them.

Turkey feathers adorned their heads, and broad brass bracelets their brown arms. They flourished their tomahawks and swooped down on the passers-by with high enjoyment of the dismay they created.

"Pull down that window! quick! Shut them out!" cried Lucy, struggling with the sash.[11]

Battles at the Magnolia Bridge over the New Basin Canal and pistols and shooting were memorialized in song. But by the early 1940s, when an interviewer caught up to "Brother" Tillman and the Creole Wild West in a bar on Mardi Gras, it was clear the violence issue was one the Indians had taken to heart. Men from the Golden Blades were also present at the bar. They said that the violence had been put down a decade earlier (c. 1930). A new song had been added to the Indian cannon which advanced this movement, "Shootin' Don't Make It."[12]

Indeed, Tillman sounded weary that day and not at all like the fierce warrior his legend might suggest. Years of hard living and jail time may have been catching up with him, though the *Picayune* noted he still led the "Wild West" in 1941.[13]

He leaned against the bar, his eyes, from which the power of vision was fast fading, troubled and brooding, his mind sad with the realization that this was probably the last time he would be able to take part in this Mardi Gras tradition. "They thought I couldn't see well enough. Well, we'll see who can see. This is my only pleasure. Oh, yes, I drink, but I don't drink for fun. I drink to hide the truth. Can you understand that? How about a drink. And let's have some music!"[14]

The Wild West period of pistols and shootings between tribes was over. Even Brother Tillman had wearied of the fighting. But the Indians' outlaw reputation had long since been burnished. It was one that has clung to them for decades despite their appearances at music festivals, recordings, and media exposure.[15] This coming out beginning in the 1970s certainly humanized their image. But not in everyone's eyes.

On St. Joseph's Night 2005, New Orleans police descended on a gathering of Indians uptown. They were ordered off the street and ordered to remove their Indian suits. Arrests were made, and the community was outraged. Big Chief "Tootie" Montana was having none of it. In July, the eighty-two-year-old Big Chief stood before the assembled city council, which had taken up the matter. He said, "Police cars coming all kinds of ways and I said, what is this? 'You all get out of the street, get on the sidewalk.' For what? We weren't doing nothing."

Then Montana collapsed. As officials scrambled to call an ambulance, the Indians in the council chambers formed a circle and sang "Indian Red" over the dying Big Chief. At his funeral, the mourners, in the hundreds, followed in a procession led by a horse-drawn hearse. Big Chief "Tootie" had died while trying to bring peace and demanding respect for the Indian culture. That change did happen, but not in a way anyone would have imagined.

KATRINA AND MARDI GRAS 2006

A month after Tootie's funeral, Hurricane Katrina and the levee failures scattered the city's inhabitants to the four winds. For weeks, residents were prohibited from returning, and when they did, many found their homes and possessions destroyed. Moreover, people lost touch with each other, often unaware if a relative had lived or died. As the struggle to return, or the decision not to, dominated the thoughts of every displaced New Orleanian, phone lines between the scattered pockets of the city's diaspora began to heat up. While the question of New Orleans's continued existence was still in doubt in some minds—Speaker of the US House of Representatives Dennis Hastert brazenly suggested that much of the city ought to be bulldozed—Mardi Gras Indians were already sewing suits in

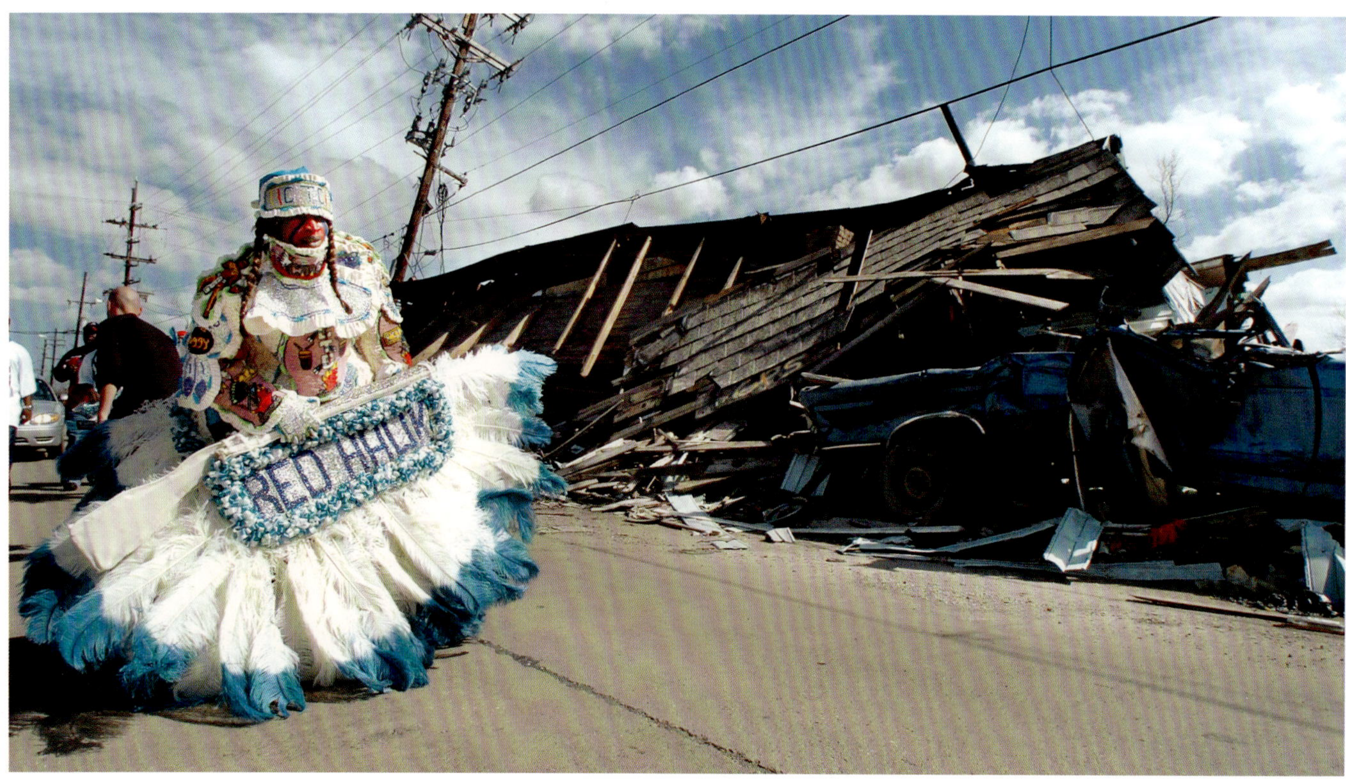

Gang Flag Alphonse Robair checks out flood damage to a lower Ninth Ward home while traveling with the Red Hawk Hunters on Mardi Gras 2006, the first after Hurricane Katrina. Photo by John McCusker/ The Times-Picayune.

Atlanta, Baton Rouge, and Houston. Outsiders questioned whether having Mardi Gras was appropriate. To New Orleanians, marking the holiday became a matter of civic pride. The message for Mardi Gras 2006 was "I will be there and I will be pretty," recalled Juan Pardo.

That February 28 morning broke with billowing white clouds against a painted blue sky. Pardo and the Golden Comanche assembled their suits at his mother's storm-damaged property on Dryades Street. It was the only location available. As Juan's brother Big Chief Wallace Pardo stepped out onto his mother's porch into the morning sunlight bathing Dryades Street, the emotion of the moment was palpable. To weary New Orleans residents, an Indian emerging on Mardi Gras morning represented not only a moment of "normality," but a faith sign that the city's cultural soul, its spirit figure, was not a victim of the flood. Over in Gert Town, Big Chief Derrick Hulin of the Golden Blades was headquartered in the parking lot of a flooded-out daquiri stand on Earhart Boulevard. There, seated in full regalia in the back of a pickup truck, he coordinated the arrival of his Indians by cell phone. He learned Flag Boy Cedric Mason was on his way in the back of another pickup.

Across town in the lower Ninth Ward, Red Hawk Hunters Gang Flag Alphonse "Dowee" Robair stood at a spot where the floodwall had failed during Katrina, spilling a 150-foot barge into a residential neighborhood. He was dressed in a white-and-blue suit with a fanned-out staff carrying the name of the Red Hawk Hunters. Spy Boy Darrell Lee Preston, dressed in bright green plumes with a purple bib and apron, stood at Robair's side as the assembled group launched into "Indian Red." Among the Indians and spectators alike there were smiles and tears. "It had to be done," Robair recalled. "It was a statement for each individual. People all over the world hearing 'is there gonna be a New Orleans?' When you heard that each individual had to say there's gonna be a Mardi Gras and I'm gonna be pretty," said Big Chief Juan Pardo.[16]

Big Chief Howard Miller remembered, "I think it was taking on more than just us, we were taking on the entire city to say we're here, this is not the end. Everybody in the city we're still here."

Despite twelve hundred deaths and 80 percent of the city flooded, New Orleans was still there and so too the bedrock of its core culture, the Mardi Gras Indian. New Orleans would not bow down. No humbow. This simpatico of all of the city's displaced people, treated as outsiders by their government and called "refugees" by their countrymen, with the outsider symbol of the proud and defiant Mardi Gras Indian was a unique moment. The common connection to place shared by Indians and displaced residents alike against the backdrop of mass disaster finally transformed the Indian image from lawless outlier to venerated, local icon. The Mardi Gras Indian had become the civic standard-bearer.[17]

And police-Indian relations, long a flash point, experienced a sea change. At Indian events, when the Indians take to the streets like Super Sunday and St. Joseph's Night, policing has had a much gentler touch. Gone are officers on horseback and sirens blaring over Indian music. On Super Sunday 2016 the police shut down the streets as they would for any

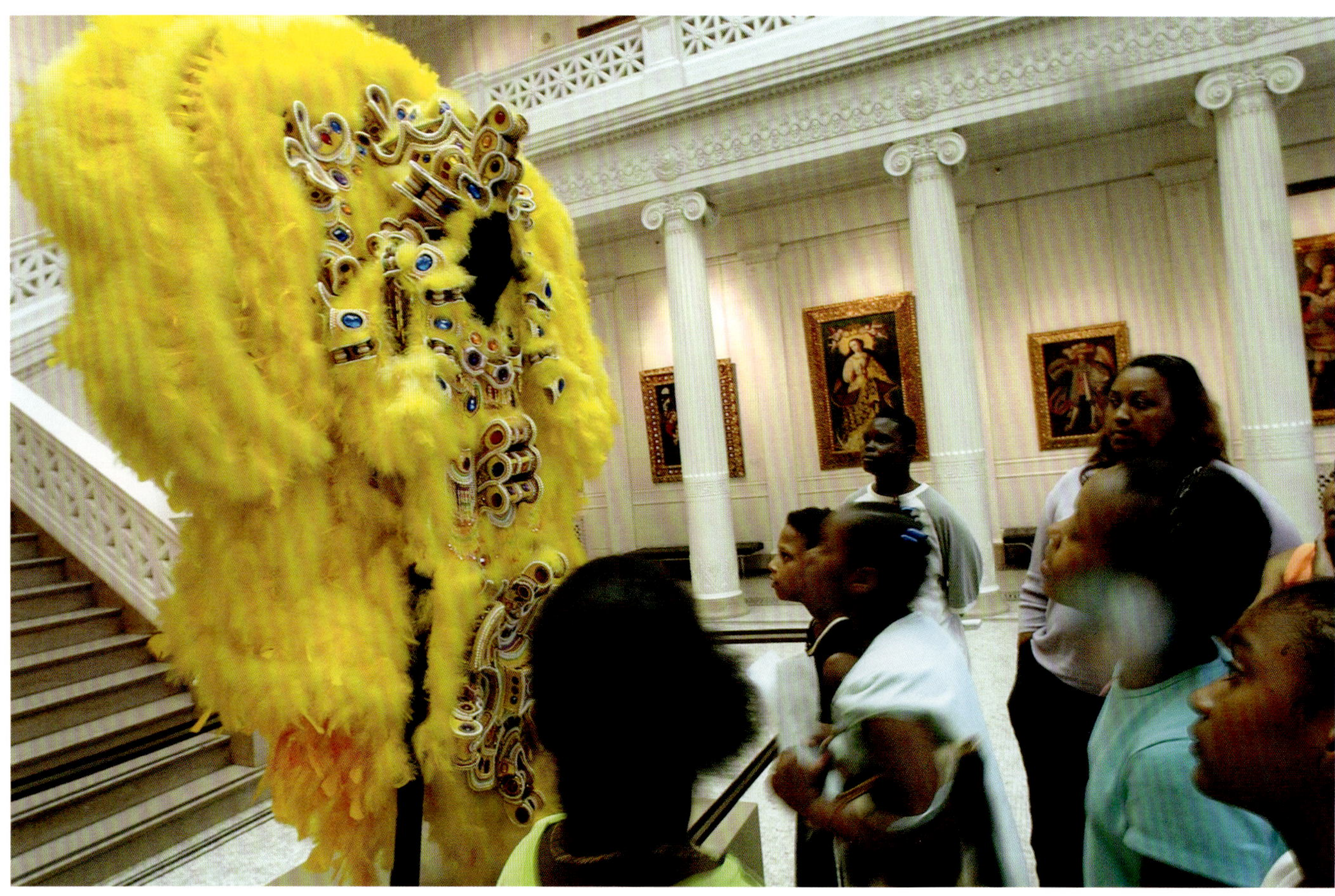

Visitors look over a canary yellow suit made by the Big Chief Allison "Tootie" Montana (1922–2005) of the Yellow Pocahontas Mardi Gras Indians. The suit is one that he made in 1993 and was displayed at the New Orleans Museum of Art to honor Montana after his passing. Photo by John McCusker/The Times-Picayune.

(Right) Wild Mohicans with Big Chief Kentrell Watson Sr., *center*, uptown, Super Sunday, 2014. Photo by John McCusker.

event and the NOPD district commander Robert Bardy was on site to make sure things went smoothly. It was the antithesis of St. Joseph's Night 2005 that prompted Montana to appear before the city council.

"We got on the same page and I give a lot of credit to Chief (Robert) Bardy. He was the first one. I never wanted to talk to the police because they had never shown us anything but disrespect. He said I want to know about you and your culture, what goes on. He wanted to help and make things go smooth. And from him beginning to understand about our culture it was passed on to other officers. A lot of these police are not from New Orleans. They don't know nothing about this," Miller observed.[18]

But this full civic embrace of the Mardi Gras Indian does not resolve the challenges and struggles ahead. Rents have skyrocketed in the decade

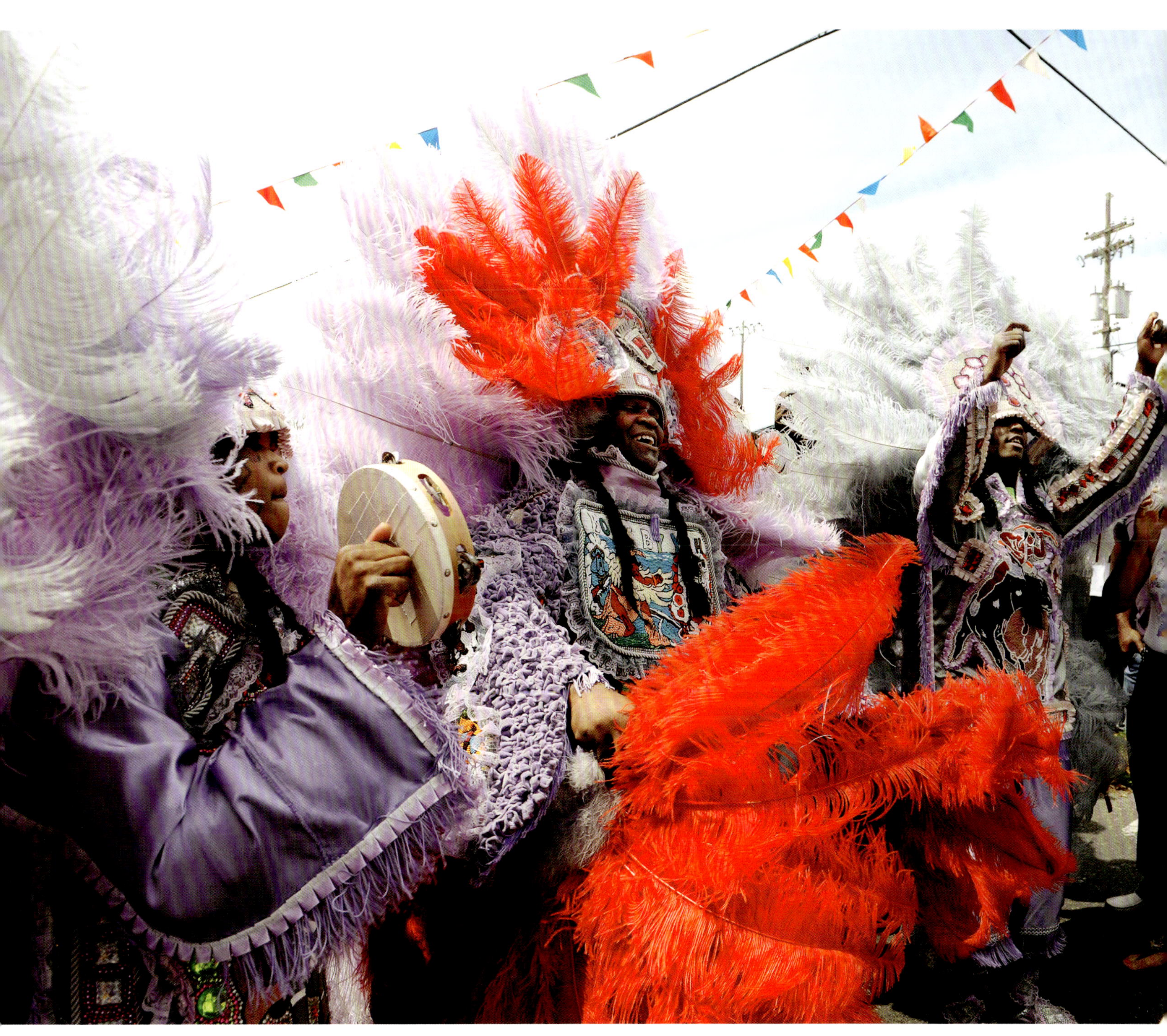

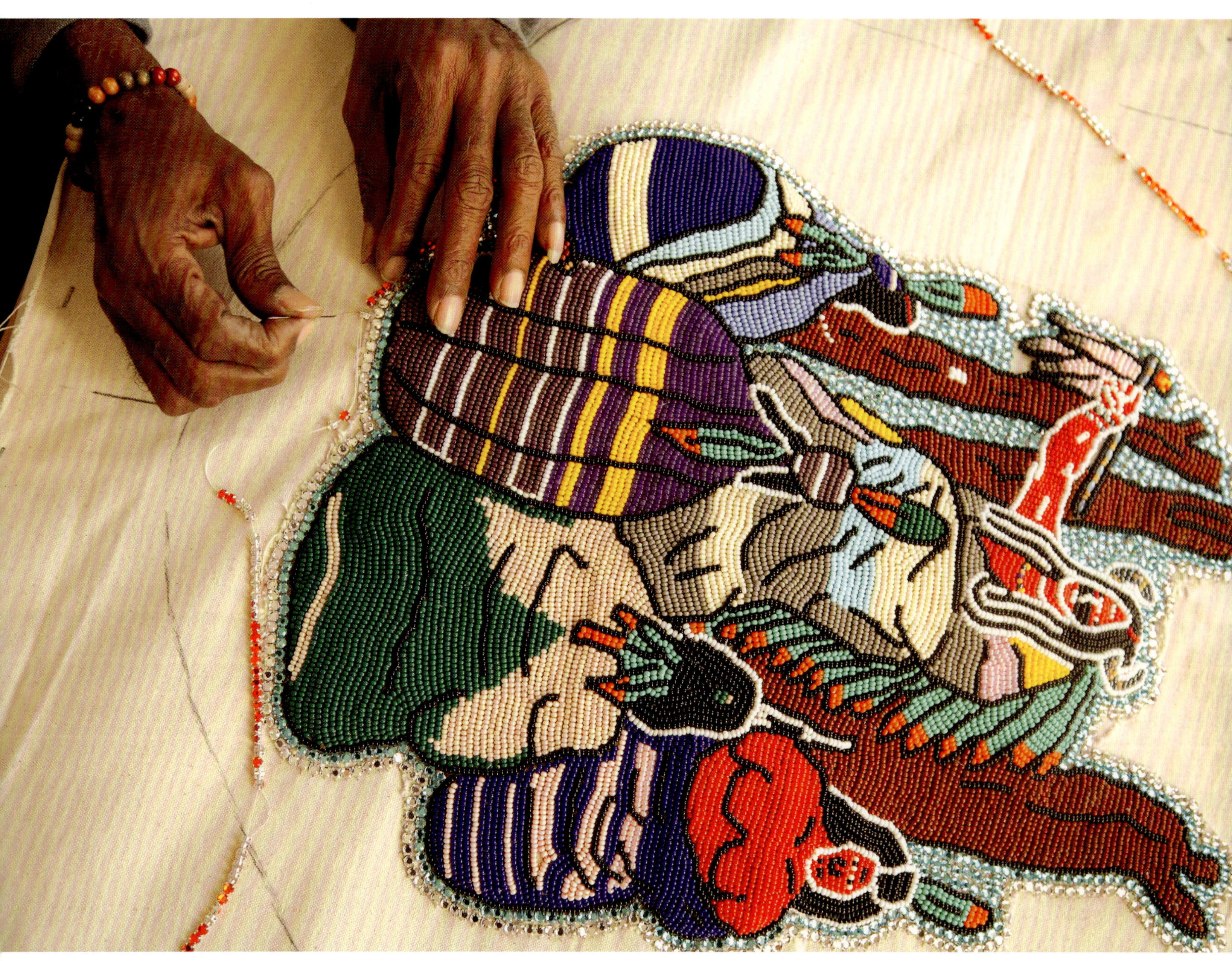

Detail of Howard Miller's beadwork for a patch for his 2019 Mardi Gras Indian suit. Photo by John McCusker.

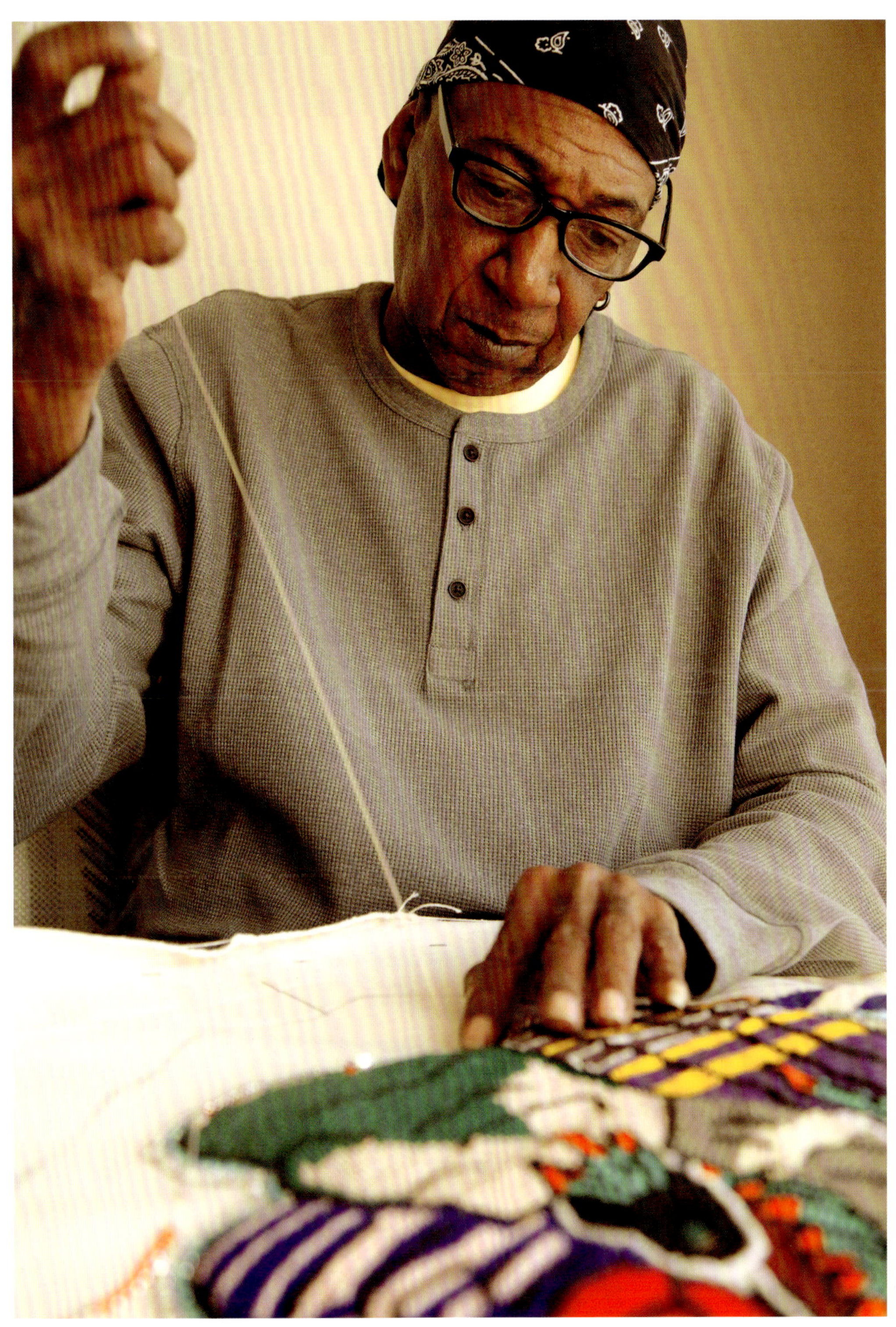

Creole Wild West Big Chief Howard Miller sews his Indian suit for Mardi Gras 2019. Photo by John McCusker.

after Hurricane Katrina in longtime Indian hot spots, like Central City and the Seventh Ward. A century of grassroots neighborhood culture finds itself uprooted by upscale renovation, displacing many of the people who make New Orleans what it is. "We are finding ourselves in Shrewsbury, Kenner, Bunche Village, Bridge City (all in suburban Jefferson Parish), we're losing that. It's not the same. You can see the culture watered down and not be what it was. Kids don't get interested anymore because it's not a neighborhood thing," said Miller. Miller grew up in Central City where his family lived over a neighborhood bar at Melpomene and Rampart streets. From his window, Miller observed Indians, brass bands, and marching clubs. "On the corner I saw it all, the Indians, I saw it all on that corner! They had a bar on every corner of old Rampart Street. My first time being where it was all black except for the shop owners. That was so cool to me. All I could say is yes," Miller remembered.

That was forty years ago. Today that neighborhood fabric is frayed and fading. The native population loss affects not only the Indians, but the brass band and second-line processions that have traveled the streets of Central City since Reconstruction. When the people who created and supported the institutions of local culture are gone, what will be left? Will New Orleans culture be a victim of its own success?

Mardi Gras Indians have faced many challenges in their history: from the collapse of Reconstruction to a century of sustained harassment from police and the public. They stopped the violence within the culture and turned their suits into works of art. These challenges demanded grit, determination, and creativity. Indians have never shown a lack of those qualities. But the forces facing Big Chief Howard are beyond any one Indian's control. Like the Native Americans they have honored for so long, Mardi Gras Indians are being driven from the ground of their ancestors. With faith in spreading an uplifting spirit to his neighborhood and a refusal to bow down to these forces, Big Chief Howard sews, his spirit stirred by each bead as it is pulled into place.

On a recent afternoon, Miller waited on the porch of the Creole Wild West headquarters on Second Street for the arrival of two teenagers he was teaching to sew. When the boys arrived, they had another young man in tow. As the other two parked their bikes on Miller's lawn, the third paused outside the wrought-iron fence where it met the sidewalk. "I wanna be an Indian!" called out the new arrival. "You wanna be an Indian?" Miller asked. The young man nodded. "Come on up here," Miller called back and soon the four were sewing together. And so the passing of the torch continues. Will this boy one day be a Big Chief, leading his tribe through the city streets as Indians have done for at least the last century and a half? Only time will tell. As for today, Mardi Gras is always next year.

CONCLUSION

New Orleans is a special place that has enabled people to create new forms of self-expression. In turn, these sounds and ceremonies have led to new forms of consciousness, making the city into a social resonance chamber which helps people experience new dimensions of personal and collective identity. One of the crucial actions we can take in this social setting is the radical act of truly listening, which, of course, is an integral part of music, since we must listen to each other carefully as we play music together. Listening is the lesson implicit in the everyday act of conversing, especially when we are greeting each other. In the beginning and in the end, with all its simultaneous complexity and simplicity, *Jockomo* also means asking about each other, or saying "Hello!"

However evanescent and infinitesimal it seems, all of the possibilities of future interaction are contained in the simple act of greeting, and the sung expression "Jockomo" grew out of a long history of greetings in the lower Mississippi River valley. Depending on the circumstances, initial contact could simply be a fleeting gesture, or it could be a very long process as it was in calumet ceremonies, with singing, dancing, and a lot of skin contact, even the act of people carrying each other. This had existential significance, to say the least. A lot was riding on this specific interaction, as it could lead to destruction and devastation, or living harmoniously together. In short, it meant war or peace. After three hundred years of shared experiences in New Orleans, in the context of Mardi Gras Indians, greeting can take the form of meeting on the street, singing, dancing, and

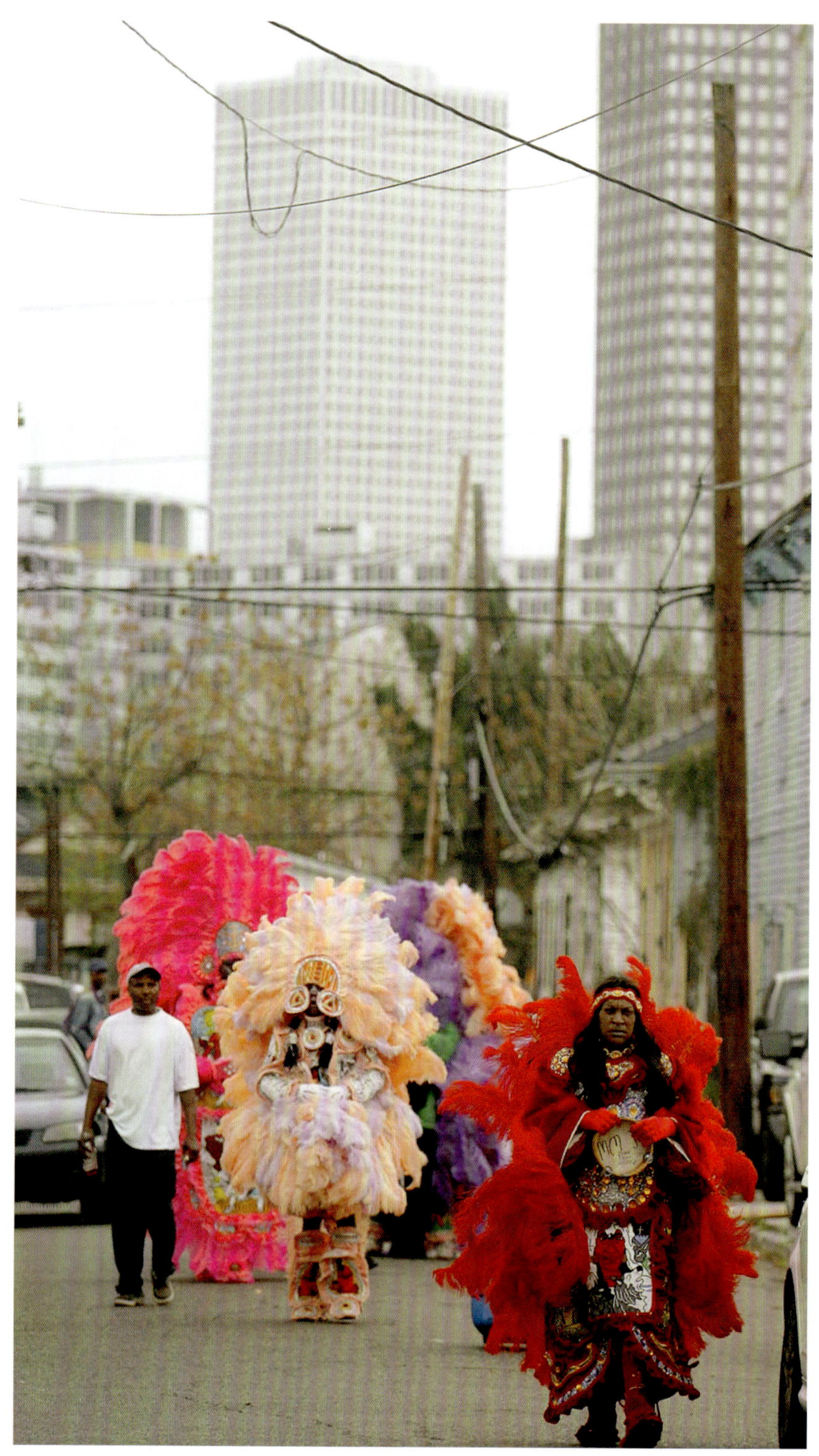

Members of the Creole Wild West, including Deirdre Lewis, *front right*, walk down LaSalle Street on Mardi Gras 2011. Photo by John McCusker.

seeing who is the "prettiest." Speaking, singing, and gesturing are different modes of greeting, but they also lead to transformation, and New Orleans has helped many people realize this over time.

This opens many questions. What constitutes the "radical act of truly listening"? Listening is a kind of introspection as well as a gathering of knowledge of one's surroundings. As Haunani-Kay Trask reminds us, "Not merely a passageway to knowledge, language is a form of knowing by itself; a people's way of thinking and feeling is revealed through its music."[1] As we encounter different sounds, they become part of us. We learn to speak other languages, and we change ourselves in the process. *Balbancha* can be understood to mean "a place of strange languages," associated with *balbaha*, or "unintelligible talk."[2] A related term is the Choctaw phrase *balbaha toba*, to become one who speaks a foreign language.[3] In other words, by learning other languages, we convert "unintelligible talk" into the primary means by which we render the cosmos intelligible, and we embrace others as we face the unknown within ourselves.

Listening is by nature improvisatory. We do not know beforehand what is going to enter our ears, yet in a kind of natural miracle, we make sense of all these sounds, as it were, on the fly. Sometimes we do not even have exact knowledge of the things we speak and sing. As someone in Congo Square once shouted, "Sing what you think you hear": as we sing new words, we plunge into the unknown of possible being. Speaking *chichicois* or singing *Jockomo*, we connect ourselves to people who came before us, or those who stand before us, and we point each other toward a new way of being.

Listening is a loosening of the pores. We can learn to listen with all of our senses. As Spirit of the Fi-Yi-Yi tribe Big Chief Victor Harris notes, "God gave us five senses, that's your education." By listening in this holistic manner, we remember that we all participate in the natural world. In late nineteenth-century New Orleans, John Watkins wrote about his experiences with the Choctaw people, and what other members of the English-speaking population could learn from them:

> I have frequently been present when some of the hunters returned from their excursion to the La. swamp. They were proud of their success, and were fond

> of relating their adventures, the perils they had encountered and the number of deer and bear they had killed—During the recital no interruption occurred nor was a question asked; but when the speaker came to a pause and sufficient time had been given, for the collection of such little fragments as had been overlooked or forgotten in the narration, then, and not till then, did the conversation become general. They were good talkers and patient listeners, and in the latter trait they might be imitated with advantage by those who affect a higher order of civilization and intellectual culture.[4]

With these words, Watkins is urging fellow English-speaking citizens—people who were behaving as though they had "a higher order of civilization and intellectual culture"—to learn to listen from others who offer a humane and fulfilling way of interacting.

The transformations described in these pages are simultaneously unique and universal. They could only have happened in the lower Mississippi River valley and culminated in *Balbancha*, yet they show a process of intersubjectivity that can happen anytime and anywhere human beings share sounds and grow together. There is always the possibility of moving beyond what we think we know, and discovering within each other a greater, more encompassing being. Despite the horrors of things that have happened in past time—and the horrors of what people still might do to each other—there is the real hope of discovering ourselves through social interaction. The simple act of listening is a key to opening up ourselves. By making ourselves vulnerable, we make ourselves sensitive to new possibilities.

When we see and hear others, who might they be? Who are we, as a group and as individuals? Who might we become together? Remembering that "history" is first and foremost a kind of inquiry, we allow ourselves to be curious about how people share their experiences over time, not only in the sense that past and present are in constant interaction, but that language and music include time itself as a fundamental ingredient of their substance. If we learn to listen to each other and move "in time" together, we can rediscover aspects of ourselves and others that might not be obvious.

The Mardi Gras Indian cultural system is an abundant river, fed by many streams and bayous, opening up many questions about the connections between people and place. There is no doubt that Mardi Gras Indians are fundamental to the New Orleans cultural landscape. Many layers of struggle—memories of destruction and dispossession, but also reclamation and re-creation—are woven into their actions. They are filled with a spirit that is both defiant and creative, with a special reverence for Native Americans, West Africans, and their own complex ancestries that defy simple categorization. Even though the public imagery of indigenous people has been saturated with centuries of misunderstanding, and generations have been caught up in the machinery of social classification, gleams of the human spirit come through the singing and marching in the streets, and the ancient council fires at night are reflected in the imagination of "fire on the bayou." With the currents of costumes, colors, and sounds, the Mardi Gras Indian cultural system helps the larger community of New Orleans and the rest of the world remember how everything flows, including our ideas about where we come from and where we're going. Indeed, the improvisational call-and-response singing, though rooted in centuries past, is contemporary with each performance or telling. This requires you to listen to another's voice before adding your own: a lesson for us all.

On the other hand, in contrast to this fluidity and responsiveness, people can hold fixed ideas of history and develop cultural productions to sustain them, which tend to be monotonous and strangely dangerous. We can see that an uncritical faith in progress led to the genocidal myth of Manifest Destiny, and locally, it inspired the theme of Comus in 1877, a Carnival procession that interpreted the march of history as the fulfilment of racial hierarchy. Such an unflinching ideological commitment to progress—which weds the movement of time with the development of a particular social arrangement—comes from a flattened view of history as a strictly linear process.

However, if we combine the notion of linear movement with circular movement in time, as in the calendrical cycles that come alive as Carnival celebrations, we can begin to understand how the old and new exist side by side. Big Chief Juan Pardo has put it this way: "For everyone, I imagine, there are similarities in the experiences (of others and ancestors), and then there are experiences that are unique to the individual. That heart of steel thing comes into play. When you finally do put it (Indian suit) on, you're wearing all this knowledge at one time."[5] This is the lesson learned by Charlevoix nearly three hundred years ago, upriver from New Orleans, when he heard the Acolapissa drum and then thought to inquire about its origins. By seeing the cycles within the line—the turning helix of time—we can also realize that even the best-laid plans, like the notion of "progress," can go terribly wrong unless we engage in the humane practice of listening to everyone around us, as we cycle in and out of life.

Paradoxically, even though certain cultural traditions have ancient elements, they somehow allow us to express ourselves in incredibly novel ways. New Orleans is known for its collective improvisation in music, and perhaps with greater attention paid to its linguistic history, we might learn to appreciate more its collective improvisation in language and identity. People around the mouth of the Mississippi River have learned to speak many languages, a linguistic heterophony that produces new languages, which reflect the new experiences of people who have learned to live together.

We sing what we think we hear—"Jockomo"—and then we listen and sing again.

APPENDIX I

Nineteenth-Century Mardi Gras Indians

Walter Brown (1874–?) A member of the visiting Third Ward Indian party arrested in Algiers in 1895, Brown lived at 652 South Franklin Street in 1900. He married Susan (last name unknown) in 1899 when he worked as a teamster.[1]

Lawrence Clementine (1887–1900) Clementine was shot to death by John Henry Lewis in a humbug between the Red, White, and Blue and the Chickasaws in the back of town on Mardi Gras 1900.[2] He had reportedly asked Lewis to bow down and kiss the ground.[3] Clementine's father was named John and he grew up in the Carrollton neighborhood with his mother, Mary Burke, and two brothers.[4] He worked as a cotton screwman.[5] Lawrence grew up in Gert Town on Short Street at Oleander.[6]

"Becate" Baptiste Eugene (1873–c.1926?) "Becate" Baptiste Eugene was the third of ten children of New Orleans–born parents and lived his life in the Seventh Ward.[7] He was tall and slender and worked as a plasterer. His father, Jean Baptiste Eugene (1842–1892), had fought in the Civil War in the Corps d'Afrique and later the Seventy-Third United States Colored Infantry.[8] After the war Jean Baptist lived at 176 Villere Street (old numbering system).[9]

Adele (sometimes Ardele in sources) was the daughter of John Taylor, born 1830 in South Carolina, and an unknown mother, who was native to Virginia.[10] Adele worked for decades as a washerwoman and gave birth to ten kids, though only six reached adulthood. Oddly, the 1880 census taken at their home lists Jean Baptiste, Adele, and three siblings, but not Becate. He is cited elsewhere on the census with his mother presumably at her job.[11]

In 1884, when Becate was eleven, the Eugene family moved to St. Anthony Street, the setting of "Tootie" Montana's Creole Wild West founding story.[12]

He married Antoinette Pichon in 1899 and daughter Marie arrived in 1900.[13] He went on to become second chief of the Yellow Pocahontas. When he died is uncertain; the confirmed record of him is a city directory listing in 1926.

Joseph Horton (1867–1910) He was the son of Georgia native Henry Horton (1840–?) and Lucy Smith (1848–1886), who was born in Maryland.[14] Henry was a soldier in the Corps d'Afrique and later the Seventy-Eighth US Colored Infantry.[15] Joseph grew up on Bertrand Street in the back-of-town while Henry labored as a carpenter and Lucy a washerwoman. The family was listed as black on the 1870 census, but as white in 1880.[16] Joseph married Alice Perry (1877–?) in 1898 and they lived in the Third Ward.[17] He was arrested numerous times for involvement in shootings and petty thefts.[18] He died in 1910.[19]

Henry Jerry (1869–1940) He was the child of Ellen Jerry, a washerwoman, and Samuel Jerry, who served in the Corps d'Afrique and later the US Colored Infantry.[20] Samuel died of a fever in 1870, when Henry was one.[21] Henry lived with his mom and a steamboat deckhand named Dennis Kennedy later that year when the census was taken. At various times, Henry worked as a plasterer and a carpenter.[22] He lived with Emma Jepson (1877–1937) beginning in 1887, and resided with her at 237 South Claiborne Avenue before moving to 1517 Gasquet Street (now Cleveland) by 1900. He married Lillie Robertson (1875–?) in 1898, but shows up twice on the 1900 census, at Emma's house and at Lillie's.[23] Jerry and Emma later lived at 719 Magnolia in 1922 and in his final years at 427 LaSalle.[24]

He was in and out of the pages of the *Picayune*, and the court system, much of the 1880s and 1900s, for everything from disturbing the peace, accidentally shooting a woman, beating a woman, and fighting, to witnessing a murder.[25] He died in 1940.[26]

Henry Lean (1837–?) Lean joined the Seventh Regiment, Louisiana Colored Infantry in New Orleans July 1863. He later worked as a steamboat fireman in Gretna in 1879, and was arrested in Algiers on Mardi Gras 1895.[27] He is the oldest Mardi Gras Indian yet identified.

John Henry "Bootsey" Lewis (1876–1933) Lewis was convicted of manslaughter for the Mardi Gras homicide of Lawrence Clementine in 1900. The shooting took place at Gravier and Franklin during a humbug between the Red, White, and Blue and the Chickasaw tribes.[28] Lewis refused to bow down to Lawrence Clementine and shot him when Clementine told him to kiss the ground. Lewis was in turn shot during the incident by Willie Williams.[29] He was sentenced to three years for manslaughter but was later pardoned.[30] He shot another man in 1909 and was convicted of murder.[31] Born in Alabama, Lewis worked as a carpenter and lived with his mother, Queenie, at 2108 Phillip Street from 1918 till 1930.[32]

Henry Marigny (1878–1938) Future Yellow Pocahontas chief Henry Marigny grew up on North Claiborne Avenue in the Seventh Ward. His father, Henry (1842–1899), served as a first sergeant in the Forty-Seventh Colored Infantry in the war. His mother, Harriet, worked as a washerwoman.[33] In 1905 he married fourteen-year-old Rosie Burns and they lived with their children Henry Jr. and Octavia and Henry's mother at 1832 North Claiborne Avenue by 1910.[34] Henry and Rosie had two more children as he worked as a driver for the Robertson Music and Art Company.[35] He is listed as a driver as late as 1932 at 2511 Bourbon Street.[36]

Edward McKinley (dates unknown) McKinley was arrested in Algiers on Mardi Gras 1895. Edward McKinley is listed in the city directories in the 1920s on General Pershing and later Bordeaux Street near the river. His last appearance is in 1952 when he is listed as a clergyman at 2812 Magnolia Street.[37]

John Smith (1874–?) One of the men arrested in Algiers in 1895. There were several men by this name in the city at that time but the most likely candidate lived in the Third Ward, which is where the other Indians with Smith that day were from. His parents were born in Arkansas and Smith lived at 719 Dryades Street in 1910 and he is listed as a musician and a widower. A decade later he lived at 420 Franklin Street.[38] He moved to South Loyola Street in 1940 when he worked as a street paver.[39]

Milton Sparks Jr. (1869–1928) Sparks was born in the Seventh Ward in 1869 and grew up on Annette Street. He was one of the five children of Fanny Smith (1847–1893) and Milton Sparks Sr. (1838–1895).[40] His father fought with the 117th Colored Infantry in Virginia and later Texas during the Civil War. After mustering out in 1867, Milton Sr. bought a house on Annette Street and worked as a cotton screwman and later became president of the Screwmen's Benevolent Association. He founded the Jerusalem Mutual Aid and Benevolent Association in 1873.[41] These societies sponsored brass band parades annually as well as musical funerals for deceased members. He is cited in the program for the ceremonial funeral parade held for President James Garfield after he was felled by an assassin in 1881.[42] Sparks Sr. was also involved in politics and was an organizer for the short-lived Greenback Workers Party in 1882, which sought to elect former Corps d'Afrique general Henry N. Frisbie as governor of Louisiana.[43]

Milton Jr. left home that same year and was injured in a mishap at his construction job.[44] He married Mary (last name unknown) in 1895, and moved to Third Street in Central City by 1900.[45] Sparks shows up in police reports as early as 1888 for fighting, assault, and being the victim of a stabbing.[46] In 1892 he fought off a pair of muggers on Camp Street, engaging them in a gun battle. In 1904, he was struck by a streetcar while masking as an Indian on Mardi Gras.[47] The 1910 census finds him as an inmate at Orleans Parish Prison.[48] He died in 1928.[49]

Robert Sam Tillman (1871–1898) Tillman was the son of Ervin, sometimes spelled Irvin (1845–1903), and Alice Mahaley (1844–?) and grew up in uptown New Orleans in Central City. Ervin's parents had come from Maryland originally but Ervin was born in Virginia about 1845.[50] Alice's parents were originally from Maryland and Virginia, though she was born in Louisiana about the same time as Ervin.

By 1880 when Robert was nine, the Tillmans were living with their three sons and one daughter at 356 Fourth Street (old numbering) near the intersection of South Rampart Street. Ervin worked as a laborer while Robert and the other kids attended school. Robert married Maria Dupre in 1896 and worked as a mason.[51] His brother Cornelius played drums in cornetist Buddy Bolden's band, credited with being the first group in New Orleans to play jazz. Cornelius was also the father of legendary Indian Cornelius "Brother" Tillman (1898–1959). Robert Sam Tillman was brutally murdered in 1898 in a street corner dispute.[52] He was remembered by Paul Longpré and others as being a leader of the Creole Wild West.[53]

Willie Williams (1870–?) Williams shot John Henry Lewis, who had just shot Lawrence Clementine in the humbug between the Red, White, and Blue and the Chickasaws in 1900.[54] He lived in the Third Ward and was a member of the Unexpected Social Club on Dryades near Perdido.[55] He was tried in 1900 for shooting with intent to murder over the Lewis shooting.[56] Williams was himself shot the next year in the same neighborhood.[57]

APPENDIX II

Mardi Gras Indian Music

Mardi Gras Indian music is a style of playing and performing both fundamental and complex. It is a combination of call-and-response mantras against improvisational lead singing, anchored by the steady, syncopated beat of drums or tambourines. This conversational river has produced ripples influencing, to varying degrees, all New Orleans music that followed. Jelly Roll Morton, the first great composer of jazz music, remembered in 1938 the voices he heard in the streets while he was growing up:

> That's the sound of the Indians. That would be some of the boys when they would be traveling in the city of New Orleans. Now that's during the Mardi Gras, they prepare for the Indian tribes I never known any more than four or five tribes in the whole city. . . . They would dance and they would sing and they would go on just like the regular Indians.[1]

Indeed, Morton said he himself had been a Spy Boy with the Indians during his youth in New Orleans over a century ago. The import of the culture in Morton's personal biography underscores its role as one strand in the braided stream of influences that brought forth jazz from New Orleans. Morton talked in detail about the musical milieu of the New Orleans he knew: the cultivated music of the French Opera House, the barrelhouse blues and ragtime of cornetist Buddy Bolden, regal brass band parades and funerals, and the great pianists Tony Jackson and Porter King. He placed the Mardi Gras Indians into that picture because he thought they belonged.[2] In the century since Morton's experiences, Mardi Gras Indian music has continued to influence New Orleans music and, on occasion, American popular music in general.

In the 1970s, artful funk band arrangements around Indian themes by Willie Turbinton in collaboration with Big Chief Bo Dollis and the Wild Magnolias created what is often referred to as "Indian funk" music. In a similar vein, the Meters and the Neville Brothers recorded with the Wild Tchoupitoulas tribe in 1977, producing Indian themed tunes like "Hey Pocky Way" and "Brother John." Indian funk music, complete with performing Mardi Gras Indians in feathers, has since become a familiar feature of the New Orleans music scene. So, too, has the fusion of contemporary brass bands and Indian music. The Indians and the city's brass bands have coexisted together for well over a century, yet it is only in recent decades that these two cultural standard-bearers have combined their sounds. This convergence demonstrates the New Orleans music scene to be as dynamic as it ever was, with Indians continuing to contribute to ongoing innovations.

Jelly Roll Morton's early twentieth-century jazz to twenty-first-century brass band/Indian fusion music is a pretty far cast, but the Indian tradition has been and continues to be fundamental to New Orleans music culture, influencing generations in the essentials of time, groove, beat, counter rhythm, and improvisation.

Some Indian songs reach back over a century and connect participants to their ancient past ("Indian Red," "Iko Iko," and "Two-Way Pocky Way"). Other standard songs, like "Shoo-Fly" and "Li'l Liza Jane," were published as sheet music and enjoyed popular national success. But any suggestion that these form a fixed, traditional canon, trapped in the amber of pious repetition, is itself a distortion. Indeed, new songs continue to be added, often memorializing noteworthy battles and legendary individuals, as the Indians continue their procession through time ("Brother John," "Let's Go Get 'Em"). This diversity of songs, where old and new tunes reside comfortably together, speaks to the dynamic nature of Indian music. The following are a sampling of songs associated with Mardi Gras Indians.

"INDIAN RED"

Eugene Honore (1892–1931) composed "Indian Red' and was a real Choctaw Indian according to fellow Yellow Pocahontas member Vincent Trepagnier. Trepagnier said Honore spent part of his time camped out in the woods with the Choctaw outside Baton Rouge. Honore's people hailed from Pointe Coupee Parish, and his grandfather Louis Honore (1823–1901) fought in the Civil War. Honore's family moved to the French Quarter before he was born.[3] Trepagnier said Honore's mother was called "Miss Choctaw."[4] Honore lived in the rear of a French Quarter building in 1910 with his aunt and uncle before marrying Viola

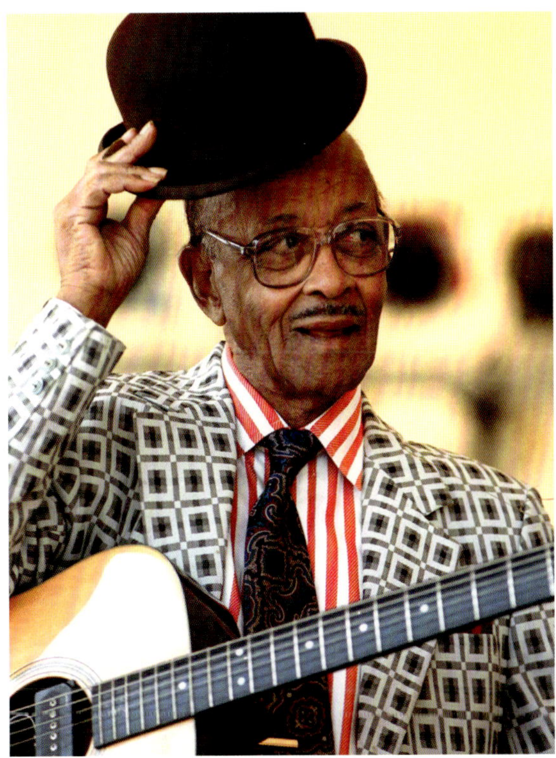

New Orleans jazzman Danny Barker (1909–1994) played with Cab Calloway's orchestra, Louis Armstrong, and Jelly Roll Morton. He was a member of the Barbarin music clan, which included drummers Paul, Louis, and Charles Barbarin, horn players Isidore and Lucien Barbarin, and singer Esther Bigeou. A noted raconteur, composer, educator, and author, Barker was a living encyclopedia of the city's folklore and culture. In 1947 he was the first to record Indian music commercially. Photo by John McCusker.

in June 1911. Viola's mother came from Fausse Pointe, in Iberia Parish in the vicinity of the ancestral home of the Chitimacha.[5]

In the 1920s, after a stint in Orleans Parish Prison, he worked as a chauffeur while living at 1215 Burgundy Street.[6] At the time of his death in 1931, Honore and Viola were living at 1004 Toulouse Street.[7] His 1892 birth would place the creation of "Indian Red," if he was indeed the composer, back to circa 1910 at the earliest. That the song went on to be universally embraced decades after the first Indians took to the streets demonstrates this is an organic tradition that continues to innovate and develop its practices. Trepagnier also credited Honore with developing Indian song structure. "Indian Red" does not follow the typical call-and-response structure exclusively, as parts are sung in unison while other passages highlight the lone voice of the Chief (see lyrics on p. 10). It is also performed at a much slower tempo than other songs. Whether as the composer of "Indian Red," or as someone with Native American ancestry that advanced music making, Honore is remembered as a significant Mardi Gras Indian and leader of the Creole Wild West.

In 1947, New Orleans guitarist Danny Barker (1909–1994) made a recording of "Indian Red" and "Chocko Mo Feendo Hey," and credited himself and Howard Mandolf as composers. The same session also produced "Tootie Ma Is a Big Fine Thing" and "Corinne Died on the Battlefield," which featured Indian-style vocal responses. They were the first commercial records featuring Indian music. Growing up, Barker lived on Chartres Street, not far from Eugene Honore's Toulouse Street home in the French Quarter. Honore, standing seven feet tall, would have been hard to miss on the narrow sidewalks.[8] Barker came from the musical Barbarin family, which included baritone horn player Isodore and drummers Paul and Louis. Barker was steeped in the music and folklore of the city. When he departed New Orleans in 1929 for New York, he must have brought "Indian Red" and the other tunes along with him. "Indian Red" has since been recorded by the Wild Tchoupitoulas in 1977, the Neville Brothers in 1978, and Dr. John in 1992.

"IKO IKO"

Iko Iko, Iko-Iko ah ne
Jockomo feeno ah na ne
Jockomo feena ne

In an 1879 account in the *Daily Picayune*, members of the crowd in the presence of a costumed Indian at Mardi Gras were quoted as calling out "Chick-a-ma-feeno." That makes it the oldest known Mardi Gras expression still in use today. With origins in Mobilian Jargon (detailed in chapter 2), an indigenous trade language that was spoken by many cultural groups, the phrase is a strand connecting today's Indians with their ancient past according to their belief system.

James "Sugar Boy" Crawford and His Cane Cutters waxed "Iko Iko" under the title "Jock-A-Mo" in 1953. In an interview with *Offbeat* magazine, Crawford recalled writing the tune:

> It (Jockomo) came from two Indian chants that I put music to. "Iko Iko" was like a victory chant that the Indians would shout. "Jock-A-Mo" was a chant that was called when the Indians went into battle. I just put them together and made a song out of them. . . . Lloyd Price just added music to it and it became a hit. I was just trying to write a catchy song.[9]

But Crawford also explained that the chant was originally "chockamo":

> It wasn't my idea to call the song "Jock-A-Mo"—Leonard Chess did that. If you listen to the song, I'm singing C-H-O-C-K, as in Chockamo. Not J-O-C-K, as in Jock-A-Mo. When Leonard listened to the session in Chicago, he thought I said "Jock-A-Mo." When I saw the record for the first time I said, "That's not the title, it's 'Chock-A-Mo.'"

The song became an international hit for the Dixie Cups in 1965.[10] Dr. John scored a hit with his version of "Iko Iko" in 1972.

"SHOO-FLY (DON'T BOTHER ME)"

> Call: My song's about young ladies fair
> Response: Shoo-fly, don't bother me
> Call: who wear "short" clothes and frizzled hair
> Response: Shoo-fly, don't bother me[11]

These lyrics to "Shoo-Fly" were published in 1868 in a South Carolina newspaper while in 1869 the St. Charles Theatre in New Orleans boasted in an advertisement that "Shoo-Fly, Dont Bodder [*sic*] Me" will be performed.[12] That same year a theatrical notice in New York declared: "'Shoo Fly' is tickling Chicagoans. 'Shoo Fly' is buzzing lively in Cincinnati. 'Shoo Fly' is also the sensation of the hour in this city. 'Shoo Fly' is a plantation song, in which the singers jump up and down in a very spasmodic manner. . . . Shoo Fly is an original negro melody and was picked up from some 'contrabands' shortly after the war by a troupe of itinerant minstrels. It is now sung in our theatres, minstrel halls and parlors, and is whistled by boys in the street, hummed by businessmen in their office and is played by nearly every brass band and orchestra in the city. So much for native music."[13]

The song is credited to T. Brigham Bishop (1835–1905), a white, northern minstrel and composer who claimed to have led a black infantry unit in the Civil War.[14] The idea for the song came from that experience, he said.

"Shoo-Fly" may have originated as a "tramping" or marching song. As the soldiers marched, their sergeant would send out a call to which the unit would respond in just the same way a Big Chief sings with his gang. The rhythm is different but the form is the same.

Bishop's version was published as sheet music in 1869. Another possible "originator" may have been another white minstrel, Cool Burgess, "the king of negro comedy," who toured extensively as a negro "delineator" from the 1860s till his death in 1905.[15] Burgess also performed it with Rollin Howard (1840–1879), who is mentioned as an arranger on competing sheet music crediting Billy Reeves and Frank Campbell as composers that same year.[16] The La Rue Minstrels claimed to be the originators of "Shoo-Fly" when they performed in New Orleans in 1870.[17] Indeed, they had been founded by Burgess, who left the partnership in 1867.[18] "Shoo-Fly" was ubiquitous nationally by then, which likely fostered its entry into the Indian song collection if it was not there already. "Shoo-Fly" enjoyed a resurgence among soldiers during the Spanish-American War in 1898 and the song remains a staple in the Indian repertoire as well as that of New Orleans brass bands.

"LI'L LIZA JANE"

ohooooooo lil Liza, lil Liza Jane
ohooooooo lil Liza, lil Liza Jane
Hair as black as coal in de mine
Lil Liza Jane
Eyes so large an big an fine
Lil Liza Jane
Ohooooooo lil Liza, lil Liza Jane
Ohooooooo lil Liza, lil Liza Jane[19]

"Liza Jane" was a typical stage name in the nineteenth century and it appeared in numerous songs including R. Hughes's "Good-bye Liza Jane" in 1871.[20] In 1867 minstrels performing in San Francisco offered "Little Ole Liza Jane."[21] There were also country and folk music songs invoking "Liza Jane" in the title or lyrics.[22] The sheet music to "Li'l Liza Jane," in the form it's known today, was not published until 1916 with a Countess Ada de Lachau named as composer. The song is almost certainly older.

"Oh, Little Liza, Little Liza Jane" was remembered by Lucy Thurston as being sung before the Civil War on Robert Dickey's plantation in Covington, Louisiana, across Lake Pontchartrain from New Orleans where she was enslaved.[23] Some sources suggest "Lil Liza Jane" was a composition by Stephen Foster and was a "Civil War Song."[24] Jelly Roll Morton recorded "Lil Liza Jane" in his Lomax interviews about his New Orleans memories. Whatever its origins and history, in 1917 "Lil Liza Jane" became a hit performed across the country.[25] Soldiers headed to France to fight in World War I sang it as a camp and tramping song and it was almost as popular as "Over There."[26]

"TWO-WAY POCKY WAY"

Two-Way Pocky Way
On tendais
Two-Way Pocky Way
On tendais
Two-Way Pocky Way

This is probably the best known and most widely sung Indian song that has been in place at least since Jelly Roll Morton's childhood remembrances from the previous turn of the century.

Tootie Montana said, "Two Way Pocky Way" means "That's what I say," or "See what I mean?" Paul Longpré interpreted it as "You go dis-away or You go datta-way.' Either one."[27]

NOTES

CHAPTER 1. INDIAN RED

1. Jason Berry, Jonathan Foose, and Tad Jones, *Up from the Cradle of Jazz: New Orleans Music since World War II* (Lafayette: University of Louisiana at Lafayette, 2009), 229. Michael P. Smith, *Mardi Gras Indians* (Gretna, LA: Pelican Publishing, 1994), 13.

2. Author interview, Howard Miller, August 9, 2017, New Orleans.

3. The song then follows a path where each member of the tribe is introduced: Spy Boy, Wild Man, Big Chief. The men take on their identities with a vow to honor their purpose, tribe, and the "Indian nation" (all tribes).

4. Angela Pulley Hudson, *Real Native Genius: How an Ex-Slave and a White Mormon Became Famous Indians* (Chapel Hill: University of North Carolina Press, 2015).

5. Author interview, Juan Pardo, August 7, 2017, New Orleans.

6. Ibid.

7. Jelly Roll Morton, *Complete Library of Congress Recordings*, Audio CD (Rounder Records, 2005).

8. Author conversation, Robert "Robbe" Lee, 1997.

9. Author interview, Howard Miller, August 9, 2017.

10. Author interview, Victor Harris, August 30, 2017.

11. Author interview, Juan Pardo, July 2017.

12. Author interview, Howard Miller, August 9, 2017.

13. Author interview, Juan Pardo, July 2017, New Orleans.

CHAPTER 2. BALBANCHA

1. William A. Read, *Louisiana Place Names of Indian Origin: A Collection of Words* (1927; rpt. Tuscaloosa: University of Alabama Press, 2008), 43; see also Ives Goddard, Patricia Galloway, Marvin D. Jeter, et al., "Small Tribes of the Western Southeast," in

Handbook of North American Indians, volume 14, Southeast, ed. Raymond D. Fogelson (Washington, DC: Smithsonian Institution, 2004), 176. Caillot says straightforwardly, "The river, which we call the Mississippi and the natives call Balbancha"; Marc-Antoine Caillot, *A Company Man: The Remarkable French-Atlantic Voyage of a Clerk for the Company of the Indies*, ed. Erin M. Greenwald, trans. Teri F. Chalmers (New Orleans: The Historic New Orleans Collection, 2013), 78.

2. Richard Bailey, *Speaking American* (Oxford: Oxford University Press, 2012), 100.

3. Among our most important sources on indigenous cultural practices are the *Jesuit Relations*, a series of reports written by French missionaries of the Society of Jesus over four decades in the middle of the seventeenth century, from 1632 to 1673. See Allan Greer, ed., *The Jesuit Relations: Natives and Missionaries in Seventeenth-Century North America* (New York: Bedford/St. Martin's, 2000).

4. Patricia Galloway, *Practicing Ethnohistory: Mining Archives, Hearing Testimony, Constructing Narrative* (Lincoln: University of Nebraska Press, 2006), 7.

5. Ibid., 26.

6. Richebourg Gaillard McWilliams, trans. and ed., *Fleur de Lys and Calumet: Being the Pénicaut Narrative of French Adventure in Louisiana* (Baton Rouge: Louisiana State University Press, 1953), 106–7.

7. Philomena Hauck, *Bienville: Father of Louisiana* (Lafayette: Center for Louisiana Studies, 1998), 69; Richard Campanella, *Bienville's Dilemma: A Historical Geography of New Orleans* (Lafayette: Center for Louisiana Studies, 2008), 110. Of course, the term "city" refers to what was envisioned in 1718 rather than the actual status of New Orleans at that time. For several years, New Orleans was little more than an outpost that developed slowly and fitfully until it became the capital of the French colony in 1721.

8. George E. Lankford, *Looking for Lost Lore: Studies in Folklore, Ethnology and Iconography* (Tuscaloosa: University of Alabama Press, 2008), 115–16; Ian W. Brown, "The Calumet Ceremony in the Southeast and Its Archaeological Manifestations," *American Antiquity* (April 1989): 315. The term "calumet" is related to the French word for reed ("chalumeau"), which often served as the pipe stem.

9. Brown, "The Calumet Ceremony in the Southeast and Its Archaeological Manifestations," 311.

10. Ibid., 316.

11. Ibid., 314.

12. In Caillot, *A Company Man*, 112–13.

13. Dayna Bowker Lee, "The Enslavement of American Indians in Colonial Louisiana" (New Orleans: Jean Lafitte National Park and Preserve, 2009); Daniel H. Usner Jr., *Indians, Settlers, and Slaves in a Frontier Exchange Economy: The Lower Mississippi River Valley before 1783* (Chapel Hill: University of North Carolina Press, 1992), 24.

14. Rev. William Ingraham Kip, trans. and ed., *The Early Jesuit Missions in North America* (New York: Wiley and Putnam, 1847), 241–42.

15. Antoine Simon Le Page du Pratz, *Histoire de la Louisiane* (Paris, 1758). *Histoire de la Louisiane* is a rich resource of information about life during the early days of the

French colony. However, this famous work was profoundly shaped by an enslaved Chitimacha woman. After settling temporarily on "Bayou Tchoupic," Le Page du Pratz "'bought from a neighboring settler a native slave in order to be certain of a person to cook for us . . . We did not understand one another yet, my slave and I, but I made her understand by signs, which the natives understand easily; she was of the nation of the Tchitimachas, with whom the French had been at war for several years.'" Unfortunately, her name is never mentioned in *Histoire*, but we are indebted to her for many of the details that inform our understanding of events at the beginning of the history of New Orleans: "[A]lthough this young woman's story does not dominate the book, she is referred to several times as the source of information on Indian traditions." In fact, she translated and explained to him the proceedings of the calumet ceremony he witnessed. See Galloway, *Practicing Ethnohistory*, 102.

16. Le Page du Pratz, *Histoire de la Louisiane*, 107–8; English translation by the author, reviewed by Russell Desmond.

17. This particular note (but not the preceding passage) was translated by James M. Crawford, *The Mobilian Trade Language* (Knoxville: University of Tennessee Press, 1978), 177–78; the English text here represents a translation by the author, loosely guided by Crawford's previous translation and also reviewed by Russell Desmond.

18. McWilliams, *Fleur de Lys and Calumet*, 6. Angle brackets are used throughout this article to indicate exact spellings in manuscripts. A likely pronunciation of <chichicois>. given in the International Phonetic Alphabet, is [ʃiʃikʷa]. See also Caillot, *A Company Man*, 112–13.

19. Crawford, *The Mobilian Trade Language*, 65.

20. See Emmanuel Drechsel, *Mobilian Jargon* (New York: Oxford University Press, 1997).

21. Emmanuel Drechsel, "An Integrated Vocabulary of Mobilian Jargon, a Native American Pidgin of the Mississippi River Valley," *Anthropological Linguistics* 38, no. 2 (Summer 1996): 286.

22. Lankford, *Looking for Lost Lore*, 115: "There is good archaeological evidence, in fact, that widespread trade networks had existed in eastern North America for well over two millennia by the time of the arrival of the French"; Crawford, *The Mobilian Trade Language*, 66–67.

23. Translation adapted by the author from Pierre François Xavier de Charlevoix, *Charlevoix's Louisiana: Selections from the HISTORY and the JOURNAL*, ed. Charles E. O'Neill (Baton Rouge: Louisiana State University Press, 1977), 160.

24. Sophie White, *Wild Frenchmen and Frenchified Indians* (Philadelphia: University of Pennsylvania Press, 2012).

25. Ibid., 120.

26. Ibid.

27. Pierre F. X. de Charlevoix, *Histoire et description générale de la Nouvelle France, avec le Journal historique d'un voyage fait par ordre du roi dans l'Amérique septentrionale* (Paris, 1744), vol. 3, 166–67. One of the French words used for "drum" in his original

account is spelled <quaiffe> (using the long "s" common in eighteenth-century typography), an unusual variant of the more standardized spelling of *caisse* "box" (cognate with Spanish *caja* and Portuguese *caixa*), related to *caisse claire* "snare drum." The original text is ". . . on y battit la quaiffe . . ." (437).

28. While we have no definitive evidence, the use of this particular word <quaiffe>, which is similar to the French term for the snare drum, carries the suggestion that two drumsticks may have been used to play this drum, a practice that was observed by Pénicaut over two decades earlier among indigenous groups living near the Gulf Coast.

29. Edward G. Gray, *New World Babel: Languages and Nations in Early America* (Princeton: Princeton University Press, 1999), 125; quote from Pierre François Xavier de Charlevoix, *Journal of a Voyage to America, 1761*, ed. Louise Phillips Kellog (Chicago: Caxton Club, 1923), vol. 1, 55.

30. Tracy Neal Leavelle, *The Catholic Calumet: Colonial Conversions in French and Indian North America* (Philadelphia: University of Pennsylvania Press, 2012), 1; although the visitors to New Orleans are referred to as the "Illlinois," this name represents a loose coalition, a "cover term for several subgroups" speaking Algonquian languages, including the Peoria, Kaskaskia, Tamaroa, and the Cahokia. See David J. Costa, *The Miami-Illinois Language* (Lincoln: University of Nebraska Press, 2003), 2.

31. See George Edward Milne, *Natchez Country: Indians, Colonists, and the Landscapes of Race in French Louisiana* (Athens: University of Georgia Press, 2015). In the words of Marc-Antoine Caillot, who met some of the survivors, "everything was on fire and covered in blood at Natchez" (Caillot, *A Company Man*, 124). Father Le Petit offers an explanation of the visit in New Orleans: "The *Tchikachas* [Chickasaws], a brave nation but treacherous, and little known to the French, have endeavored to seduce the Illinois Tribes from their allegiance: they even sounded some particular persons to see whether they could not draw them over to the party of those Savages who are enemies of our Nation. The Illinois have replied to them that they were almost all 'of the prayer' (that is, according to their manner of expression, that they are Christians); and that in other ways they are inviolably attached to the French, by the alliances which many of that Nation had contracted with them, in espousing of their daughters . . . At the first news of the war with the *Natchez* and the *Yazous*, they came hither to weep for the black Robes and the French, to offer the services of their Nation to Monsieur Perrier [governor of Louisiana], to avenge their death'" (Reuben Gold Thwaites, ed., *The Jesuit Relations and Allied Documents*, vol. 68 (Cleveland: The Burrows Brothers Company, 1900: 201–3).

32. Leavelle, *The Catholic Calumet*, 1. Chief Chicagou was a particularly well-traveled representative of his people: just five years earlier, in 1795, he participated in a delegation of the "Illinois Confederacy" (Cahokia, Kaskaskia, Michigamea, Moingwena, Peoria, and Tamaroa) to Paris, France, where he addressed King Louis XV in person. The syncretic musical practices of the Kaskaskia were observed a generation earlier, in 1711, by Pénicaut: "The Revered Jesuit Fathers have translated the Psalms and the hymns from Latin to their language. At Mass or Vespers the Illinois sing the stanzas in turn with the French that

live among them; for example, the Illinois sing one stanza of the Psalm or the hymn in their language, and the French the following stanza in Latin, and so on with the remaining ones, and in the key in which they are sung in Europe among Catholic Christians" (McWilliams, *Fleur de Lys and Calumet*, 139).

33. Leavelle, *The Catholic Calumet*, 124.

34. Ibid., 125. Taking place while the French were conducting their campaign against the Natchez, this presentation of the calumet was certainly also an indication of military alliance. As practiced by many indigenous groups in the Mississippi River valley, "the ceremonies associated with the calumet facilitated trade and diplomacy among friends by expressing a commitment to violence against common enemies" in Brett Rushforth, *Bonds of Alliance: Indigenous and African Slaveries in New France* (Chapel Hill: University of North Carolina Press, 2012), 30.

35. Robert Michael Morrissey, *Empire by Collaboration: Indians, Colonists, and Governments in Colonial Illinois Country* (Philadelphia: University of Pennsylvania Press, 2015).

36. Ibid., 10.

37. Ibid., 7–8. This included an overlapping of European and indigenous slavery systems. "As the region's Natives encountered French traders and eventually settlers in the second half of the seventeenth century, they greeted them with rituals and gifts to signal their friendship and to invite the newcomers into an alliance. Among the most significant of these gifts were enslaved enemies, offered as a sign of trust and evidence of Native power" (Rushforth, *Bonds of Alliance*, 11).

38. Kathleen DuVal, *The Native Ground: Indians and Colonists in the Heart of the Continent* (Philadelphia: University of Pennsylvania Press, 2006), 4. As used by DuVal, the term 'native ground' pertains to the Arkansas River valley, but it could also be applied to other areas where indigenous people had more control over the circumstances of interaction with Europeans. At the same time, we must keep in mind that cycles of warfare, slave raids, and shifting alliances show how a dynamic hierarchy of control existed among Native groups, which in turn was exploited by the European colonial powers: "the French insistence on mediating, rather than taking sides in, disputes between Native groups registers as a cynical attempt to exert authority rather than an example of French accommodation to Native cultural demands" (Rushforth, *Bonds of Alliance*, 12).

39. There is a strongly gendered aspect to indigenous Christianity in the Illinois Country: "Numerous French observers commented that the Christian message attracted women far more than men among the Illinois . . . Kaskaskia and other Illinois women, like Marie Rouensa, discovered in Christianity a comforting source of spiritual renewal and a viable outlet for their social energy" (Leavelle, *The Catholic Calumet*, 158).

40. Leavelle, *The Catholic Calumet*, 160. Of course, for every story of conversion, we must consider the political or social factors: "Female Christian converts often defied their families and communities" (172). Marie Rouensa's father also had other things in mind besides spirituality: "Chief Rouensa of the Kaskaskias certainly hoped to strengthen his relationships with the French" (174).

41. Thwaites, *The Jesuit Relations and Allied Documents*, 209–11.

42. Morrissey, *Empire by Collaboration*, 36. At the same time, it must be noted that, among the groups of the Illiniwek (Illinois) coalition, many Kaskaskia had converted to Christianity by the fourth decade of the eighteenth century while most Peoria still remained aloof to the missionaries' efforts.

43. Ibid., 38.

44. Leavelle, *The Catholic Calumet*, 106; please note that the grapheme <8> could be used to represent the phonemes o, u, and w (Greer, *The Jesuit Relations*, vi).

45. Leavelle, *The Catholic Calumet*, 106.

46. Ibid., 108.

47. Ibid., 31. The significance of the calumet among the Illiniwek had many dimensions: "Miami-Illinois-speakers called the calumet 'ap8agana,' and its shaft 'ap8acanti,' referring to the feathers with which the shaft was wrapped, drawing manit [sic], or spiritual power, from these beings that lived between heaven and earth and therefore bridged the two worlds. The smoke, too, linked the sky world with land, drawing upon the power of the sun, which had grown the tobacco, by ingesting and then offering back the smoke from the plant. Indians sometimes made calumets in pairs, one painted green and the other blue to represent the earth and sky, emblematic of the calumet's power to bring otherworldly power to bear on worldly matters. Alliances confirmed in a calumet ceremony thus represented far more than practical political agreements. They were sacred bonds, and those who violated them risked disaster" (Rushforth, *Bonds of Alliance*, 31–32).

48. Usner Jr., "American Indians in Colonial New Orleans," 171.

49. Ibid., 179.

50. Ibid.

51. Ibid.

52. *Louisiana State Gazette* (New Orleans, LA), September 20, 1826, p. 1.

53. Usner, *American Indians in the Lower Mississippi Valley*, 168.

54. Brian Klopotek, "Of Shadows and Doubts: Race Indigeneity, and White Supremacy," in *Indivisible: African-Native American Lives in the Americas*, ed. Gabrielle Tayac (Washington, DC: Smithsonian National Museum of the American Indian, 2008), 87.

55. Ibid., 88; Jerah Johnson, "Colonial New Orleans: A Fragment of the Eighteenth-Century French Ethos" in *Creole New Orleans: Race and Americanization*, ed. Arnold R. Hirsch and Joseph Logsdon (Baton Rouge: Louisiana State University Press, 1992), 80: "Indians disappeared from sight in New Orleans not because they died out or moved away, but because, in the words of an 1880s observer, they 'melted away into mulattoes.' The Indians became New Orleanians by gradually blending into the city's African community. An overwhelming number of black families in New Orleans today have in their genealogies several not very remote Indian ancestors."

56. *Daily Delta* (New Orleans, LA), May 21, 1853, p. 6.

57. *Daily Picayune* (New Orleans, LA), August 11, 1838, p. 3.

58. *Daily Picayune*, January 12, 1859, p. 5.

59. *Daily Picayune*, December 10, 1850, p. 4.

60. Usner, *American Indians in the Lower Mississippi Valley*, 120.

61. Ibid., 120–21.

62. Ibid., 121.

63. *Daily Picayune*, December 5, 1910, and July 12, 1897, p. 10; *Times-Democrat*, May 7, 1899, p. 28.

64. *Times-Democrat*, August 31, 1907, p. 3.

65. *Daily Picayune*, August 4, 1882, p. 2.

66. *Daily Picayune*, May 17, 1839, p. 2.

67. H. F. Gregory, "Music Holds the People Together," in *Remaining Ourselves: Music and Tribal Memory*, ed. Dayna Bowker Lee (State Arts Council of Oklahoma, 1995), 14–15.

68. Ibid.

69. Greg O'Brien, *Choctaws in a Revolutionary Age: 1750–1830* (Lincoln: University of Nebraska Press, 2002), 49.

70. McWilliams, *Fleur de Lys and Calumet*, 109–10.

71. Blaise D'Antoni, *Chahta-Ima and St. Tammany's Choctaws* (Mandeville, LA: St. Tammany Historical Society, 1986), 58–59.

72. Ibid., 59.

73. Ibid., 61.

74. Dagmar Renshaw LeBreton, *Chahta-Ima: The Life of Adrien-Emmanuel Rouquette* (Baton Rouge: Louisiana State University Press, 1947), 206; D'Antoni, *Chahta-Ima and St. Tammany's Choctaws*, 61.

75. Cyrus Byington, ed., "John R. Swanton" and "Henry S. Halbert," *A Dictionary of the Choctaw Language*. Smithsonian Institution, Bureau of American Ethnology, Bulletin 46 (Washington, DC: Government Printing Office, 1915), 10. In Byington's dictionary, a monumental achievement reflecting nearly half a century of experience among the Choctaws, the entry *achukma fehna* is defined as "very good; rare." Chahta-Ima's reply thus indicates an appreciation for something outstanding or excellent.

76. Robert D. Spratt, Notes on Choctaw Indians, their language, etc. Manuscript. William Stanley Hoole Special Collections, University of Alabama Library, 59. Byington's dictionary describes *chukma* ("good; well; healthy") as being "usually written *achukma*." Since this can refer to someone's state of health or well-being, *chukma* and its variants in other Muskogean languages throughout the southeastern United States would often be spoken while people were greeting each other.

77. Drechsel, *Mobilian Jargon*, 68–69.

78. Given the origins of this song lyric, it is not surprising that there are variations in spelling and pronunciation. Please note that the song recorded by Danny Barker has been spelled differently in scholarly articles. See George Lipsitz, *Time Passages: Collective Memory and American Popular Culture* (Minneapolis: University of Minnesota Press, 1990), 250.

79. The connection between this particular lyric in the song "Iko Iko" and Mobilian Jargon was first noted by Geoffrey Kimball, who is cited in Drechsel (*Mobilian Jargon*). The original chant had "Chockomo" (or "Chock-a-mo") instead of "Jockomo." The latter

was based on a different interpretation of the initial consonant. Please see description of "Iko Iko" in Appendix II.

80. LeBreton, *Chahta-Ima*, 260–61.

CHAPTER 3. POOR LO

1. Michael Goldfield, *The Color of Politics: Race and the Mainsprings of American Politics* (New York: New Press, 1997), 39–45.

2. Neal Salisbury, *Manitou and Providence: Indians, Europeans, and the Making of New England, 1500–1643* (New York: Oxford University Press, 1982); Karen Ordahl Kupperman, *Indians and English: Facing off in Early America* (Ithaca, NY: Cornell University Press, 2000).

3. Thomas Patterson, *A Social History of Anthropology in the United States* (Oxford: Berg, 2001), 11–12.

4. Benjamin L. Carp, *Defiance of the Patriots: The Boston Tea Party and the Making of America* (New Haven, CT: Yale University Press, 2010), 157; Philip J. Deloria, *Playing Indian* (New Haven, CT: Yale University Press, 1998).

5. Carp, *Defiance of the Patriots*, 157.

6. Alan Trachtenberg, *Shades of Hiawatha* (New York: Hill and Wang, 2004), 14.

7. Paul Reddin, *Wild West Shows* (Urbana: University of Illinois Press, 1999), 6–7.

8. Ibid.; Stanley Weintraub, *Victorian Yankees at Queen Victoria's Court: American Encounters with Victoria and Albert* (Newark: University of Delaware Press, 2011), 36–37.

9. *Daily Picayune*, June 17, 1843, p. 2.

10. *Daily Picayune*, December 6, 1843, p. 1.

11. Henry Wadsworth Longfellow, *Evangeline* (New York: Maynard, Merrill, & Co., 1893 [1847]), 92.

12. *Daily Picayune*, February 23, 1891, p. 4.

13. Washington Irving, *Selected Prose*, ed. Stanley Williams (New York: Holt, Rinehart and Winston, 1950), 376–77.

14. Ibid.

15. Nathaniel Hawthorne, *Great Short Works of Nathaniel Hawthorne*, ed. Frederick C. Crews (New York: Harper & Row, 1967), 246.

16. Angela Pulley Hudson, *Real Native Genius: How an Ex-Slave and a White Mormon Became Famous Indians* (Chapel Hill: University of North Carolina Press, 2015), 96.

17. Robert F. Berkhofer, *The White Man's Indian: Images of the American Indian from Columbus to the Present* (New York: Vintage, 1979), 88.

18. Robert M. Lewis, ed., *From Traveling Show to Vaudeville: Theatrical Spectacle in America, 1830–1910* (Baltimore: Johns Hopkins University Press, 2003), 11.

19. Ibid., 317.

20. *Daily Picayune*, March 8, 1850.

21. *Daily Picayune*, November 11, 1854.

22. Lewis, *From Traveling Show to Vaudeville*, 69.

23. Robert Toll, *Blacking Up* (New York: Oxford University Press, 1974), 250.

24. Lynn Abbott and Doug Seroff, *Out of Sight: The Rise of African American Popular Music, 1889–1895* (Jackson: University Press of Mississippi, 2002), 106.

25. *Daily Picayune*, September 8, 1890.

26. *Daily Picayune*, December 13, 1900.

27. Lewis, *From Traveling Show to Vaudeville*, 105–6.

28. Berkhofer, *The White Man's Indian*, 90.

29. Ibid.

30. *Daily Picayune*, July 8, 1851, p. 1.

31. Ibid.

32. Hudson, *Real Native Genius*.

33. Berkhofer, *The White Man's Indian*, 95.

34. Hudson, *Real Native Genius*, 97.

35. *Daily Picayune*, March 30, 1837, p. 5.

36. *New Orleans Item*, September 18, 1904, p. 12.

37. *Daily Picayune*, January 17, 1876, p. 2.

38. *Daily Picayune*, February 19, 1888, p. 12.

39. Ibid.

40. *Times-Picayune*, January 1, 1916, p. 15.

41. *Times-Picayune*, January 1, 1916, p. 6.

42. Ibid.

43. Lewis, *From Traveling Show to Vaudeville*, 241.

44. Ibid., 237.

45. Ibid.

46. Ibid., 238. The name of this Cheyenne warrior, Heova'ehe, has been mistranslated as "Yellow Hand" in several historical accounts.

47. Ibid., 239.

48. Ibid., 241–42.

49. Usner, *American Indians in the Lower Mississippi Valley*, 124–25.

50. Ibid., 125.

CHAPTER 4. CHICK-A-MA-FEENO: AN IDENTITY EMERGES

1. "Maskers Visit Algiers," *Daily Picayune*, February 27, 1895, p. 2.

2. The word "humbug" is a New Orleans colloquial term used by Mardi Gras Indians to denote a fight, disagreement, or contentious issue.

3. Usner, *American Indians in the Lower Mississippi Valley*, 87.

4. Washitaw Nation.

5. Berry et al., *Up from the Cradle of Jazz*, 235.

6. Year: 1880; Census Place: New Orleans, Orleans, Louisiana; Roll: 462; Family History Film: 1254462; Page: 674B; Enumeration District: 054; Image: 0330. Year: 1900;

Census Place: New Orleans Ward 7, Orleans, Louisiana; Roll: 572; Page: 18B; Enumeration District: 0066; FHL microfilm: 1240572s.

7. While it cannot be said with absolute certainty that this was the house that became 1313–15 St. Anthony when the numbering system changed in 1893, the extended family lived at the latter address into the 1960s.

8. Berry et al., *Up from the Cradle of Jazz*, 237.

9. "Indians Parade in Regalia, Ritual," Anita Schrodt, *Times-Picayune*, February 8, 1975, p. 46.

10. "Gray's victim dead," *Times-Democrat*, March 23, 1898; "Held for Murder," *Daily Picayune*, March 16, 1898.

11. "Combined Shows Viewed by 25,000," *Indianapolis Star*, August 6, 1907, p. 11; *Clarion-Ledger*, September 30, 1917, p. 11.

12. "Dr. W. F. Carver's 'Wild West,'" *Daily Picayune*, February 18, 1884, p. 5. "Buffalo Bill To-Night," *Times-Democrat*, November 13, 1908, p. 9. "Amusements," *Daily Picayune*, January 24, 1885, p. 4. *Times-Democrat*, October 25, 1908, p. 23.

13. US Census, Year: 1880; Census Place: New Orleans, Orleans, Louisiana; Roll: 463; Family History Film: 1254463; Page: 165B; Enumeration District: 081; Image: 08131900; Census Place: New Orleans Ward 11, Orleans, Louisiana; Roll: 574; Page: 11A; Enumeration District: 0114; FHL microfilm: 1240574. Year: 1910; Census Place: New Orleans Ward 10, Orleans, Louisiana; Roll: T624_523; Page: 8A; Enumeration District: 0169; FHL microfilm: 1374536; New Orleans, Louisiana Birth Records Index, 1790–1899; Volume: 121; Page: 627.

14. Reid Mitchell, *All on a Mardi Gras Day: Episodes in the History of New Orleans Carnival*, 1st ed. (Cambridge, MA: Harvard University Press, 1995), 19.

15. Caillot, *A Company Man*, 134–35; Sophie White, "Massacre, Mardi Gras, and Torture in Early New Orleans," *William and Mary Quarterly* 3rd ser., 70 (July 2013): 497–538.

16. Caillot, *A Company Man*, 135.

17. New Orleans (LA) and Cabildo, *Records and Deliberations of the Cabildo,* AB301, 1779–84, vol. 2, New Orleans Public Library – Central – Louisiana Division. 47–48.

18. Daniel Rasmussen, *American Uprising: The Untold Story of America's Largest Slave Revolt*, rpt. ed. (New York: Harper Perennial, 2012).

19. Robert Tallant, *Mardi Gras . . . As It Was* (Gretna, LA: Pelican Publishing, 1989), 104.

20. Ibid., 100.

21. Ibid., 100.

22. Michael Smith, *Mardi Gras Indians* (Gretna, LA: Pelican Publishing, 1994), 81.

23. Smith, *Mardi Gras Indians*, 83.

24. Tallant, *Mardi Gras . . . As It Was*, 104.

25. Ibid., 104.

26. Ibid., 104.

27. "First Municipality Council," *Daily Picayune*, February 17, 1846, p. 2.

28. Celebratory flour throwing was practiced in European carnivals for centuries. In America it was a longstanding Halloween prank. The influx of Irish immigrants in

this period may have played a role in making it a crossover practice to the Mardi Gras celebration.

29. "Mardi Gras," *New Orleans Crescent*, March 8, 1848, p. 2.

30. "Mardi Gras," *Daily Picayune*, February 8, 1842, p. 2.

31. *Weekly Picayune*, February 14, 1842.

32. Tallant, *Mardi Gras . . . As It Was*, 103.

33. Mitchell, *All on a Mardi Gras Day*, 24.

34. James K. Hogue, *Uncivil War* (Baton Rouge: Louisiana State University Press, 2006), 2–3.

35. Ibid., 44.

36. Ibid., 6.

37. Errol Laborde, Peggy Laborde, and Mitchel Osborne, *Mardi Gras: Chronicles of the New Orleans Carnival* (Gretna, LA: Pelican Publishing, 2013), 163.

38. James Gill, *Lords of Misrule: Mardi Gras and the Politics of Race in New Orleans* (Jackson: University Press of Mississippi, 1997), 128.

39. Gill, *Lords of Misrule*, 137.

40. *Times-Democrat*, February 25, 1903, p. 7.

41. "Yesterday's Maskers," *Daily Picayune*, February 10, 1875, p. 8. "Mardi Gras Maskers," *Daily Picayune*, February 12, 1903, p. 10.

42. Louis Armstrong, *Louis Armstrong, in His Own Words: Selected Writings* (New York: Oxford University Press, 2001), 212.

43. *Commercial Bulletin*, Ash Wednesday 1838.

44. Charles Lyell, *A Second Visit to the United States of North America, Volume* 2 (New York: Harper & Brothers, 1849), 91.

45. "Ash Wednesday," *Daily Picayune*, March 1, 1854, p. 2.

46. Tallant, *Mardi Gras . . . As It Was*, 107.

47. "Hebrew Ball at Mechanics Institute," *Daily Picayune*, February 26, 1869.

48. "The Relics of Mardi Gras," *Daily Picayune*, March 2, 1870.

49. "Scenes from the Streets," *Times-Democrat*, February 22, 1871, p. 10.

50. "Mardi Gras," *Morning Star and Catholic Messenger*, February 26, 1871, p. 1.

51. "Street Scenes," *Daily Picayune*, February 18, 1885.

52. "We See a New Moon," *Daily Picayune*, February 22, 1885.

53. "A Romance of Mardi Gras in the Olden Time," *Daily Picayune*, February 15, 1891, p. 13.

54. "Rex has Come," *Daily Picayune*, February 25, 1879.

55. Elise Kirsch, *Downtown New Orleans in the Early Eighties: Customs and Characters of Old Robertson Street and Its Neighborhood*, 1951. A pamphlet in the New Orleans Public Library.

56. "The Coon Carnival," *Times-Democrat*, February 28, 1900.

57. Other named individuals (Harry Conners, John Smith, R. J. Jones) had no obvious ties to other Indians or had names too common to identify definitively.

58. Hogue, *Uncivil War*, 25.

59. John N. Chamberlin, *Captaining the Corps d'Afrique*, ed. John Bisbee (Jefferson, NC: McFarland & Co., 2016), 46.

60. Hogue, *Uncivil War*, 25.

61. "Amusements," *Daily Picayune*, March 21, 1865.

62. "Official," *Times-Democrat*, July 15, 1864.

63. Chamberlin, 55, quoting Philip S. Foner, *Life and Writings of Frederick Douglass: The Civil War, 1861–1865*, vol. 3 (New York: International, 1952), 365.

64. "A Mysterious Political Movement. Ex-Soldiers of the Corps d'Afrique Propose to Run their Old Commander," *Daily Picayune*, May 17, 1872.

65. Hogue, *Uncivil War*, 7–8.

66. William J. Schafer and Richard B. Allen, *Brass Bands and New Orleans Jazz* (Baton Rouge: Louisiana State University Press, 1977).

67. "Greenbackers," *Times-Democrat*, October 3, 1882.

68. *Daily City Item*, July 29, 1892, p. 4.

69. Schafer and Allen, Brass Bands and New Orleans Jazz.

70. Rachel Breunlin, Ronald W. Lewis, and Helen Regis, *House of Dance and Feathers: A Museum by Ronald W. Lewis* (New Orleans: University of New Orleans Press, 2009), 65.

CHAPTER 5. REBIRTH: OUTLIER AS ICON

1. *Complete Library of Congress Recordings*, Audio CD (Rounder Records, 2005).

2. "The Coon Carnival," *Daily Picayune*, February 28, 1900.

3. Ibid.

4. "Negro Indians go on War Path," *Times-Picayune*, February 14, 1923, p. 2.

5. *New Orleans Item*, October 29, 1923, p. 6. *Daily States*, June 27, 1916, p. 6.

6. Al Kennedy and Herreast Harrison, *Big Chief Harrison and the Mardi Gras Indians* (Gretna, LA: Pelican Publishing, 2010), 149.

7. Ibid., 149.

8. "Claiborne Merchants Compliment Police," *New Orleans Item*, February 12, 1911, p. 4.

9. "The Ball," *Daily Picayune*, February 23, 1898.

10. Tallant, *Mardi Gras . . . As It Was*, 107.

11. "In the French Part of Town," *Times-Democrat*, March 2, 1897, p. 16.

12. "Gumbo Ya-Ya," *Goodreads*, https://www.goodreads.com/work/best_book/9932-gumbo-ya-ya-a-collection-of-louisiana-folk-tales (accessed August 8, 2017).

13. *New Orleans Item*, February 21, 1941.

14. Robert Tallant, Lyle Saxon, and Edward Dreyer, *Gumbo Ya-Ya. A Collection of Louisiana Folk Tales*, 1st pbk. ed. (Gretna, LA: Pelican Publishing, 1987).

15. A decade back, in a rare incident, one Indian struck another with an object. The offender was prohibited from masking for a period.

16. Author interview, Juan Pardo, July 2017.

17. A similar case could be made for the New Orleans brass band funeral tradition. Within weeks of the flood, city brass bands were again playing funerals for the departed. There were even symbolic funerals held to put away the sorrow of the storm and take up living again. The Black Men of Labor, a social aid and pleasure club, held a funeral in Algiers on All Saints' Day 2005 while another "healing" march was held in Treme and the French Quarter. *Times-Picayune*, November 2, 2005, p. B1.

18. Author interview, Howard Miller, August 7, 2017.

CONCLUSION

1. Haunani-Kay Trask, "From a Native Daughter," in *The American Indian and the Problem of History*, ed. Calvin Martin (New York: Oxford University Press, 1987), 172.

2. John Watkins, Louisiana Special Collections, Tulane University (97), 10.

3. Byington, *A Dictionary of the Choctaw Language*, 87.

4. John Watkins, Louisiana Special Collections, Tulane University (97), 3/3.

5. Author interview, Juan Pardo, August 7, 2017.

APPENDIX I: NINETEENTH-CENTURY MARDI GRAS INDIANS

1. Year: 1900; Census Place: New Orleans Ward 3, Orleans, Louisiana; Roll: 571; Page: 10B; Enumeration District: 0022; FHL microfilm: 1240571.

2. "John Henry Lewis Indicted," *Daily Picayune*, June 27, 1900.

3. Ibid.

4. Year: 1880; Census Place: New Orleans, Orleans, Louisiana; Roll: 464; Family History Film: 1254464; Page: 455C; Enumeration District: 090.

5. US City Directories, 1822–1995 [database on-line]. Provo, UT, USA: Ancestry.com.

6. Ibid.

7. Year: 1880; Census Place: New Orleans, Orleans, Louisiana; Roll: 462; Family History Film: 1254462; Page: 674B; Enumeration District: 054; Image: 0330.

8. US Civil War Soldier Records and Profiles, 1861–1865, Historical Data Systems, Ancestry.com. US Civil War Pension Index: General Index to Pension Files, 1861–1934, Ancestry.com. US Civil War Soldiers, 1861–65, National Park Service, Ancestry.com.

9. Soards New Orleans 1869, US City Directories, Ancestry.com.

10. Year: 1880; Census Place: New Orleans, Orleans, Louisiana; Roll: 461; Family History Film: 1254461; Page: 450C; Enumeration District: 046; Image: 0706.

11. US Census, New Orleans, Year: 1880; Census Place: New Orleans, Orleans, Louisiana; Roll: 461; Family History Film: 1254461; Page: 450C; Enumeration District: 046; Image: 0706.

12. New Orleans, Louisiana Directories, 1890–1891, Ancestry.com.

13. US Census, New Orleans, Year: 1900; Census Place: New Orleans Ward 7, Orleans, Louisiana; Roll: 572; Page: 18B; Enumeration District: 0066; FHL microfilm: 1240572.

14. US Census, New Orleans, Year: 1870; Census Place: New Orleans Ward 5, Orleans, Louisiana; Roll: M593_521; Page: 212B; Image: 341410; Family History Library Film: 552020.

15. US Civil War Pension Index: General Index to Pension Files, 1861–1934, Ancestry.com.

16. Year: 1870; Census Place: New Orleans Ward 5, Orleans, Louisiana; Roll: M593_521; Page: 212B; Image: 775; Family History Library Film: 552020. US Census 1880, New Orleans, Year: 1880; Census Place: New Orleans, Orleans, Louisiana; Roll: 459; Family History Film: 1254459; Page: 555A; Enumeration District: 023; Image: 0768.

17. Louisiana Vital Records; Volume: 20; Page: 852 New Orleans, Louisiana, Marriage Records Index, 1831–1964.

18. "Discharged," *Daily Picayune*, June 8, 1900; p. 11. "Joseph Horton Assault," *Times-Democrat*, February 10, 1905.

19. Orleans Death Indices 1908–1917; Volume: 150; Page: 690.

20. The National Archives at Washington, D.C.; NAI Title: General Index to Civil War and Later Pension Files, c. 1949–c. 1949; NAI Number: 563268; Record Group Title: Records of the Department of Veterans Affairs, 1773–2007. 1870 US Census Year: 1870; Census Place: New Orleans Ward 3, Orleans, Louisiana; Roll: M593_520; Page: 475A; Image: 203566; Family History Library Film: 552019.

21. Orleans Death Indices 1804–1876; Volume: 47; Page: 531, New Orleans, Louisiana, Death Records Index, 1804–1949.

22. Year: 1900; Census Place: New Orleans Ward 3, Orleans, Louisiana; Roll: 571; Page: 11B; Enumeration District: 0023; FHL microfilm: 1240571. Year: 1870; Census Place: New Orleans Ward 3, Orleans, Louisiana; Roll: M593_520; Page: 475A; Image: 151; Family History Library Film: 552019 Year: 1870; Census Place: New Orleans Ward 3, Orleans, Louisiana; Roll: M593_520; Page: 475A; Image: 151; Family History Library Film: 552019.

23. Year: 1900; Census Place: New Orleans Ward 3, Orleans, Louisiana; Roll: 571; Page: 11B; Enumeration District: 0023; FHL microfilm: 1240571. Year: 1900; Census Place: New Orleans Ward 3, Orleans, Louisiana; Roll: 571; Page: 6A; Enumeration District: 0025; FHL microfilm: 1240571.

24. Year: 1930; Census Place: New Orleans, Orleans, Louisiana; Roll: 802; Page: 25A; Enumeration District: 0042; Image: 182.0; FHL microfilm: 2340537.

25. *Daily Picayune*, February 19, 1886, p. 7; *Daily Picayune*, September 12, 1887, p. 8; *Daily Picayune*, September 18, 1887, p. 6; *Daily Picayune*, April 18, 1894, p. 16; *Daily Picayune*, August 27, 1884, p. 3.

26. US Headstone Applications for Military Veterans, 1925–1963.

27. Soards Directory, 1879. Historical Data Systems, comp. US Civil War Soldier Records and Profiles, 1861–1865 [database on-line]. Provo, UT, USA: Ancestry.com,2009.

28. "Grand Jury," Daily Picayune, June 27, 1900, p. 8.

29. Times-Democrat, June 12, 1901, p. 8.

30. Times-Democrat, June 12, 1901, p. 8.

31. "Justice Figures. Work of the Criminal Courts During the Year Shows That Few Guilty Men," *Daily Picayune*, September 1, 1909.

32. US World War I Draft Registration Cards, 1917–1918, Louisiana; Registration County: Orleans; Roll: 1684922; Draft Board: 09.

33. Marigy's mother's name is given as Harriet on some documents and Marinet on others. Registration State: Louisiana; Registration County: Orleans; Roll: 1684919; Draft Board: 06; Year: 1910; Census Place: New Orleans Ward 7, Orleans, Louisiana; Roll: T624_521; Page: 6A; Enumeration District: 0113; FHL microfilm: 1374534.

34. Year: 1910; Census Place: New Orleans Ward 7, Orleans, Louisiana; Roll: T624_521; Page: 6A; Enumeration District: 0113; FHL microfilm: 1374534.

35. Year: 1920; Census Place: New Orleans Ward 7, Orleans, Louisiana; Roll: T625_621; Page: 6A; Enumeration District: 118; Image: 319. World War I draft registration; Registration State: Louisiana; Registration County: Orleans; Roll: 1684919; Draft Board: 06.

36. US City Directories, 1822–1995, New Orleans, p. 915.

37. New Orleans, Louisiana, City Directory, 1952. New Orleans, Louisiana, City Directory, 1923.

38. Year: 1920; Census Place: New Orleans Ward 3, Orleans, Louisiana; Roll: T625_618; Page: 7A; Enumeration District: 34.

39. Year: 1940; Census Place: New Orleans, Orleans, Louisiana; Roll: T627_1418; Page: 8B; Enumeration District: 36–39.

40. New Orleans, Louisiana Birth Records Index, 1790–1899; Volume: 56; Page: 449.

41. Louisiana, *Actes Passés À La Session de La Législature de L'état de La Louisiane* (W. Van Benthuysen & P. Besancon, Jr. State Printers, 1872).

42. New Orleans (LA) General committee of arrangements of the funeral ceremonies in honor of James Abram Garfield, *A History of the Proceedings in the City of New Orleans: On the Occasion of the Funeral Ceremonies in Honor of James Abram Garfield, Late President of the United States, Which Took Place on Monday, September 26th, 1881* (A. W. Hyatt, printer, 1881).

43. "Greenbackers," *Times-Democrat*, October 3, 1882.

44. *Times-Democrat*, October 3, 1882, p. 3, http://www.newspapers.com/image/130946041/?terms=%22milton%2BSparks%22.45 (accessed April 30, 2017). Year: 1870; Census Place: New Orleans Ward 7, Orleans, Louisiana; Roll: M593_522; Page: 587B; Image: 370401; Family History Library Film: 552021. Year: 1880; Census Place: New Orleans, Orleans, Louisiana; Roll: 462; Family History Film: 1254462; Page: 588B; Enumeration District: 051; Image: 0158; Year: 1900; Census Place: New Orleans Ward 11, Orleans, Louisiana; Roll: 574; Page: 9B; Enumeration District: 0115; FHL microfilm: 1240574.

46. "Stabbed in the back," *Times-Democrat*, November 10, 1888; "First recorder's court," *Daily Picayune*, January 4, 1894; "Criminal District Court," *Times-Democrat*, August 22, 1899.

47. "Masker struck by streetcar," *Times-Democrat*, February 17, 1904, p. 10.

48. Year: 1910; Census Place: New Orleans Ward 3, Orleans, Louisiana; Roll: T624_520; Page: 4A; Enumeration District: 0032; FHL microfilm: 1374533.

49. Orleans Death Indices 1918–1928; Volume: 197; Page: 1062.

50. Year: 1880; Census Place: New Orleans, Orleans, Louisiana; Roll: 463; Family History Film: 1254463; Page: 165B; Enumeration District: 081; Image: 0813. Louisiana, Marriages, 1718–1925.

51. US City Directories, 1822–1995 [database on-line]. Provo, UT, USA: Ancestry.com, 2011. *Times-Picayune*, January 17, 1894, p. 11.

52. "Sam Tillman Murder," *Daily Picayune*, March 16, 1898.

53. Berry et al., *Up from the Cradle of Jazz*, 237.

54. *Daily Picayune*, February 28, 1900, p. 10.

55. *Daily Picayune*, January 8, 1899, p. 12.

56. "First City Criminal Court," *Times-Picayune*, March 1, 1900, p. 13.

57. *Daily Item*, December 20, 1901, p. 2.

APPENDIX II. MARDI GRAS INDIAN MUSIC

1. *Complete Library of Congress Rec*ordings, Audio CD (Rounder Records, 2005).

2. Some have looked with skepticism upon Morton's Indian claims, but a look at New Orleans geography and Morton's places of residence should dispel any doubt that he would be familiar with the culture. Later, Morton lived in central city uptown, a few blocks from Robert Sam Tillman, leader of the Creole Wild West.

3. 1910 US Census: Baton Rouge Ward 1, East Baton Rouge, Louisiana; Roll: T624_513; Page: 14A; Enumeration District: 0017; FHL microfilm: 1374526. Year: 1880; Census Place: New Orleans, Orleans, Louisiana; Roll: 461; Family History Film: 1254461; Page: 381C; Enumeration District: 044; Image: 0565. Year: 1900; Census Place: New Orleans Ward 6, Orleans, Louisiana; Roll: 572; Page: 5B; Enumeration District: 0057; FHL microfilm: 1240572. Year: 1880; Census Place: New Orleans, Orleans, Louisiana; Roll: 461; Family History Film: 1254461; Page: 381C; Enumeration District: 044; Image: 0565.

4. Berry et al., *Up from the Cradle of Jazz*, 238.

5. 1880 US Census: Fausse Pointe, Iberia, Louisiana; Roll: 454; Family History Film: 1254454; Page: 381B; Enumeration District: 029; Image: 0144.

6. WW I draft records. Registration State: Louisiana; Registration County: Orleans; Roll: 1684918; Draft Board: 05. Year: 1920; Census Place: New Orleans Ward 3, Orleans, Louisiana; Roll: T625_618; Page: 2A; Enumeration District: 36; Image: 1220.

7. Year: 1930; Census Place: New Orleans, Orleans, Louisiana; Roll: 803; Page: 1B; Enumeration District: 0079; Image: 790.0; FHL microfilm: 2340538.

8. *Daily Picayune*, December 11, 1864, p. 1.

9. "BackTalk: An Interview with James 'Sugar Boy' Crawford," *OffBeat Magazine*, http://www.offbeat.com/articles/james-sugar-boy-crawford/ (accessed May 4, 2017).

10. In 1967 as part of a lawsuit settlement between "Sugar Boy" James Crawford and the Dixie Cups, the trio were given part songwriting credit to the song.

11. "Shoo Fly Don't Bother Me," *Fairfield Herald*, March 4, 1868, p. 4.

12. *Fairfield Herald*, March 4, 1868, p. 4. "Amusements," *Daily Picayune*, December 24, 1869, p. 5.

13. "Musical and Theatrical Notes," *New York Herald*, December 15, 1869, p. 7.

14. "Shoo Fly; Walk Round from the Negro Farce of the Cook," *Duke Digital Collections*, http://library.duke.edu/digitalcollections/hasm_b0408/ (accessed April 27, 2017).

15. *Madison County Monitor*, January 19, 1906, p. 4. *Bessemer Herald*, November 11, 1905, p. 2.

16. "A Steamboat Bully," *Daily Picayune*, March 16, 1898, p. 9.

17. "St. Charles Theatre," *Daily Picayune*, April 25, 1870, p. 1, at Newspapers.com.

18. William L. Slout, ed., *Burnt Cork and Tambourines: A Source Book for Negro Minstrelsy* (San Bernardino, CA: Borgo Press, 2007), 44.

19. Lucy Thurston, age 101, interview WPA Writers project. Lyrics to 1917 version, P.D.

20. P. 4.

21. "Little Old Liza Jane," *San Francisco Chronicle*, February 7, 1867, p. 1.

22. Newman Ivey White, *American Negro Folk-Songs* (Cambridge, MA: Harvard University Press, 1928), 172–75.

23. Lucy Thurston, age 101, interview WPA Writers project.

24. "Stephan Foster Liza Jane Civil War Songs," *Sheboygan Press*, January 30, 1929, p. 6.

25. "Kenneth Clark leads club women in song," *Arkansas Democrat*, May 3, 1918, p. 11; "Soldiers' Minstrel Matinee and night," *Wilmington Morning Star*, August 24, 1918, p. 5.

26. "Yip-I-Addy," *Des Moines Register*, April 21, 1918, p. 12.

27. Berry et al., *Up from the Cradle of Jazz*, 244.

INDEX

Page numbers followed by *n* indicate endnotes.

About the Authors

Shane Lief was born and raised in New Orleans. Over the past decade, he has presented papers at the annual meetings of the American Musicological Society, the American Anthropological Association, the Society for German-American Studies, and the Louisiana Historical Association. When not teaching or writing about the history of languages, he plays music and leads a percussion band that marches in Mardi Gras parades.

John McCusker is a New Orleans native who worked as a photojournalist for three decades at the *Times-Picayune* and later the *New Orleans Advocate*. He was part of the team that shared the 2006 Pulitzer Prize for Journalism for covering Hurricane Katrina. He is author of *Creole Trombone: Kid Ory and the Early Years of Jazz*, published by University Press of Mississippi, and founder of the Cradle of Jazz Tour.